Finance for a Better World

Finance for a Better World

The Shift toward Sustainability

Edited by

Henri-Claude de Bettignies

and

François Lépineux

palgrave
macmillan

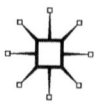

First published 2009 by
PALGRAVE MACMILLAN

Palgrave Macmillan in the UK is an imprint of Macmillan Publishers Limited,
registered in England, company number 785998, of Houndmills, Basingstoke,
Hampshire RG21 6XS.

Palgrave Macmillan in the US is a division of St Martin's Press LLC,
175 Fifth Avenue, New York, NY 10010.

Palgrave Macmillan is the global academic imprint of the above companies
and has companies and representatives throughout the world.

Palgrave® and Macmillan® are registered trademarks in the United States,
the United Kingdom, Europe and other countries

ISBN-13: 978–0–230–55130–5   hardback

This book is printed on paper suitable for recycling and made from fully
managed and sustained forest sources. Logging, pulping and manufacturing
processes are expected to conform to the environmental regulations of the
country of origin.

A catalogue record for this book is available from the British Library.

Library of Congress Cataloging-in-Publication Data
Finance for a better world : the shift toward sustainability/edited
       by Henri-Claude de Bettignies and François Lépineux.
            p. cm.
    Includes bibliographical references and indexes.
    ISBN 978–0–230–55130–5
1. Banks and banking. 2. Social responsibility of business.
       3. Sustainable development—Economic aspects. I. Bettignies, Henri-
    Claude de. II. Lépineux, François, 1968–
    HG1601.F46 2009
    332.1—dc22
2008041044

10   9   8   7   6   5   4   3   2   1
18 17 16 15 14 13 12 11 10 09

Printed and bound in Great Britain by
CPI Antony Rowe, Chippenham and Eastbourne

Contents

List of Figures

List of Tables

Notes on the Contributors

Pasquale Arena is Associate Professor of Business Economics, Vice-president of the management and control program and delegate of the Dean for business ethics at the Faculty of Economics, University of Catania, Italy. He is a member of the Italian Academy of Business Economics, of the Italian Society of Accounting History, and of the Italian Society of Accounting and Business Administration. Co-founder of SPES and co-founder and member of the Board of EBEN Italian Chapter, he is also a member of the Scientific Committee of the PhD in Business Economics at University of Catania. He has been a member of the Scientific Committee of the Research Conference 2007 *Finance and Society in Ethical Perspective*. His areas of research focus on Business Ethics, Corporate Social Responsibility, Business Economics, Public Management and Governance and Accounting History. With regard to Business Ethics and CSR he has edited *Corporate Social Responsibility: Scientific Development and Implementation*, 2006 by Aracne and he is also the author of the paper "The Contribution of Ethical Codes in the Development of CSR". His research work is currently oriented towards understanding the potential role of the collective dimension in corporate and public governance and in various organizational contexts.

Henri-Claude de Bettignies is the EU Chair Distinguished Professor of Global Governance and China-Europe Business Relations, CEIBS, in Shanghai where he has created the Euro-China Centre for Leadership and Responsibility (ECCLAR). He is also the AVIVA Chair Emeritus Professor of Leadership and Responsibility and Emeritus Professor of Asian Business at INSEAD. Between 1988 and 2005, with a joint appointment at Stanford University (Graduate School of Business), he shared his time equally between Europe, California and the Asia Pacific region. Professor de Bettignies started the development of the Ethics initiative at INSEAD, and pioneered a new approach (AVIRA) to enlighten business leaders. Over a 16-year period the AVIRA program brought together 900 Chairmen and CEOs from 60 countries, keen to enrich their vision and enhance their "responsible" leadership competence. Henri-Claude teaches MBAs, E-MBAs and executives at CEIBS and at INSEAD in the areas of ethics and CSR, HR management and corporate transformation.

On the editorial Board of five academic journals he has published many articles and five books on management in Japan, in Asia, and on business ethics.

Paul H. Dembinski is Professor at the University of Fribourg, where he teaches International Competition and Strategy, and Ethics in Finance and Business. Since 2002, he has also taught at the Tischner European University in Krakow, Poland. He is also the initiator and Director of Foundation of the Observatoire de la Finance (1996) www.obsfin.ch. The mission of the Observatoire de la Finance is to promote awareness of ethical concerns in financial activities and the financial sector. Paul H. Dembinski is also the founder and editor of the bilingual journal entitled *Finance & the Common Good/Bien Commun* (1998). Since 2006 he has held the "Ethics and Finance" chair at the Catholic Institute of Paris. A political scientist and economist by training, Paul H. Dembinski has written a dozen books and some 60 scientific articles in the field of internationalization of enterprises, globalization, competition, ethics and finance. His latest book, called *Finance, Servant or Deceiver?*, will be published by Palgrave Macmillan in spring 2009.

Ali Fatemi is the Chairman of the Finance Department at DePaul University where he also holds a position as a Professor. Previously he held positions at Kansas State University and Wichita State University, and has been a Visiting Scholar at UCLA and at the University of Maastricht. He also has had teaching assignments at Ritsumeikan University, Erasmus University, Tilburg University, Justus Liebig University, Johann Wolfgang Goethe University, Europa Universität Viadrina, Bahrain Institute of Banking and Finance, and the Czech Management Center. He is a graduate of Oklahoma State University, where he received his PhD (1979) and his MBA (1975). Professor Fatemi has published in leading academic journals including: *Journal of Finance, Journal of Business Research, Journal of Economic Psychology, Global Finance Journal, Pacific-Basin Finance Journal, Financial Services Review*, and *Japan and the World Economy*. His current research deals with issues related to mergers and acquisitions, executive compensation, dividend policy, and corporate governance. He was the editor of *Journal of Applied Finance* (2000–7), and has served as a member of the editorial board or a reviewer for a variety of domestic and international finance journals, including *European Financial Management, Global Finance Journal, The International Journal of Finance* and *Managerial Finance*.

Iraj Fooladi holds the Douglas C. Mackay Chair in Finance at Dalhousie University. He is also the president of the Administrative Sciences Association of Canada (ASAC). He was the co-editor of the *Canadian Journal of Administrative Sciences* for the six-year period Jan. 2000–Dec. 2005. He also serves as Associate Editor and on the editorial board of other finance and economics journals such as the *Journal of Applied Finance* and *Studies in Economics and Finance*, and *Workplace Review*. His current research interests include bond portfolio strategies, investors' behavior under uncertainty, and socially responsible investments. Dr Fooladi has published in various refereed finance and economics journals, and has received awards for his writings from reputable academic associations such as the Western Economics Association and the Financial Management Association. Dr Fooladi's teaching interests include Managerial and Corporate Finance, Investment, and Portfolio and Money Management. His teaching in the regular and executive programs outside Canada includes countries such as the United States, New Zealand, the Philippines, Jamaica, and Saudi Arabia. Dr Fooladi has provided consulting to various private companies as well as to government departments.

Isabelle Guérin is a Research Fellow at the Institute of Research for Development (IRD, France); Head of the Research Program "Labor, finance and social dynamics" at the French Institute of Pondicherry (South India); and leader of the project "Rural microfinance: do processes matter?" for the French National Agency for Research (ANR, program "*Les Suds, Aujourd'hui*"). She is a socioeconomist specializing in interactions between household behavior, vulnerability and social justice. Her areas of specialization are: (1) household survival and livelihood strategies, with a focus on indebtedness, over-indebtedness, debt bondage and on gender dimensions of vulnerability; (2) collective action and NGOs interventions, with a focus on microfinance, empowerment programs, and linkages with public policies. Her latest publications include *India's Unfree Workforce – Of Bondage, Old and New* (forthcoming, co-edited with J. Breman and A. Prakash); *Microfinance Challenges: Empowerment or Disempowerment of the Poor?* (2005, co-edited with J. Palier); and "Women and Money: Multiple, Complex and Evolving Practices", *Development and Change*, Vol. 37, No. 3, pp. 549–70.

Leo Johnson is the Co-Founder of Sustainable Finance, sustainability advisors to over 50 leading global banks and businesses. He is the author of the IFC publication, *Beyond Risk – Sustainability and the Emerging Markets Financial Sector*, and winner of the IFC Corporate Award for his work advising the financial sector on the Equator Principles. On behalf of SFL, he was a Judge and is the Technical Adviser to the *Financial Times* for the FT Sustainable Banking Awards. He is a Judge and Sustainability Adviser for the 2008 Prix Pictet Award, and sits on the Advisory Board of Triple Bottom Line Investing. Leo Johnson was a Scholar of New College, Oxford, and has an MBA from INSEAD, and an MSc in Environmental and Resource Economics from UCL, where he was Dow Scholar. He has worked with Banco Real as a sustainability adviser from 2002 to the present.

Adam Kanzer is Managing Director and General Counsel of Domini Social Investments and Chief Legal Officer of the Domini Funds. For the past ten years, he has directed Domini's shareholder advocacy department, where he has led numerous dialogues with corporations on a wide range of social and environmental issues. He currently serves as co-chair of the Contract Supplier Working Group at the Interfaith Center on Corporate Responsibility, focusing on improving working conditions in corporate global supply chains. He is a frequent speaker and commentator on socially responsible investing. Prior to joining Domini in 1998, Mr Kanzer was a litigator for four and a half years with the firm of Cahill Gordon & Reindel in New York City. In October 1997, Mr Kanzer volunteered as an international observer of the South African Truth and Reconciliation Commission. Mr Kanzer holds a BA in Political Science from the University of Pennsylvania and a JD from Columbia Law School.

François Lépineux is Professor and Head of the Center for Responsible Business at Rennes School of Business (in Brittany, France), and Research Fellow at INSEAD. After graduating from HEC Paris School of Management in 1990, he has carried on various research and consulting activities, and received a PhD in Management Science at the Conservatoire National des Arts et Métiers (CNAM, Paris). He is co-author of the book *Sustainable Development and Corporate Governance* (2003, in French) and has produced a number of other publications. His areas of interest include the relationship between business activities and the search for the common good, ethical issues in the financial services industry, as well as stakeholder theory, the emergence of a global civil society and the shift in the social contract. François Lépineux is co-founder and past President (2002–5) of ADERSE (Association pour le Développement de l'Enseignement et de la Recherche sur la Responsabilité Sociale de l'Entreprise), the French academic association for the development of education and interdisciplinary research on CSR.

Céline Louche is Assistant Professor at Vlerick Leuven Gent Management School (Belgium). She teaches and researches into the area of Corporate Social Responsibility (CSR). In her work, she explores the way processes of change take place, and is interested in the construction of the CSR field with a special focus on CSR as a factor of innovation and value creation, but also in SRI, and in stakeholder processes. She is the author of several articles, both academic and general, and has contributed chapters to several books. Recent articles include: "Socially Responsible Investment in Japan: Its Mechanism and Drivers" (2008); "Understanding the CSR Landscape in Belgium" (2008); "Investissement socialement responsable: différences entre Europe et Etats-Unis (2006); and "From Financial Corporate Governance towards Responsible Corporate Governance" (2006). Before joining Vlerick, Céline Louche worked for five years as a Sustainability Analyst for SRI at the Dutch Sustainability Research Institute. She is a member of the Academic Board of EABIS, of the scientific committee of the International Network for Research on Organizations and Sustainable Development, and of the SRI advisory committee of Dexia Asset Management.

Steven D. Lydenberg is Chief Investment Officer for Domini Social Investments (USA). He has been active in social investing for 30 years as Director of Corporate Accountability Research with the Council on Economic Priorities; Investment Associate with Franklin Research and Development Corporation (now Trillium Asset Management); and Director of Research with Kinder, Lydenberg, Domini & Co. (now KLD Research & Analytics). Mr Lydenberg is the co-author of *Rating America's Corporate Conscience* (1986) and *Investing for Good* (1993) – a guide for socially responsible investors – and co-editor of *The Social Investment Almanac* (1992). His is also the author of *Corporations and the Public Interest: Guiding the Invisible Hand* (2005). He holds degrees from Columbia College and Cornell University and is a Chartered Financial Analyst (CFA).

Solène Morvant-Roux, PhD in economics, is a microfinance project leader at Farm Foundation (www.fondation-farm.org) and postdoctoral Research Fellow at the Institut de Recherches pour le Développement, France. As a PhD candidate she lived for one year in Mexico as a research fellow of the Centre d'Etudes mexicaines et centroaméricaines (CEMCA). She also has short-term field experience in different developing countries such as Morocco, Togo, Guinea and Madagascar. Her research interests deal with microfinance in rural areas and focus on financing agricultural activities, debt, social institutions and migration. Her recent publications include: "Microfinance Institution's Clients Borrowing Strategies and Lending Groups Financial Heterogeneity under Progressive Lending: Evidence from a Mexican Microfinance Program", *Savings and Development*, No. 2 (2007), pp. 193–217, and "Quelle microfinance pour l'agriculture des pays en développement?", *Exclusion et liens financiers* (2008, editor).

Marc Roesch, Agronomist and PhD in Agro-Economics from Montpellier University. After working during more than 20 years in Africa, especially in Agronomic Research, he was in charge of the Training Service of CIRAD (Centre International de Recherche Agronomique pour le Développement). Since 1999 he has returned to research and is particularly interested in socioeconomic aspects of agriculture finance. His research fields are mostly oriented on all aspects related to microfinance and rural economy at the household level. In India for three years, his main specialization has been on household economy and particularly indebtedness.

Christel Scholten is a Manager of the Sustainable Development Department of Banco Real in Brazil. She joined the team in 2003 after working at the ABN AMRO head office in Amsterdam for two years and is responsible for integrating sustainable development into various aspects of the organization, from strategy and governance to policies, processes and educational programs. Since 2008, her focus has been on designing and delivering educational programs on sustainability for clients and other stakeholders. Christel is Canadian and has lived in several other countries including Mexico, The Netherlands, and Bangladesh where she spent time working in the area of microfinance with organizations such as the Grameen Bank and BRAC. She has a Bachelor of Commerce from the University of Saskatchewan (Canada), and a Master of Science in Responsibility and Business Practice from the University of Bath (UK). She was very involved in the international youth organization AIESEC, is an active member of Pioneers of Change, and serves on the board of The Shire, a learning centre in Canada for the study and practice of how to build a sustainable human future.

Jean-Michel Servet, born in Lyon (France) in 1951, trained in economics, sociology and anthropology. He is currently Professor at the Graduate Institute of International and Development Studies (Geneva), and associated to the French Institute of Pondicherry (India), to the Institute of Research for Development (Paris), and to the CERMI (Solvay Institute – Brussels). Jean-Michel Servet is the author of close to 200 publications, including several books and a large number of articles in scientific journals, focusing on economic, finance and social development. As a socioeconomist developing the conceptual approach of Karl Polanyi, he published in 2006 a 500-page book on microfinance (in French): *Banquiers aux pieds nus*. He is also a historian of economic and financial thought, and contributes on a regular basis to newspapers and journals in France and Switzerland on economic and social development issues. Every year, he is invited by nongovernmental organizations and companies to give lectures on these topics.

Cheon Kheong Tan was a Research Associate at INSEAD (Singapore). He holds an MBA from Nanyang Technological University (Singapore) and a Bachelor of Social Sciences degree with Second Class Honours (Upper Division) in Economics from the National University of Singapore. His research areas include Leadership and Responsibility, Corporate Social Responsibility, Asian Business and International Management.

Federica Viganò holds a PhD in Philosophy from the universities of Milan and Berlin (Freie Universität) and a Laurea in Philosophy from Università Statale of Milan (Italy). She is Senior Researcher at the Fondazione Istud. Her research interests cover Corporate Social Responsibility and Sustainability issues. She is interested in CSR in a systemic logic perspective: CSR as a vehicle of social justice, redistribution and democracy. She is currently exploring innovative approaches such as the capability tools based on A. Sen's viewpoint, particularly useful to operationalize qualitative but increasingly important dimensions linked to the overarching question of development (diversity, intangible dimension, reputation, culture). She teaches Cultural Economics at the universities of Bolzano and Genoa. She has contributed to the book: *Rhetoric and Realities: Analyzing Corporate Social Responsibility in Europe* (2008).

David Wheeler is Dean of the Faculty of Management, Dalhousie University, Nova Scotia. He has published more than 70 articles and book chapters and has done numerous television and radio broadcasts on environmental and social issues and business. He was principal author of *The Stakeholder Corporation* – the first business text to be endorsed by a former UK Prime Minister; an advisor to the UK Government on governance aspects of the Company Law Review; a member of the UK Government Advisory Committee on Consumer Products and the Environment and the Reference Group for Canada's National Report to the World Summit on Sustainable Development (Rio+10); and co-founder of the UK business-led *Committee of Inquiry – a New Vision for Business* that reported directly to Prime Minister Tony Blair in November 1999.

Andy White is a Managing Director at Innovest Strategic Value Advisors, the number one ranked firm for sustainable investment research. His principal focus is corporate governance and its impact on companies' and investors' financial performance. Prior to joining Innovest, he was Managing Director of Research for Core Ratings/Fitch, a successor company to Global Risk Management Services in London. His responsibilities there focused on leading the SRI research team, developing and enhancing its research methodology, and developing new analytical products. Prior to that, Mr White spent several years as a senior researcher on corporate governance and social responsibility at Pensions & Investment Research Consultants (PIRC). His duties at PIRC focused heavily on engaging with both companies and institutional investors on a variety of proxy voting issues. Mr White has also worked as a business analyst in industry, with both Cape Plc in London and BASF AG in Germany. He has written for a number of financial journals including the FT and contributed a chapter to a recent book entitled *Cut Carbon, Grow Profits* (2007). He holds an MA in Environmental Management from the University of Central England as well as an Honors BA in European business studies.

1
Introduction

Henri-Claude de Bettignies and François Lépineux

The subprime crisis that erupted at the very heart of global capitalism showed the destructive power of an economic system that has no moral compass. Over US$10 trillion in assets might be destroyed; millions of poor families have been evicted from their homes while millions have also lost their jobs in the shrinking economy. Worst yet, the malaise has spread around the world – although it has had less impact in Asia (partly because governments have learnt their lesson from the East Asian financial crisis of 1997). The crisis has its roots in the wrong assumptions about human nature that underpin our current paradigm of capitalism and its dominance in the globalization process. Milton Friedman's model, Adam Smith's "invisible hand" – assuming that when an individual pursues his own interest ("rational" decision makers) he is contributing to the greater good of all – do not seem to produce the Common Good.

Smith's assumption worked well in a world of limited resources where economic decisions were made by individuals based on rational calculations of their interest but keeping an eye out for the greater good of all, but this is no longer the case in the "New Economy" where people are "spoilt for choice" (pushed by effective marketing), making their purchase decisions on the basis of emotion as much as reason. Unscrupulous operators can exploit human frailties for profits (as illustrated in the subprime mess by the "ninja" loans extended by bankers to people with "no income, no job, no asset"), while old-fashioned greed fuels the drive for shareholder value maximization or incentive pay based on short-term results. By entrusting the functioning of our complex global financial system to self-interested talented individuals, the economy may be hijacked by them to serve their own interest. Hence, unregulated free market capitalism shows the endogenous causes of its dysfunctions in the system itself, and tinkering with it through increasing regulatory oversight is merely applying a band aid to an illness that requires surgery.

We have already learnt that for an economic system to achieve the Common Good, it must not only be efficient, it requires a moral compass: it needs values to discipline purpose. The observation of today's "global village" puzzles many who wonder how in a world so effective in creating wealth, we are so ineffective in distributing it; how in a planet with finite resources and a vulnerable nature we remain so wasteful and obnoxious to Gaia... Not making sense of the world we live in, unable to decipher what is happening in our daily life, is bound to increase our anxiety (with all its consequences), to induce self-centered behavior, egoism and an erosion of the sense of the "community." Remembering LTCM, Barings or Enron, Main Street has more difficulties than Wall Street to make sense of Bear Stearns, Société Générale, EADS, or Fanny Mae. It is not so much the complexity of sophisticated financial products, the globalization of the world of finance, that makes people worried about the future, it is also the noise – and the evidence – about the deterioration of our planet and its ecosystem, the growing gap between rich and poor, etc. Society is looking for meaning as yesterday's values and lighthouses seem to have been submerged into the wild globalization tempest.

Now, the poor cannot afford to eat; only the rich become really richer; food and particularly water wars are spreading; and a "globalization" process that does not make the world better is the easy villain. Globalization associated with – if not led by – the financialization of our planet induces the question: is it possible to use and manage finance to improve life for the community living on our planet? This is what this collection of essays – from academics and practitioners – tries to explore, challenging definitions and ideological prejudices, questioning dominant paradigms, models and theories, bringing empirical evidence to challenge common beliefs, and proposing paths to explore. Are the current tools of microfinance, SRI, CSR, really the effective paths to fight against poverty, to bring the long-term view or to account for all stakeholders, in order to reach the objectives of sustainability they claim to contribute to achieve? In the fast-coming microfinance bandwagon, is the arrival of private players under the pressure of profitability going to pervert microfinance – as Muhammad Yunus feared in his recent Nobel Prize Award speech – and is microfinance really fighting against poverty or fighting against finance exclusion?

Would Socially Responsible Investment (SRI) – where we encounter so many different definitions (and not only between US, Japan or Europe) – contribute to put pressure on corporate behavior as boards see their institutional investors walking the talk to align their investment patterns to their values? Are we going to see both convergence and divergence in SRI coexisting, making it more difficult to anticipate what SRI will become tomorrow? Will (some) shareholders' values – or, for instance, attitudes toward human rights issues – be effective (through their whistle-blowing impact) to influence corporate behavior toward responsibility (and sustainability) as in the example given by Reverend Leon Sullivan's Principles that contributed to bringing apartheid to an end? If SRI is controversial – as is microfinance – the same observation is valid for CSR, often a mere instrument used to build brand, enhance reputation, and decrease risk – in short, "instrumentalized" for image development and legal protection. Unless we find cases like Banco Real in Brazil, where leadership was a key factor in the full implementation of a CSR approach throughout the whole organization, the road to sustainability may remain only paved with good intentions.

Scenarios for the future are not optimistic. The issue is not whether to be pro- or antiglobalization. We cannot escape globalization any more than we can escape gravity. Globalization, beyond being our current dominant paradigm, is the train we, willingly or not, boarded. It has sped across both territories we know and lands we do not. The problem is that it has no driver. Unregulated globalization, characterized by the lack of cooperation within the so-called "international community" (in reality, not a "community" at all), by a battlefield of egos, has little chance of producing the sustainable world future generations would have the right to expect. We have created a world where growing income gaps are undermining social fabrics (at the macro level and at the national level) while fanning protectionist temptations; where abusing our reliance on nonrenewable resources – scrambled more recently by greedy emerging economies – accelerates environmental deterioration and fuels climate change; where an excess of liquidity on the global scale generates banking irresponsibility and turns the financial planet into a casino; and where we realize more than ever the extreme fragility of our international financial system (the recent subprime crisis being a symptom).

Only dreamers see the next stage of globalization producing a better world for our children. A realistic view of our planet today makes it imperative to work on the creation of a new culture, or rather a new civilization. This collection of essays is a small step on the narrow path we need to explore for that purpose. On that path we will need to develop a new generation of leaders *aware* of the interdependence between the way we run financial resources on this planet and its impact on sustainable development; men and women of character with a long-term *vision* of the "world community." We will need to stimulate *imagination* to increase our capacity for social innovation and we must encourage all leaders in business (as well as in government and in civil society) to internalize *responsibility* in making decisions and taking *action*. Strategic courage will remain an ingredient of responsibility, much beyond the domain of finance. If those five attributes of awareness, vision, imagination, responsibility and action remain in short supply, our grandchildren will blame us, legitimately. It will be too late.

Part I
Microfinance and Socially Responsible Investment: Evolution and Impact on Human Rights

2
Microfinance, Financial Inclusion and Social Responsibility

Isabelle Guérin, Marc Roesch, and Jean-Michel Servet

> There is nothing more misleading than good intentions because they give the illusion of being goodness itself.
>
> Emmanuel Bove, *Le Pressentiment*, Le Castor Astral, Paris, 2006 [1935], p. 105.

> The higher a monkey climbs, the more butt he'll show.
>
> Belizean proverb

Introduction

While one can observe an extension and intensification of financialization in all modern societies, including the so-called "developing countries," access to financial services is usually not thought of as a fundamental human right.[1] Yet, financial instruments play a more and more essential role, whether in the risk management of daily life, to increase one's income or to smooth resources and expenses. But the international community has its eyes fixed mainly on the Millennium Objectives of the fight against poverty adopted by the United Nations in 2000;[2] on its first indicator, the increase of per capita income; and on the associated objective of a decrease by half of the proportion of the population living on less than a dollar a day by 2015. Among all the objectives adopted, there is no comprehensive indicator of the use of financial services. Also, there is no financial indicator among the human development criteria of the United Nations Program for Development. Yet the proposed indicators are diversified and even reach beyond the strictly economic domain. There are, for example, references made to health care, education, environment, to women's participation in public life and to housing conditions.[3] Certainly, these indicators are thought to increase the productive capacities of the people. This omission of the financial dimension contrasts with the more and more intense media coverage of microfinance, from the time of the first Microcredit Summit in 1997 until the climax of the Nobel Prize awarded to Muhammad Yunus and the Grameen Bank in 2006. Such an omission has serious consequences, in particular the fact that the issue of social responsibility in the financial sector does not attract much attention. This kind of debate is much more frequent in domains such as nutrition, health care, education and environment, which are considered fundamental needs for survival in a so-called democratic society.

However, we think that a study on social responsibility in matters of finance is absolutely essential, for several reasons. It is first of all indispensable in order to avoid illusions about the supposed virtues and merits of microfinance in the fight against poverty. Microfinance is often considered a tool in the fight against poverty, while it has to be understood first and foremost as a tool against financial exclusion. This clarification is essential and the term "financial inclusion" seems to us much more appropriate than "microfinance." To equate microfinance with the fight against poverty is extremely dangerous; we will emphasize this several times. Not only is microfinance, unfortunately, poorly equipped to really fight against poverty, but even more so, this confusion of objectives leads many players (not only microfinance organizations, but also commercial banks and investors) to adopt practices not very compatible with effective action in the fight against poverty. To question the social responsibility of the players involved in the fight against financial exclusion is therefore also indispensable to avoid improper practices.

Social responsibility in matters of financial inclusion, what does that mean? This chapter intends to start the debate by offering some lines of thought. Firstly, it is essential to question the diversity of financial needs and the diversity of the populations targeted. This line of questioning should be the first step in any study concerning social responsibility. To be satisfied with cultural or ideological prejudices, as is still often the case, leads to favoring microcredit (while other services like insurance, savings and remittances are often essential), to focus on entrepreneurship as an ultimate objective of microfinance (while in reality very few poor people can turn themselves into entrepreneurs) or to focus only on the "poor" (while other population categories often urgently need financial services). Secondly, it is equally essential to question the economic and social impact of microfinance services as well as the appropriateness of the means employed in light of the objectives pursued. It is not enough to offer financial services in order to "do good." Microfinance services are positive when they bring about long-term improvement of the well-being as well as the individual and collective capabilities of the people. They are negative when, conversely, they have the effect of reducing – directly or indirectly – the well-being and capabilities. Microfinance providers cannot content themselves with offering just any kind of financial service under the pretext that access is limited and ignore how people use their services and the consequences of it. It is also their responsibility to think about the objectives, the appropriateness of these objectives and the means employed to achieve them. Thirdly, this question of social responsibility concerns not only microfinance service providers, but indeed all stakeholders and players in the chain of microfinance service providers. By imposing too many constraints, financing and refinancing modes (donors, social investors, commercial banks, etc.) often have a serious impact on the nature of the supply. The same can be said about supervising and regulatory agencies, and more generally with all public authorities (at the local, national and international levels). Lastly, technical advisers (experts, evaluators, researchers) also have an undeniable responsibility when they promote and approve this or that "model."

Our reflection is conducted in six stages. First of all, we condemn the naive talk about the so-called merits of microfinance, by focusing especially on the myth of the poor entrepreneur. A second section deals with the diverse needs of the targeted populations. A third section describes the recent efforts in the area of social rating and the social performance analysis of microfinance organizations. These initiatives represent undeniable progress, while demonstrating several limitations, such as denying the responsibility of all the stakeholders in the microfinance chain. The fourth section stresses the necessity of not only considering all the players, but also clarifying their role precisely by considering their institutional status and their own constraints. The last two sections deal with the role of commercial institutions. If their increasing influence is not necessarily "bad" in itself (contrary to many prejudices), it can nevertheless lead to many improper practices (section 2.5). So it is necessary to identify very precisely the particular responsibilities in the microfinance sector that they can handle, by emphasizing the risks taken when one privatizes social responsibility (which would replace government intervention – see section 2.6).

2.1   Microcredit and the myths about the needs of microfinance clients

Since the first Microfinance Summit in Washington in 1997, the supposed effectiveness of small loans in the fight against poverty has had a lot of media coverage, and the granting of these loans[4] has been regarded as a historical turning point for humanity. Ten years later, in October 2006, this euphoria has been stimulated by the awarding of the Nobel Peace Prize to Muhammad Yunus and the Grameen Bank, which he founded 30 years earlier. This extended media coverage had the merit of drawing attention to the problems of financial exclusion. But reflection on the real financial needs of the populations has been limited. The laurels which were awarded to microcredit have today multiplied so that it is often mistaken for goodness itself. In such a context it seems presumptuous to question its supposed merits. If microcredit is by nature good, how is it possible to put into question the social responsibility of those who spread this financial technique? On the contrary, they should be considered de facto benefactors of humanity even if some of their credit agents behave in the field like belligerent loan sharks (Perry 2002; Fernando 2006; Fouillet et al. 2007).

It seems to us not only completely wrong, but also irresponsible and dangerous to pretend, like Jacques Attali, president of Planet Finance, that "poverty could be globally eradicated by the general and professional development of microfinance which will also represent in the future a tremendous market for commercial banks" (AEF 2006: 115). In the short term, such a belief can allow some microfinance operators and their promoters to easily attract funds. It can also allow opportunistic and even rent-seeking behaviors. However in the long term, none of the stakeholders (microfinance providers, but also investors, donors, public authorities, etc.) have an interest in maintaining such an illusion. It becomes imperative to denounce the illusions and myths of microcredit.[5] The supposed merits of microcredit are generally based on the myth of the "poor entrepreneur." It would be enough to give "capital" to the poor through microfinance in order to let the entrepreneurial potential, present in every human being, unfold. The complexity and the diversity of microfinance impact studies have largely contributed to reinforcing this myth. Scientific rigor demands costly and lengthy procedures which are generally not adapted to the constraints and needs of the practitioners; the context and intervention modalities limit the range of the comparison and make any generalization difficult (Wampfler et al. 2006). Yet, all the impact studies based on thorough fieldwork give the same results: microcredit smoothes income, facilitates the management of household budgets and stabilizes small businesses, and in this it is very useful. But microcredit does not fight poverty and cannot pretend to. At most, this financial tool can increase the range of choices and opportunities available to the poor, stabilize and diversify their all too often irregular sources of income, and improve an often laughable productivity record.

In many countries, the poor have access to a range of informal financial services (family, neighbors, life insurance, private lenders, savings accounts, employers, etc.[6]). Such services are costly and sometimes dangerous because they are a source of strong dependence, even bondage (Guérin 2006), but they exist. What is mostly lacking is the technical and commercial capacities giving access to viable markets, and in many cases the market itself. To imagine that the market can expand ad infinitum because of a global demand induced by micro-loans is equally utopian. When credit is used to buy goods manufactured outside the area where the borrowers live (medicine, for example), there is virtually no increase in local income and resources flow out of the community. Only local currencies (like the WIR system operating in Switzerland since the 1930s, but the development agencies do not support such systems), would allow a local growth in income through an "endogenization" of credit. This small contribution of microcredit to additional productive investments and the income drain on the local economies also explain why microcredit can lead to over-indebtedness since in many cases microcredit does not create any additional income.

There are several limitations to micro-entrepreneurship. Low profit margins are a very common occurrence, with strong variations from one sector to another (for example, animal breeding): the success obtained here is absolutely not transposable elsewhere. There are many examples of rapid saturation of local markets and substitution effects (each new business is a threat to a neighboring business). This occurs mostly because of the lack of local purchasing power (because there are no clients), but also because of the lack of competitiveness in relation to manufactured products, or because of mimicking behavior leading to a surplus of some goods although their demand is low (lacking experience, and being afraid to take risks in developing a new product, entrepreneurs imitate their neighbors). Also, the strongly hierarchical functioning of the local markets is a constant problem. Monopolies or quasi-monopolies are often the case and the position of petty entrepreneurs looks like disguised outsourcing, with often very precarious working and living conditions. Finally, let us note the difficulty of the poor to switch to entrepreneurship because of a lack of competence, of social network, a lack of access to information or because of psychological and social attachment to agriculture or paid employment, which are considered not only a source of dependence but also of protection.[7] One forgets too often that in many Southern countries the majority of the population remains dependent on agriculture, from a material point of view as well as psychological – this can be observed in South Asia and in Africa (World Bank 2007). Agriculture is not a regular activity and the income it generates can fluctuate greatly from one year to another, notably because of weather conditions. Following a natural disaster, a drought, flooding or cyclone, the family's investment potential is reduced, the workforce unemployed, the debt burden and bondage increased, etc. But then microfinance responds very poorly to the demands and risks of agricultural activities (Cirad 2002; Morvant-Roux 2006). More generally, the successes realized by microfinance on a domestic level imply very specific dealing with local conditions of production and consumption as well as geographical constraints: high population density with purchasing capacity, specialization in products of integrated commodity chains where purchasing is guaranteed, producers' cooperatives or associations facilitating access to the market, etc.

To become an entrepreneur, even on a very small scale, means first of all to take a risk. And yet, the most materially deprived people live in a very vulnerable situation. This is the reason why a high percentage of microcredit is used to cover emergency spending (health care, nutrition and housing, ceremonies, repaying old and costly debts). In this microcredit is useful, but these expenses prevail over investments and risk-taking behaviors and they do not generate wealth, contrary to common belief. The success stories of various borrowers which are naively posted on Internet sites are media instruments and not serious proof. Why is it that Bangladesh, the market most saturated by the microcredit supply (and where the 20 largest microcredit institutions are located, operating for more than 20 years, affecting 21 million families – that is to say 105 million people out of a total population of 147 million inhabitants), remains one of the "least developed countries"? The poverty rate officially measured by the percentage of the population earning less than a dollar a day is still 36 percent in 2000, as it was in 1992. The statistics published at the last Microcredit Summit suggest that Bangladesh is approaching the Millennium Objectives (Daley-Harris 2006). But no statistics on income are mentioned. What is stressed is the decrease in the fertility rate and the increased political participation of women. These results are very good news, but they do not at all demonstrate that poverty is declining in the economic sense of the term (which is the first indicator of the Millennium Objectives). Is this "progress" in "human" development a consequence of microcredit, or is it rather the result of demographic and political changes in the Bangladeshi society, in which case it cannot be attributed to greater financial inclusion?

Failing to increase the income of the poorest substantially, microcredit can lead to their over-indebtedness and create more drama than hope among the most destitute. In India for example, at the beginning of 2006, the country witnessed a wave[8] of suicides by women, clients with a heavy debt burden who had been harassed by unscrupulous credit agents (Fouillet 2006; Roesch 2006). The Indian case, sometimes accused of being the "bad boy" in matters of microfinance, is probably the most poignant but not exceptional: some areas of Bangladesh and Bolivia (Navajas et al. 2000) also record numerous examples of over-indebtedness due to microcredit.

2.2 Clarifying the objectives of microfinance: What is the target population? What are the services?

Financial inclusion as wide as possible (a condition of socially sustainable development) implies first of all the ability to clarify microfinance objectives and to truly make the distinction between the fight against poverty (to which microfinance cannot pretend) and the fight against financial exclusion. This clarification of objectives and of the targeted populations is a first step towards social responsibility. Financial institutions (particularly commercial banks) can find a niche in the microfinance sector without having to cloak themselves in the dignity of the fight against poverty. Many people who are not poor do not have access to essential financial services. In any case, an increasing number of microfinance organizations, under the pressure of profitability, distance themselves from clients with low income, especially those with very low income (Balkenhol 2007). It is therefore a mistake to confuse the fight against poverty with the fight against financial exclusion if we want to understand the position of the different stakeholders of the sector and the consequences of their intervention.

According to the data compiled by Claessens (2006), a bank or savings account is used, on average, only 26 percent of the time in countries with average or low per capita income, with very important variations between urban and rural areas. In countries with very low per capita income, this percentage does not exceed 10 percent, while it is close to or even exceeds 90 percent in most countries with high per capita income. For example, there is less than one banking institution per 100,000 inhabitants in Ethiopia, Honduras and Madagascar. In comparison, Austria, Belgium or Spain have more than 50. The percentage of households having a bank or postal account in Denmark is more than 99.1 percent; in Tanzania it is only 6.4 percent. Among 900 million

Africans, only 4 percent have a bank account and 1 percent have received a bank loan (Claessens 2006). The percentage of the population having a bank account is 10 percent in Egypt and 40 percent in the Philippines (van Oosterhout 2005: 66). Even in countries where the average per capita income is the highest in the world, there are people who have very limited access (almost nil) to financial services, indispensable for survival in their own country. But it is true that in most European countries, in Japan, the United States, Canada, Australia and New Zealand, the poverty line and the financial exclusion line usually merge (Gloukoviezoff 2006).

In other words, in developing countries, the population which does not have access to financial services is much larger than the "poor" population. To understand this, let us imagine a three-tiered pyramid. At its base are the populations permanently below the famous poverty line. Contrary to common belief, microcredit is only rarely concerned with such clients.[9] Above this poverty line (second category) are the populations which are chronically poor: they enter and exit poverty regularly. For them, savings and insurance services are often more useful than microcredit. Finally, the third category (between the "chronically" poor and the top of the pyramid) represents the populations which are not financially excluded. They are often small producers, entrepreneurs and employees. Generally, they are the ones who can really benefit from microcredit.

Many instruments are now available to evaluate the degree of poverty of microfinance clients. Yet, because of the lack of human and financial resources, and perhaps also because this would damage their image as an institution "at the service of the poor," very few microfinance organizations apply rigorous criteria for a precise definition of the supposed poverty and vulnerability of their clients. Many merely declare that they are active in rural or suburban areas with populations which have a very high proportion of low per capita income. That is why there is so much confusion about the targets of microfinance for many players far from the field. This confusion is problematic for a very simple reason: it amounts to denying the strong social inequalities which characterize societies with a high rate of poverty, including those on the local level, thus reinforcing the obvious risks of inequality. For instance, as far as microcredit for "productive" activities is concerned, cases of loan misuse by the better-off are not uncommon, and the very widespread exclusion of agricultural activities from long-term financing to the benefit of trade and transport. When microfinance targets above all clients above the poverty line, and in the absence of any additional measures for providing basic services to the poorest, there is a strong risk of reinforcing inequalities. This is demonstrated, for example, in various case studies brought together by Jude Fernando (2006).[10] Microfinance alone can therefore not pretend to be an ethical form of solidarity.

2.3 Performance and social rating

For some microfinance providers, thinking about the social dimension of microfinance is not new, even if the usage of the term "social responsibility" is much more recent. In the English-speaking world, the debates of the 1990s focused mostly on the opposition between "minimalist" and "maximalist" microfinance, the first limiting itself to the supply of financial services, the second integrating financial services in an altogether larger range of services supposed to guarantee a better impact on the clients and therefore often considered more "social" than the former. The debates were for a long time (and still are in part) focused on the degree of poverty of the target population, the "pro-poor" microfinance organizations being considered more "social" than the others. Different evaluation methods to measure the degree of a client's poverty have thus emerged during the 2000s.[11] In the French-speaking world, the thinking on the social dimension of microfinance seems to have been more innovative; for example, with the distinction between microcredit and "solidarity-based finance" introduced during the 1990s by practitioners as well as by some researchers.[12] At the practitioner's level, the solidarity-based finance project, supported by the Fondation pour le Progrès de l'Homme (led by the Cerise network and bringing together microfinance organizations from all the continents), has played a leading role in spreading this notion. Defined by the players as having the mission "to use the financial instrument for sustainable development," solidarity-based finance wants to differentiate itself from "pre-banking" microfinance (which confines itself to the fight against financial exclusion), as much in regard to its mission, vision, identity and capacity as to its behavior (Chao-Beroff and Prébois 2001). The necessity of taking into account local social networks (getting inspired by them and reinforcing "positive" social capital), becoming aware of the complexity of the client's needs, and finally coordinating with other forms of development policies are some of the declared priorities.

More recently, and again at the initiative of the Cerise network, the debate has shifted to "social performance," adopted today at the international level by most of the networks involved in microfinance. Breaking with the dual approaches used up to now (social versus commercial or banking; "minimalist" versus "maximalist"; the fight against poverty

versus the fight against banking and financial exclusion), Cerise proposes to assess the social performance of microfinance organizations not
in terms of agenda or results only, but in terms of coherence between
the agenda, the means employed, the action fulfilled and finally the
results – effects and impacts (Lapenu and Doligez 2007). The proposals
of Labie (2006), when he asks questions about the conditions necessary for an "ethical" microfinance, go in the same direction. Noting
that microfinance organizations have various objectives and constraints,
he suggests analyzing the legitimacy and ethical dimension of microfinance interventions and particularly their operating mode (more or
less commercial approach, more or less cooperative and participatory,
shareholder versus stakeholder, etc.), not in the absolute, but here again,
according to the objectives and the intervention environment. For example, the issue of subsidies, the allocation of profits (if any), the degree
of client "participation" – these are choices which are not "good" or
"bad" in themselves, but which are contingent on the objectives and
the socioeconomic, cultural and local political characteristics.

This type of approach, very demanding since it implies a minimum of
analysis which has to be constantly updated, seems particularly appropriate to us because it avoids hasty and dogmatic judgments. To evaluate
the degree of social responsibility by referring to legal status makes no
sense; we will come back to this later. It is the same for the announced
objectives, which in no way reveal the actual results obtained. Recent
research conducted in the Indian context based on empirical, in-depth
studies shows how the setting up of a finance system able to redistribute
wealth in a sustainable way is not only a very complex task, but evades
any established model (Guérin et al. 2007). In the Indian case, the so-
called "community-based" approach is not necessarily more egalitarian
than the one which is called "capitalist" (we use here the terms used
by the practitioners), even if the former pretends to have more ambitious political and social objectives than the latter. The difficulty of
conceiving and proposing quality services, really meeting the needs of
the populations, is the deciding factor here, but then it implies specific capacities which the microfinance organizations lack, whether or
not they are in the "community-based" movement. Bringing into play
"participation," often claimed as a determining factor of social viability
and therefore of the microfinance organizations' social performance (in
particular through so-called "community-based" initiatives), proves to
be very ambiguous, and does not necessarily contribute to the empowerment of the populations, nor to a better quality of financial services.
The political action of the microfinance organizations (lobbying, actions

and voices for basic rights, etc.), often desirable from a normative point of view, is sometimes also ambiguous since it can easily transform itself into the instrumentation of the populations.

Following the pioneering work of Cerise, many initiatives dealing with the issue of social performance have seen the light. Cerise and the Imp-Act Consortium have each separately worked out management and measuring tools for social performance meant to be used by the microfinance organizations, the ultimate objective being a self-evaluation and then a modification of their own practices in order to improve their social impact. The first tests of the tools worked out by Cerise among a sampling of diverse microfinance organizations (whose common goal is to question their own practices, and this is far from being systematic among microfinance practitioners), confirm the importance of a pragmatic, noncategorical or statutory approach. These tests also highlight characteristics related to status, size and geographic location or to implementation in a rural or urban environment, but without any emerging hierarchy (Lapenu and Doligez 2007). For example, NGOs have a tendency to distinguish themselves by a more pronounced targeting of the poorest cooperatives by the attention they grant to the "social capital" of their members, while commercial microfinance organizations put more emphasis on social responsibility toward their staff. One can also observe that the small microfinance organizations look first of all at developing their targeting strategy, while the bigger ones want to diversify their actions in favor of an "enlarged" social strategy: targeting the quality of the services and the reinforcement of social capital.

Parallel to the self-evaluation initiatives of social performance, two working groups were formed in 2005 whose aims are to combine and coordinate these different experiences. The first one (Social Performance Task Force) brings together a group of players interested in the social performance of microfinance (practitioners, researchers, donors, investors, rating agencies) whose aim is to develop exchanges on this subject. The second, organized by the donors (CGAP Donor Working Group on Social Performance), has given itself the mission of strengthening coordination between the backers, taking into account social performance and working on benchmarking indicators. These two groups came to a common definition of social performance in microfinance. This definition enlarges the concept of social performance beyond the mere targeting of the poor to integrate notions of social responsibility and development of "capabilities."

The conceptual framework developed by Cerise and used by the Social Performance Task Force has four dimensions. The first deals with the degree of poverty and financial exclusion of the targeted population. The second with the quality of the services (judged according to their speed, proximity, transparency, adaptation to needs, and access to nonfinancial services). The third is about establishing relations of trust with the clients and strengthening their "social and political capital." It is evaluated according to the following criteria: transparency and information sharing; involvement and participation in meetings and decision-making; access to training programs; and supervision of the organization's functioning. The question of "empowerment" is also discussed, measured in terms of specific training, participation of the clients in collective action, etc. The fourth dimension is specifically called "social responsibility of the institution" and is aimed at the employees (training, social protection, etc.), the clients (evaluation studies, adaptation of the services, life insurance, measures in case of natural disasters) and finally the local community (compatibility with local sociocultural values, etc.).

Let us finally mention the growing interest expressed by microfinance information platforms (especially the Microfinance Information Exchange – MIX) and by rating agencies (PlanetRating, M-Cril, Microfinanza) on this question: they are also currently testing indicators of social performance, meant to be coupled with financial indicators intended for social investors. In microfinance, as in other areas, the reliability and importance of social rating naturally raise many questions: the difficulty of collecting data (what is the degree of reliability of self-evaluation or of quick audit procedures?), excessive and arbitrary simplification (in matters of indicator choice as well as in their judgment), normative judgments not necessarily adapted to local sociocultural circumstances, etc. As stressed by Lapenu and Doligez (2007) in their assessment of the recent initiatives of social performance (both have contributed much to the development of the tools elaborated by Cerise on social performance), it is too early to measure the real impact of these initiatives: is it an opportunity effect which eases the stakeholders' conscience through a so-called "objective" demonstration of social impact, or rather an instrument at the service of new forms of governance and regulation?

One should distinguish here between rating and self-evaluation. The initiatives of the rating agencies are meant to be entirely standardized and more or less imposed by the investors on the microfinance organizations; one fears that they will contribute not only to strengthening the standardization of practices, but also to reinforcing the media aura around microcredit. The perspective that has been gained today in the area of social responsibility from social and environmental rating methods of the corporate sector is hardly encouraging. It is well known that most of the enterprises merely issue a social and environmental assessment, without altering their practices or changing their strategies (Alberola and Richez-Battesti 2005). The self-evaluation initiatives of the microfinance organizations (stemming from a voluntary initiative where the indicators are revised according to each context, while fitting into a common grid allowing comparison), are no doubt promising with regard to the evolution of the practices and regulation modes via consultation processes and public debate. If such efforts are very praiseworthy, they have nevertheless the drawback of limiting themselves to microfinance providers. However, all the players in the financial chain are concerned: clarifying the role of the various stakeholders seems to us an essential condition of any effort in terms of social responsibility.

2.4   Clarifying the role of the stakeholders

We have said repeatedly: microfinance is not by nature a "good" or "bad" action. It all depends on the conditions under which it is applied. In the same way, there are not in the area of microfinance "good" players and others (for example, commercial banks) who would be by nature, or more precisely because of their status, harmful or corrupting these good intentions. To study social responsibility in matters of microfinance, it is therefore indispensable to clarify the activity and role of the different players according to their own institutional capacity. Here too, one should compare the declared goals of the institutions and the precise impact of their interventions. The confusion about the status of the players and their respective, effective roles is widespread. Some come from private organizations with nonlucrative goals; others from the public sector, local, national or from bilateral or multilateral cooperation, applying administered programs; others, finally, from financial institutions with lucrative goals. These different players can act together and complementarily or by subsidiarity. This brings us to the simplistic, classic opposition between public and private, state and market. Having or promoting a particular status (for example, nonlucrative) does not guarantee that the practices are supportive. On the other hand, having a commercial status is altogether compatible with attracting public subsidies and private funds covering huge deficits, as it can be with solidarity modes of intervention.

Today, one can observe a growing interest in microfinance by the "market" and private investors. It is here that supply and demand meet. On the one hand, capital holders seek new opportunities all the time (whether loans, capital share or risk coverage). On the other hand, the demand for financial services by the populations is growing and micro-finance providers, in order to meet this demand, constantly seek new financing modalities, and try more and more to free themselves from the constraints of subsidies. Muhammad Yunus, in his speech delivered at the Nobel Prize Award ceremony in December 2006, strongly criticized the commercialization of microfinance, prompted by the massive arrival of profit-making, private players in the sector. According to him, the financial interests of commercial banks would "pervert" microfinance, considered "positive" by nature. The objective of the different players of society, including financial institutions, should essentially be to eradicate poverty, microcredit being a central element in this strategy.

However, one should not be shocked because financial groups seize the opportunity to spread their services among populations that have been financially excluded up to now. Offering sound investment opportunities to their clients is their *raison d'être*. Conversely, why should we ignore the predatory behavior of some microfinance credit agents, even of some so-called nonprofit organizations?[13] And why should banks' intervention in this area be more prone to criticism than other forms of investments they make? Why should it be viewed positively that the Danone Group, in association with the Grameen Group, invests in Bangladesh to sell one of its yogurts, while the investments of some banking groups in the microfinance sector would be viewed negatively? Is it because the commercial banks take a portion of the market in a fast-expanding sector? Profit opportunities which can be socially useful exist in microfinance. Opportunities exist for investors accepting high risks and wanting to diversify their portfolios. These are profitability niches. Important opportunities exist for those seeking ethical or solidarity investments. In order to avoid misunderstanding and simplistic accusations, it seems indispensable to clarify the different types of investments and support from microfinance organizations and their various programs in order to know their precise aims, in particular regarding the income level of the clients and their degree and forms of financial exclusion. Conversely, the commercialization of microfinance can have extremely bad effects. Such effects have already been observed and must be denounced.

Before describing in detail the improper practices of commercialization, let us emphasize that the introduction of foreign investments (whether private funds in the form of investment or assistance, or public funds) is not always a priority in developing countries. A 2004 study conducted by the International Monetary Fund showed that among 44 sub-Saharan countries, 40 had cash surplus problems (Saxegaard 2006). Funds are not lacking, it is the capacity of the local financial institutions to reinject this money into the local economy which is lacking. More than North–South fund transfers, the countries among the poorest in the world (in terms of per capita income) often need more international and local guarantee funds encouraging the local banks to grant loans. The International Guarantee Funds of Geneva are an example of this; there you can find side by side the Soros Foundation, local collectives and activists from Swiss cooperative and mutual organizations. Today there are around 60 international guarantee funds like this all over the world. It is also the social responsibility of financial players to question the effects of certain forms of external financing in some countries. Finally, some subsidies and investments would certainly be more effective in promoting larger financial inclusion by supporting services other than credit, like migrant remittances and micro-insurance products, savings services and networks, as well as retirement funds. It is also a responsibility of microfinance donors and investors to question the specific financial needs of the different population categories.

2.5 The illusions and risks of the commercialization of microfinance

A tendency today aims at transforming microfinance organizations into "banks for the poor," which pleads not only for the automatic refinancing of financial markets, but also for the uncapping of interest rates. But this position is unrealistic if one wants to impose it on all models of microfinance. Who is going to believe that the deregulation of interest rates is the right solution to develop small loans for the benefit of the poor? In Peru, some microcredit institutions give loans at 5 percent a month (meaning 60 percent a year) and yet they cover only populations above the poverty line in urban areas. They let the subsidized NGOs intervene in very poor rural areas where the population density is low and illiteracy high. In Brazil, microfinance players demand that limits be set on the interest rates offered.

The productive and profitable use of microcredits spearheads the justification of the so-called "liberation" of interest rates. But this idea is wrong for situations where microcredit is used for "social" expenses and where there is no increase in income. It is also wrong for agricultural activities where profitability (rough margin on the investment) hardly reaches 8 percent per farm for vegetable production and 15 percent for animal breeding. To imagine that in the near future it will be possible to make the investments profitable for a great number of microfinance institutions is a mistake; in the long run, the whole sector will be weakened when it realizes that it is unable to attain this objective. Subjected to immediate constraints, many players choose to lie or to lie to themselves and to benefit from a fashionable, positive image in relation to other, more traditional forms of intervention. These are less attractive since they cannot make believe that tomorrow the poor will be able to repay.

To pretend that the lender's risk is low because the repayment rate is high is to ignore the fact that many organizations (among them the Grameen Bank of Bangladesh) reschedule many loans, or authorize the repayment of late monthly installments with a new loan. One should not get bogged down in the observation of individual risks (that some organizations cover with insurance and obligatory savings – that is to say by drawing considerably on the income of these populations), but analyze the collective risks related to the climatic, political, economic, etc. conditions which severely hit some regions and which make some microfinance institutions which seemed recently solid suddenly collapse when outside support does not cover the internal deficit.

To believe that microfinance could be very profitable leads one to adopt strategies hardly compatible with the objective of reducing inequalities, necessary to the very decrease of poverty itself. The concentration of microfinance supply in areas with solvent clients (sometimes they are almost middle class), is a common strategy and spatial inequalities in the microfinance supply at the national level are also very common. In India, two states from the south (Andhra Pradesh and Tamil Nadu), classified among the wealthiest, contain almost three-quarters of the supply (Fouillet 2007). In many African countries, the microfinance supply is concentrated in areas with very heavy urban density (Cirad 2002). The rural areas are deserted even if they are the poorest, while some urban areas are subjected to fierce competition very prone to over-indebtedness. This is particularly evident in Benin (Martinez 2007). In Mexico, the rural areas of the poorest districts were so neglected by microfinance providers that in 2001 the federal state, supported by the World Bank, set up a program to support and structure intermediary financial services (Arredondo Casillas 2001).

2.6   Do financial institutions, especially commercial banks, have a responsibility to fight poverty? Can one privatize it?

We have highlighted as much as possible the current confusion between the fight against poverty and the fight for financial inclusion. Rejecting this confusion is especially important for those who do not want to confuse the social responsibility with the social performance of an institution. Why should a financial institution intervene directly in the fight against poverty? Is not its primary social responsibility to contribute to the financial inclusion of the population, without discrimination, and to make sure its actions do not increase poverty? Financial institutions, including banks, play a major role in financial inclusion for two reasons: certainly, because their purpose is to offer financial services and often they exercise a monopoly in this field (particularly regarding savings), but also because the financial exclusion that they induce can systematically generate risks. They have to act so that their actions will not have side effects, by providing for one group of people while not contributing to the deterioration of the living and survival conditions of the other; for example, by facilitating over-indebtedness.[14] But, if financial institutions have a responsibility in matters of financial inclusion, it is difficult to understand why they should have a particular responsibility in the fight against social exclusion and poverty. Insofar as financial services have a determining role in contemporary society (including in developing countries and towards the poor), their responsibility today is much stronger than in the past. But this responsibility, let us repeat, is limited to providing financial services adapted to the diversity of needs and without discrimination. It seems dangerous and pointless for them to go beyond this role.

Well beyond the financial sector, one has to note that very frequently now companies from the corporate sector, in the name of this famous social responsibility, go far beyond their original operating field. Today, it is more and more frequent that large companies acquire foundations or services (often linked to communication services) in order to invest in the field of social responsibility. And microfinance can thus benefit from corporate subsidies which have nothing to do with the financial sector (for example, a car manufacturer like Ford can support projects in this field). This type of practice, which is ultimately related to private charity, varies according to the countries, their traditions and legislation. Very often, it is financial considerations (income or inheritance tax) which motivate this mobilization of resources.[15] Nevertheless, these actions, a priori generous, contain in themselves the very dangerous seed of neoliberal management of societies, and a strong incoherence in the interventions because of total decentralization of the decisions they imply.[16] We enter here into a new plutocratic world. The problem with these voluntary contributions, as well intentioned as they are, is that there is no democratic control of the resources allocated.[17] Big companies mobilize and structure themselves, notably by setting up subsidiaries, avoiding taxes and social security deductions while simultaneously investing an increasing share of the surplus they enjoy in operations which more or less escape the control of public authorities (represented by democratic institutions).

What is the risk of entrusting development financing to private sources having compassion and charity as their origin? That it is not the most useful and urgent initiatives that are taken, but those based on an empathy principle and on very partial information about the problems and needs. One counts on the sympathy of the public, but public opinion is volatile, ephemeral, fluctuating, more often motivated by emotion than reason. How then to ensure the equity and the sustainability of their actions? In some countries, for example in the US, the national preference is strong; but the corporate sector, particularly corporations of international stature, cannot limit their social responsibility to the national arena. A strong risk of this kind of tendency (if these initiatives are not supplementary to, but substitutes for, public action), is that the areas of intervention are determined by the media's construction of a positive image of the corporate sector, and not by the most urgent and overwhelming needs of the populations. Without a regulatory institution[18] assessing the impact of the actions taken, charity has to be regarded as a dangerous last resort. A recent example illustrates perfectly the limitations and improper practices followed by private charity: the sizeable influx of funds after the tsunami in South Asia, while the earthquake in Pakistan a few months later only provoked general indifference. Worse, the recent audits of the management of tsunami funds reveal a total lack of transparency in regard to management as well as in decision-making, and also interest collusion with large companies.

The main foundations finance their "social" actions thanks to financial benefits derived from investments which can provoke contradictory effects. Let us take the example of the Gates Foundation: there is no ethical assessment of the financial investments which yield the profits meant to finance the charitable actions of the Foundation. One can very well imagine that this Foundation endangers people because of the pollution generated by the companies in which it owns shares, and on the other hand, that it acts against the environmental consequences of these programs, this time through the Foundation thanks to the surplus generated by the shares. Under these circumstances the Foundation gives with one hand what it takes with the other, and in some cases gives less than what it takes. These private initiatives can also be duplicated by public initiatives. There is also the risk that this kind of financing usurps the responsibility of the states. This criticism about the intervention of United Nations organizations has already been made in the past. Such interventions contribute to weakening the foundations of democracy or to actually preventing its emergence. Democracy, contrary to what is often asserted, was not born historically from the market, but rather from the tax system. It is interesting to draw a parallel between the contemporary private charity, strongly supported by this notion of "social responsibility" and the European private charity of the nineteenth century. The difference is that at that time one had to deal with the shortcomings of a social state which did not yet exist; today, one substitutes oneself in lieu of the state, putting oneself outside any democratic control. It is not elected assemblies and democratic governments or bureaucrats who decide on the allocation of resources anymore, but those who have the financial means. That private institutions support citizen initiatives, but in so doing overstep the field of their own social responsibility (which should be determined only by their particular sector of activity), stems perhaps from good intentions. But such interventions run the risk of undermining the very foundations of democracy.

Conclusion

The craze for microcredit has the merit of drawing the attention of public authorities and financial institutions to the extent of contemporary financial exclusion, in a context where financial services have become a real necessity. Luckily today, microfinance is not limited to microcredit. Savings, insurance, remittances, are often more important services than credit (even if they are still much less developed). Nevertheless, where there is a lack of hospitals, clinics, medicine and doctors, it is not micro-insurance which by some miracle will make them spontaneously appear just by expressing this need. Therefore the question may be asked: which purpose are injunctions and subsidies to create micro-enterprises serving when there is no viable market, and when nothing is done to create one or to link the entrepreneurs to the market if it exists? To ensure the financial transfers of the migrants, there must be effective security in the transfer of information and funds. To propose services functioning very badly or which are non-existent is more a source of dysfunction than efficiency. The need for primary education and adult literacy, health care and risk prevention, clean drinking water, toilets and means of communication, are, for the poorest, more urgent than the large-scale diffusion of small loans. It would be wrong to imagine that good practices in microfinance are an answer to these problems. Microcredit cannot in the short term meet the needs of the most destitute. Some economic theories have made us believe that growing inequalities in income and property (that microcredit could provoke in populations well below the poverty line), are a first condition for a global increase in income. After 50 years of development policy and a quarter of a century of increasing economic inequalities, such theories are completely obsolete today. This means that a really voluntary policy in the fight against poverty and inequalities cannot be based exclusively on a microfinance tool.

To speak of the social responsibility of microfinance players means first and foremost to give up a generous but unfortunately dangerous and utopian vision. Microfinance is an instrument to fight against financial exclusion, and nothing else. To speak of the social responsibility of microfinance players is also to question the responsibility of all the stakeholders. Microfinance providers are obviously in the forefront, and the nonlucrative status of many of them does not exclude them from being questioned regarding their social responsibility, far from it. But the donors, investors, public authorities, experts and researchers also share a part of the responsibility. Concerning the commercial financial institutions, their involvement cannot be immediately condemned under the pretext that they are seeking profits; however, this involvement has to be seriously monitored and regulated. The social responsibility of the private sector is a necessity today as never before, but to be satisfied with charity can in no way ensure a social justice system worthy of the name. It is democracy which is at stake.

Notes

1. The study conducted in this chapter is based on the work carried out under the FIP research program on microfinance, at the IRD (UR LPED and UR *"Travail et Mondialisation"*), the IUED, and as part of the "entrepreneurship" network of the AUF. For additional studies in French, see Fouillet et al. (2007).
2. See http://millenniumindicators.un.org/unsd/mifre/mi_goals.asp.
3. See http://millenniumindicators.un.org/unsd/mifre/mi_goals.asp, objective 7, target 11.
4. We should mention that the phenomenon is not as recent as it seems, since it revives the financial services of the "mutualist" and cooperative movement of the second half of the nineteenth and the beginning of the twentieth century. On the lessons of this comparison, see Dichter (2006, 2007).
5. See in this regard Dichter (2007), Fernando (2006), Servet (2006) and van Oosterhout (2005).
6. See for example Bouman and Hopes (1994), Adams and Fitchett (1992), Guérin (2006), Servet (1995) and van Oosterhout (2005).
7. There are very few in-depth studies actually demonstrating the role of microfinance in the domain of entrepreneurship. A recent study made in India (Roesch et al. 2007) shows how much trouble paid agricultural workers experience when turning themselves into entrepreneurs.

8. About 60 according to the Indian press. Following this crisis at the beginning of the year, a regional microfinance association (The Andhra Pradesh Mahila Abhivruddhi Society, APMAS) has made an assessment of the situation. The report reveals that two-thirds of the clients from the district where the incidents happened did not know the interest rate and the calculation method of the loan they had taken. Even more serious and revealing of the bad effects of spreading microcredit, dependence on private lenders and big landowners has increased in more than a quarter of the cases following the granting of microcredit. We will not expand here on the mental and physical torture which made headline news.

9. See for example Hulme and Mosley (1996) and Gentil and Servet (2002).

10. See also Morvant-Roux (2007) for a case study in Mexico, and Guérin and Palier (2005) for various case studies in India.

11. See for instance the tools used by CGAP, Grameen Foundation, USAID.

12. See, in particular, the publication of the Walras Research Center.

13. We allude here to very badly adapted microcredit services leading periodically to the over-indebtedness of the borrowers. Over-indebtedness is often masked by a rescheduling of loans or by having recourse to other loans, particularly informal, and therefore an impoverishment of these so-called microcredit beneficiaries harassed by credit agents.

14. It is surprising to see microcredit impact studies on income focused on the average income of the local population, without questioning the eventually increasing disparities among the people and the increasing marginalization that microcredit creates for sections of the population.

15. Theses incentives are strong in the United States, while nonexistent in Sweden, for example.

16. Adam Smith himself in book V of *The Wealth of Nations* criticized this privatization of the management of society by using the example of the East India Company and by comparing the management modes of the French and English West Indies. This perfectly illustrates the fundamental distinction that needs to be made between neoliberalism and liberalism.

17. Contrary to the ancient time when the political community imposed necessary expenses on the rich – see in this regard Paul Veyne (1976).

18. Comité d'Aide au Développement (2003: 60).

References

Adams, W.A. and Fitchett, D.A. (eds) (1992) *Informal Finance in Low-Income Countries*. Westview Press, Boulder.

AEF (2006) *Rapport moral sur l'argent dans le monde 2006*. Association d'Economie Financière, Paris.

Alberola, E. and Richez-Battesti, N. (2005) "De la responsabilité sociale des entreprises: Evaluation du degré d'engagement et d'intégration stratégique," *La Revue des Sciences de Gestion*, 211–12: 55–71.

Arredondo Casillas, E. (2001) *Estudio para el Desarollo y fortalecimiento de Instituciones Financieras Rurales en las Regiones Marginadas de Oaxaca*. SAGARPA-Banco mundial, Mexico City.

Balkenhol, B. (ed.) (2007) *Microfinance and Public Policy, Outreach, Performance and Efficiency.* Palgrave Macmillan/ILO, London.

Bouman, F. and Hospes, O. (1994) *Financial Landscape Reconstructed: the Fine Art of Mapping Development.* Westview Press, Boulder.

Chao-Beroff, R. and Prébois, A. (2001) "Solidarity Finance," Working Paper of the Working Group on Solidarity Economy, http://finsol.socioeco.org/en/documents.php.

Cirad (2002) "Le financement de l'agriculture familiale dans le contexte de libéralisation: quelle contribution de la microfinance?" International Seminar on Agriculture Financing, Dakar, 21–24 January.

Claessens, S. (2006) "Access to Financial Services: a Review of the Issues and Public Policy Objectives," *The World Bank Research Observer*, 21/2: 207–40.

Comité d'Aide au Développement (2003) "Fondations philanthropiques et coopération au développement," *Dossiers du CAD*, 4/3, OECD, Paris.

Daley-Harris, S. (ed.) (2006) *State of the Microcredit Summit Campaign Report 2006.* Microcredit Summit Campaign.

Dichter, T. (2006) "Foreign Aid Policy: Old Wine in New Bottles," *Foreign Service Journal*, June, 28–34.

Dichter, T. (2007) "A Second Look at Microfinance. The Sequence of Growth and Credit in Economic History," The Cato Institute, Center for Global Liberty and Prosperity, Development Policy briefing paper 1: 1–13, February 15.

Fernando, J.L. (ed.) (2006) *Microfinance. Perils and Prospects.* Routledge, London.

Fouillet, C. (2006) "La microfinance serait-elle devenue folle? Crise en Andhra Pradesh," *Espace Finance*, Gret-Cirad, April 25.

Fouillet, C. (2007) "Spread of the SHG Banking Linkage Programme in India," International Conference on Rural Finance Research: Moving Results, held by FAO and IFAD, Rome, March 19–21.

Fouillet, C., Guérin, I., Morvant-Roux, S., Roesch, M. and Servet, J.-M. (2007) "Le microcrédit au péril du néolibéralisme et de marchands d'illusions. Manifeste pour une inclusion financière socialement responsable," *Revue du Mauss*, 29: 118–32.

Gentil, D. and Servet, J.-M. (eds) (2002) "Microfinance: petites sommes, grands effets?" *Revue Tiers Monde*, 172: 729–890.

Gloukoviezoff, G. (2006) "From Financial Exclusion to Overindebtedness: the Paradox of Difficulties of People on Low Income?" in Anderloni, L., Braga, M.D. and Carluccio, E.M. (eds) *New Frontiers in Banking Services*, Springer-Verlag, Heidelberg and Berlin, pp. 191–212.

Guérin, I. (2006) "Women and Money: Multiple, Complex and Evolving Practice," *Development and Change*, 37/3: 549–70.

Guérin, I. and Palier, J. (eds) (2005) *Microfinance Challenges: Empowerment or Disempowerment of the Poor?* "Sciences Sociales" Series, French Institute of Pondicherry.

Guérin, I., Fouillet, C. and Palier, J. (2007) "La microfinance indienne peut-elle être solidaire?" *Revue Tiers-Monde*, 190, July–August.

Hulme, D. and Mosley, P. (1996) *Finance against Poverty*, vol. 1. Routledge, London.

Labie, M. (2006) "Questions éthiques dans la gestion des organizations de microfinance", paper presented at the seminar "Ethics and Microfinance," Centre de Recherche en Ethique Économique, Lille, December 8.

Lapenu, C. and Doligez, F. (2007) "Mesure des performances sociales: les implications pour le secteur de la microfinance," *Recma*, 304: 46–62.

Martinez, O. (2007) "Microfinance et territoires dans le sud-est béninois: approche en terme de risque au travers d'une vision discriminante de l'espace." Université de Provence Aix–Marseille I, LPED, Marseille, 13 pp.

Morvant-Roux, S. (2006) "Processus d'appropriation des dispositifs de microfinance: un exemple en milieu rural mexicain." Thèse de doctorat en sciences économiques, Université Lumière Lyon 2.

Morvant-Roux, S. (2007) "Microfinance Institutions' Clients Borrowing Strategies and Lending Groups Financial Heterogeneity under Progressive Lending: Evidence from a Mexican Microfinance Program," *Savings and Development*, 2: 193–217.

Navajas, S., Shreiner, M., Meyer, R., Gonzalez-Vega, C. and Rodriguez-Meza, J. (2000) "Microcredit and the Poorest of the Poor: Theory and Evidence from Bolivia," *World Development*, 28/2: 333–46.

Perry, D. (2002) "Microfinance and Women Moneylenders. The Shifting Terrain of Credit in Rural Senegal," *Human Organization*, 61/1: 30–40.

Roesch, M. (2006) "Des dettes jusqu'à ne plus en vivre," *Bulletin d'Information du Mardi*. Gret–Cirad, Espace Finance, April 11, http://www.microfinancement.cirad.fr.

Roesch, M., Guérin, I., Kumar, S., Thanuja, M., Venkatasubramanian, M. and Ponnarasu, M. (2007) *Impact Assessment of the Peblisa Project in Tamil Nadu*. Report for the International Labor Organization, French Institute of Pondicherry.

Saxegaard, M. (2006) "Excess Liquidity and Effectiveness of Monetary Policy: Evidence from Sub-Saharan Africa," IMF Working Paper 06/115, May, 50 pp.

Servet, J.-M. (ed.) (1995) *Epargne et liens sociaux. Etudes comparées d'informalités financiers*. AEF / Aupelf-Uref, Paris.

Servet, J.-M. (2006) *Banquiers aux pieds nus: La microfinance*. Odile Jacob, Paris.

Van Oosterhout, H. (2005) *Where Does the Money Go? From Policy Assumptions to Financial Behavior at the Grassroots*. Dutch University Press, Utrecht.

Veyne, P. (1976) *Le pain et le cirque. Sociologie historique d'un pluralisme politique*. Editions du Seuil, Paris.

Wampfler, B., Guérin, I. and Servet, J.-M. (2006) "The Role of Research in Microfinance," *Revue Dialogue*, 37: 11–25.

World Bank (2007) *World Development Report 2008: Agriculture for Development*. World Bank, Washington.

3
Explaining the Take-Off of Socially Responsible Investment

Pasquale Arena

The interest with which academics, politicians, companies and the wider community are observing ethics and socially responsible investment demonstrates how relevant this issue has become. We are living through a complex cultural process which is trying to overcome the dualism of ethics and finance. Hence, academic literature has been paying more and more attention to the exploration of the relationship between finance, ethics and society, especially over the last few years. At the same time, companies and practitioners are testing new corporate social strategies. Nowadays, the role of the government is changing; both government and community need more help from companies. While companies are committed to developing socially responsible investment, ethics emerges as the most powerful instrument of moral legitimacy for companies, able to stimulate stakeholders' participation and help both companies and stakeholders to move towards the common good.

Today finance, one of the keys to a nation's economic development, must redefine itself in relation to the anthropological and social–environmental context in which it works, and which provides both opportunities and constraints. In fact, the community would like to be more involved in influencing decision-making, and although prestigious sustainability indices are valuable, they are not enough to get the approval and guarantee the participation of the community. On the other hand, ethics has to make every possible effort to develop a comprehensive, morally correct model of the individual that could affect socially responsible strategies. Can we then explain the take-off of SRI as a new social deal?

Introduction

The aim of this chapter is to try to answer the question: why has socially responsible investment (SRI) come to life? This question will encourage us to reflect on the individual and on the process of democratic management related to stakeholder theory[1] and to the interpretation of "moral legitimization," intended as a means to justify the correct strategic management of firms. The next step is to observe if social and ethical reasons, depending on the inner equilibrium of the individual and developing SRI, can help companies and stakeholders optimize[2] their decision-making, improving company equilibrium over time.

This study will highlight the socioethical dysfunctions which cause company crises and which can even challenge the very existence of the firm. The processes involved in democratic management are becoming more and more important over time, because of the growing and maturing judgment of the whole community; when it does not feel protected against certain company behavior the community reacts, sometimes violently. In other words, if the world of finance wishes to embrace a real nonfictitious social–ethical strategic vision and to prove that ethics is not at odds with financial strategies, it has also to take up the challenge of promoting a wider decisional participation. Financial institutions should take into consideration not only the ideas and interests of the stakeholders, as representatives of the individuals, but at the same time, it has to consider the ideas and interests manifested by people as individuals.

The consideration of such a view which plays a crucial role in the strategy–policies–results pathway, has to be made explicit and presented through corporate social disclosure, to prove that the best possible decisions have been taken by the company and that, consequently, they deserve the social consensus of the whole community. The roots of this consideration can be found in the ambivalence of people as human beings and as members of a specific community.

3.1   The take-off of SRI and self-respect

The gradual development of the stakeholder model has increasingly stressed the growing interest of companies towards the community.[3] Such interest has mainly emerged as a new model of common development, inspired by a shared and wider conception of ethicalness/morality; or as a prevalent atomistic conception of selfish nature deriving from the existential features of the company,[4] namely instrumental features. These two possible evaluations demonstrate that corporate strategic management has opened its vision to a broader participation, favoring the enlargement of democratic processes. More specifically, in order to grant business success, exclusive logics of observation of the well-known "competitive system" have been associated with logics of observation of another system called "social," integrating them progressively in a single set of analysis.

Why is it happening? Why is all this attention paid to the stakeholder model? How can we justify the take-off of SRI? What are the reasons behind this phenomenon? Can we detect these reasons in the roots of the philosophy of life? We think we may find the answer by looking at the complex human inner equilibrium as a sort of spiritual balance.

Trying to explain our point of view based on a thoughtful examination of the individual, we claim that the complicated balance of the human being is strongly influenced by interpersonal relationships. These intertwine differently within various contexts, and are linked to the individual's power positions. Contexts such as family, friendship, work and social groups give rise to a personal logic of respect towards others, logic which interacts at the same time with self-respect. We have to observe how mutual respect can affect a sort of "relationship of equivalence," at an interior (spiritual[5]) level among the parts, which behave in different contexts. The relationship of equivalence expresses the balance of advantages and disadvantages that each one can reach within these contexts. We have tried to schematize the main forms and contexts related to the term "respect":

1. *Respect for love* – in the family context everyone behaves as a donor. No one thinks of being rewarded for his/her work or for his/her money but everyone expects cooperation from the others. This cooperation could consist of, for example, getting satisfaction from a child doing well in an exam or assisting a family member during a stay at hospital, etc. However, the relationship of equivalence is reached with tolerance and flexibility. This is due to the high level of love among the individuals, which explains why spiritual balance is reached;

2. *Respect for affection* – in the context of friendship the mechanism of donation could be identical to the family context but, in such a case, it would be extreme. Here, instead, everyone acts regularly as a temporary donor, giving something and expecting the same courtesy in return or, in any case, to be rewarded sooner or later. It is not based on the exploitation of others but it represents a positive attitude to building and developing a working relationship or sharing recreational activities. Compared to the family context, the relationship of

equivalence is reached with lower tolerance and flexibility. The spiritual balance depends greatly on the character of the individual;

3. *Respect for interest* – in the context of the business world, it is usually difficult to find subjects acting as donors. The basic rule is one of exchange. Goods and services for money, whose amount has to exceed the sum of inputs which have been used to produce them. The level of respect for interest depends a lot on the expectations of profit. Such a level of interest ranges from aggressive forms of interest (for high profits) to other more moderate ones (for reasonable profits). The relationship of equivalence is satisfied when everybody is gratified by their own interest, which derives from the balance between advantages and disadvantages. There is low tolerance and flexibility. The spiritual balance is based on the personal interpretation of the purpose of economic activity in which he/she is involved;

4. *Respect for sensitivity* – in the social context we can identify an inner respect towards institutions, nature, people, future generations, and so on. It derives from the different perceptions of the possible damage that can be caused by one's own behavior. The relationship of equivalence appears more complicated and difficult to reach, with reference to the overall evaluation of advantages and disadvantages which could follow. The spiritual balance depends on personal convictions, beliefs and religions.

These four forms of respect are interconnected with the concept of self-respect, symbolizing the barycenter of the general spiritual balance of the human being, which emerges from thoughtful examination: giving rise to a figure that can be schematized as a four-leaved clover of spirituality. Despite the main interconnection mentioned above (respect for love in the family context, respect for affection in the friendship context, respect for interest in the business context and respect for sensitivity in the social context), these four forms of respect can also be found in other contexts. For instance, we could find forms of respect for affection or sensitivity also in the business context. Similarly, we could find forms of respect for interest in the friendship context or in the social context.

In such a problematic framework,[6] self-respect is the "equilibrium," namely the inner peace, which results from multiple interactions lived by the individual when an overall coherent moral system embraces a number of insightful moral checks and balances.

So what? Thanks to companies, civil society has been growing and widening, but it is worried about the decay in human values and wishes to optimize, with an adequate blend, both personal intangible and tangible values together with the common good. Hence, institutions have been driven to put forward recommendations on corporate social responsibility, sustainable development and socially responsible investment as well. The point is that community-matured awareness – according to several historical contexts – previously did not require as many transparent documents in order to evaluate the ethical behavior and the social–environmental choices made. As democracy expands, the community wishes to play a more important role than in the past. Public consciousness is growing into public usefulness. People, as individuals, would like to count more within the company decision-making system to reach inner peace. The individual, acting as stakeholder, would represent in this way a vehicle through which several levels of respect could be harmoniously combined. Generally speaking, the moral legitimization could be interpreted like the stakeholder capacity to give positive answers to the represented communities, whose people desire to find peace of mind, namely self-respect in the private sphere, interacting with respect in the public sphere. The increase of stakeholders promotes a wider democracy and even a greater optimization of SRI, viewing it as a contextual and qualitative dimension. Besides, the consumer, as an individual, continually tests the company's reliability through their choice of products and services. Observing the chains of financing, production and distribution, the consumer tries to obtain his/her self-respect with awareness relying on companies who they believe deserve his/her trust.

Has the take-off of SRI already started? We would say so, looking at socially responsible mutual funds, solidarity funds, pension funds, microfinance, ethical banking, charitable banks, ethical financial intermediation, savings bank foundations, insurance broker ethics, green shares, socioethical districts, etc.; but the question is, is the stakeholder model sufficient to grant the company equilibrium over time? In other words, when can SRI be considered adequate with regard to the demands of the whole community?

3.2   SRI and the decision model

As mentioned before, the stakeholder approach compared to other models has touched the heart of people, giving them the chance to participate indirectly in company decisions. In practice, attention has been focused on stronger organized power and pressure groups; on one hand, this attention would seem to allow negotiations to reach a balance and, on the other hand, to get closer to the whole community.[7] However, in this way, a wider participation of the whole community in choosing the areas and the levels of intervention would appear satisfied.

In fact, what occurs in real business life is a little different. Indeed, in the case of weak and/or missing representatives from legitimate areas of interest, the general framework of negotiation, approach and participation of the whole community would be truly differentiated. In a sense, it is also possible to reflect on the importance and the effects of the modality through which consent[8] among the parts is reached. Taking the concept to the extreme and simplifying it in a way, at least five modalities of consent management[9] can be identified:

1. *Persuasive modality* – respect is given to the opinions of the interlocutor who is able to interact among the parts. Privileging the confrontation, he/she is prone to dialogue and is determined not to dominate, he/she investigates solutions in the light of common agreement with the prospect of reciprocal improvement;
2. *Antagonistic modality* – whenever somebody in a superior position (e.g. at work context) disagrees with the point of view of a subordinate, he/she escapes the confrontation. This plunges to the roots of contractual power, trying to exploit changing positions of strength which places the negotiation in context, both temporary and permanent, of advantage over the subordinate;
3. *Emulative modality* – this modality makes the most of the skills of persuasion by putting forward positive examples of the advantages available to others. Relying on self-conviction, the emulative modality does not pursue a true confrontation nor uses a position of strength but concentrates on showing the reasonable opportunities which the interlocutor could obtain;
4. *Manipulative modality* – it utilizes persuasive levers (different from the real interests at stake) which derive from an advantageous social relational position placed on affection, friendship, trust, gratitude, etc. It is the exercise of a mediated power, far from confrontation, based on the investigation of possible exploitable areas of personal exclusive advantage;
5. *Authoritative modality* – due to a hierarchical relationship which avoids any sort of confrontation, this modality manifests itself using the levers of punishment and prize-giving to reach consent. The assumption of such a relationship is that the interlocutor is unable to contribute to reaching consent as he/she is at a lower hierarchic level.

Although considering the possible interferences among the above modalities that, evidently, must be regarded as trends, we believe that among them, the persuasive modality would seem the only one applicable in dealing with stakeholders. In the other instances, the stakeholder model would not rest on a solid base, that is, it would not be able to operate in a participatory context of the represented communities. This would debase the pillars of the theory itself, as participation is the evidence, and not only the intentions, of the recognition of moral legitimization. On the other hand, this participation also shows all its effectiveness through the fecundity it bears. Thus, why does the persuasive modality not take off? Or would it seem to function only with stronger and better organized power and pressure groups?[10]

Therefore, the theoretical model is surely a good start, we could say a landmark, and it highlights a linear route which is viable but, following progressive social–ethical maturity acquired by the whole community, it seems to us that it could be refined and compared in the light of an ethical dilemma, which originates from the ambivalence of man. This dilemma can better explain how to examine the problem more deeply and how to try to develop a reasonable solution. The questions we ask ourselves are:

1. Are we sure that the represented areas and their priority levels are actually those required by the whole community?
2. Are we sure that the areas are adequately represented?
3. And, again, are we sure that participation is real or is mediated by groups?

Such questions do not necessarily suppose preconceived negative responses, but wish to mention a possible divergence, interpretable as ethical/moral dysfunction,[11] between manifesting one's own thought of "being like an individual" as to of "being like a part of a community." Two kinds of divergences can be identified:

1. Absolute dysfunction or misunderstood ethicality – which emerges in the functioning of the democratic systems exploiting present power set-ups, information asymmetries and one's own abilities, and also in dialectic, to persuade others in order to obtain personal advantages;
2. Relative dysfunction or ethicality of belonging – which appears linked to a different ethicality/morality expressed by the group in relation to its aims as to the ethicality/morality expressed by the individual interconnected to the philosophy of life.

The investigation on the ethical dysfunction can be seen as a heuristic approach which, on the one hand, has new opportunities to seize, and, on the other, a dialogue more oriented towards the individual.

3.3 The different pathways of personal thought on SRI and respect

Following such arguments, it may be helpful to try to define using two different terms the two underlying states manifesting one's own personal thought in the two contexts: "being like a part of a community" and "being like an individual." This will be done while being aware of the difficulties and inaccuracies which arise when definitions are proposed.

In being like a part of a community, the subject refers to an organic community (i.e. stakeholders) united by relations privileging a certain interest. Such exaltation of interest, emphasizing the opinions of the same group, could result in not giving the right consideration to other significant areas, certainly for the logical and explainable circumstance of identification with the group. We are dealing with an almost exclusive dimension, which tends to dominate as a narrow mandate. The core objective of being like a part of a community is obtaining respect within the group.

In being like an individual, the subject, not referring only to an organic community, is potentially able to consider various aspects of remark/interest, a potentiality that originates from the circumstance of "morally" belonging to more organic communities. Therefore, there exists a multidimensional center that is able to mediate a wider balance. The core objective of the individual is reaching self-respect. According to the second assumption, the term "collectivity",[12] as synonymous of the whole community, may be used.

Falling in a philosophical excess and with all due reservation, we could state that the first approach would seem more oriented towards utilitarian theories, while the second would come closer to deontological theories.[13] To summarize:

1. When the company considers the needs demonstrated by stakeholders,[14] it addresses the whole (or almost the whole) community seen as a set of represented and recognized organic communities – stakeholders aim at reaching respect within their own group;
2. Whereas when the company considers aggregating in homogeneous areas the levels of interests related to the needs of single individuals,

it addresses the whole community seen as a set of single users – individuals aim at reaching self-respect.

In order to be sure that our point of view is clearly exposed, we should think of the difference between manifesting the vote openly or in secret. In the first case, it is possible to verify whether the components belonging to a group have followed the assigned directives and, as a result, the expressed opinion can be shared or not by the voter. In the second case, it is more difficult to control the votes, since it is not possible to directly identify the subjects that expressed their opinion, only the final result, the voter's personal opinion should not be affected by the group to which he/she belongs and, therefore, it should be interior and real. In other words, convergence in the final results may or may not exist but there is no doubt that the creation processes for manifesting the needs, and therefore the opinions, are different. Nonetheless, it is reasonable to suppose a divergence especially for the reasons outlined previously, which in our opinion is due to the presence of ethical external/internal group variables.

In general, such relative ethical variables are not necessarily ascribable to incorrect behaviors – which could still be present and consequently emerge in a phase of comparative observation – but to natural and matured beliefs, typical of groups. Those groups reinterpret the thought expressed by single individuals, filtering it and consequently modifying it in the areas and subareas of interest and on the levels of priority.

3.4   SRI as a contribution of companies to the whole community

It is well known that there is a certain lack of confidence towards companies.[15] Even though it is possible to distinguish different development processes in diverse economic–geographic spaces, companies are often observed as ambiguous entities with the exclusive aim of profit for their shareholders[16] or, at least, prevalently oriented toward the creation of economic value for them, for example, by offering stock options to executives. However, the above scenario shows that mediation in obsessively pursuing profit can find a compromise, on the one hand, by considering a social responsibility and SRI of the enterprise and, on the other, in envisaging a series of shared rules, which guarantee ethical behaviors.[17] The epochal turning point is just around the corner. This is a question of reorienting the route, considering that such ethical behaviors are not confined to a single dimension but can be considered as superordinate elements, which pervade both internal and external dimensions of companies. Therefore, it seems clear that ethical behaviors have their own criticality when they infer from the social responsibility (degree of accountability) of enterprises, that is, when the company itself is recognized as a virtuous entity[18] oriented to pursue transactions (quantity/efficiency) and mutual dealings (quality/efficacy) as well.

The rediscovery of the company as a social–ethical entity is a watershed and a great challenge for the future;[19] such a challenge can be met if we consider man not only through his representatives but also as a single individual. In other words, an all-embracing socioethical company has not to recover an ethical–social function but such a function[20] has to be interiorized, that is, manifesting both mental and implemented attitudes in such a way as to prove the democratic participation formulated at an individual level.[21] Only in this way can the distance between the individual and the company be reduced by taking more democratic and more shared decisions;[22] this will trigger a virtuous circle that, on the one hand, will allow the enterprise to be influenced by the individual sphere of the person and that, on the other, will allow the firm to influence the individual field of the person and reduce social unease, the possible destructive effects of which are evident to everyone. Overcoming the opportunistic logic can happen in one way only: allowing the personal free expression of ideas of one's own morality, because the latter represents the true key to life.[23]

The opening of the company to society, enlightened by ethics, has to fit in with the spiritual balance that can be interpreted as self-respect. As participation in the social context is comprised of functional interdependencies among the contexts, which are synthesized at the level of the individual, it is convenient if not necessary to foresee personal mechanisms of involvement, which grant decision-making democracy. In our opinion, the social–ethical company embraces such aspects and is as a pioneer of an integrating/approaching process of the individual to the whole world of enterprises. This is even more crucial as the consideration taken by the company regarding the thought expressed of "being like an individual" – defined as an opinion of the collectivity – appears with a triple value:

1. *Political* – favoring an approach of companies to the individual and therefore allowing recovery of a misunderstood finality;
2. *Individual* – favoring the balance of man with himself (interior) through his social integration;

3. *Ethical* – favoring the decision-making democratic nature, the risks of incurring noncorrect behaviors are reduced.

But there is more. The social policies of the company have to make use of cooperation at the moment of the implementation in order to be successful. If the proposals/decisions are exclusively connected with representative groups, they cannot be interiorized at an individual level, creating a waste of resources, inside and outside of companies. That is, the implementing part of "being like an individual" in the three afore-mentioned political, individual and ethical values manifests itself in daily individual behavior and it seems critical in its various applicable fields. This is due to the coordinating mechanism based on the volun-tariness which acts not only on the enterprise but also on the users. Moreover, the expected possible coercive mechanisms and the likely con-trol instruments prove ineffective. Who better than the collectivity – as intended in the previous definition – can indicate more adequately the guidelines of identification of the social value of the company? However the social value of the enterprise is calculated, it has to consider the levels of importance expressed by the individual.

3.5   The solutions to the dilemmas in SRI

The main problem created by the stakeholder model is that of passing from the descriptive formulation to the prescriptive one, that is, when we determine the criterion with which to balance interests and diver-gent values.[24] The doctrine warns that it is necessary to consider all the stakeholders (multistakeholder approach[25]), even the weakest and the most emarginated ones, and proposes a contract solution (with a social contract[26]) in which, on an ideal level, each stakeholder will try to exchange positions with the others, reaching decision-making unanimity.

In its enunciation, the suggested theoretical model indicates the choice of a method that gradually, despite its problematic and complex nature, pursues a settlement of interests at stake. Being inspired by the iden-tification of the method, a slight chance to bring the absolute equity (utopian) closer to a relative equity (tendency to the real) appears: the contribution of the aforementioned collectivity model.

Considering and juxtaposing the stakeholder and collectivity models, it is their integration that can illuminate us in making the final deci-sion, where the key element for careful consideration has to be sought in the opinion of "being like an individual," which represents the inner socioethical balance of man mediated by moral balance. It deals with the search for a relationship of equivalence – mentioned above – where the reflection of the individual, unlike belonging to a single community, is revealed by considering the advantages and disadvantages of belonging to more groups with whom the individual interacts at system level – we mean as a complex agent – and that allow him/her to obtain the *pax* with himself/herself originating from the *pax* with the social life. In such a manner, the tempering of stakeholders' interests and, above all taking into account the conceptual validity of the model under discussion, their moral legitimization – proved by a process of idea creation which, originating from the reflection of the single individual, presents itself as more balanced – they both can lay the foundations on a minimum respect basis and the ethical criterion of the "social contract" would be unambiguous, easily and truly viable (possible application). Even doubting the full certainty of an individual's judgment (genuineness of expression), it would, however, give a greater guarantee of acting for the right reason and according to more democratic bases of reflection inspired by the centrality of the individual and, in any case, by the positiveness of man.

3.6 Suggestions for implementation

In such a framework, the development of a social–ethical strategic vision of the enterprise would have to include the following phases, aggregating opinions for homogeneous areas and levels of priorities:

1. Demand of the whole community (collectivity) – recognition of the social–ethical demand, following the track of the manifestation of thought expressed by the collectivity (individual), to be carried out through an actual census of personal ideas. Even though we can accept advanced statistical methodologies linked to information technology, as direction indicators to follow, the aim of the survey ought to be devoted to the whole community. This is due to the fact that in all underlying conceptual logic – addressed to the recovery of the participation of the individual in the sphere of the three aforementioned values (1) political–democratic (2) individual–moral (3) ethical–behavioral – the whole process has to pass through the metabolizing of being an individual as an active part of the whole community and not as a subject who is isolated or not deeply interested. In any case, we argue people should have the right to express their beliefs in those countries which are defined as democratic;

2. Demand of several communities – recognition of the social–ethical demand, following the track of the manifestation of thought

expressed by the community, to be carried out through a census among the representative groups (stakeholders);

3. Integration/weighting of the two emerging demands by companies in order to define the social–ethical demand;
4. Formulation of the social–ethical supply by the company;
5. Determination of the point of optimization between demand and supply with the identification of critical areas to prioritize when allocating resources, adopting policies and codes of behavior and the achieving of objectives in relation to the social–ethical value.

It is useful to specify that in phase (3) (integration/weighting of the two demands) the bases of the data to be weighed and the "weights" (the demand of the collectivity or the demand of the communities) can be exchangeable. The choice will depend on company consideration of the level of maturity (ability to discern the area), and level of ethicality (ability to behave correctly), since both levels are reached in relation to the local contexts. Facing a context considered mature and ethically correct, the initial base can be one of the community weighed by one of the collectivity as the levels of social and ethical sensitivity seem advanced (the interest groups are increasingly approaching more comprehensive considerations). In a less mature and ethically less correct context, the initial base is changed with that of the collectivity weighed by that of the communities (as the judgment of the individual seems less influenced by partisan pressures).

3.7   SRI as a growing trend generating a variety of choices

Finance must direct SRI in the right way: inspiring the socioethical vision of the company, seen as a reasonable interface between the understanding among SRI (company decisions) and social, ethical and environmental issues (cultural and personal values of whole community/collectivity). In other words, finance should improve understanding of the world through real-life values, rediscovering its neglected genetic code.

This pathway can likewise prove useful, apart from corroborating the moral legitimization and the social contract's tangible possibilities of success, for its illuminating ability to signal areas and levels of interest of the whole community (collectivity). This happens when thought is manifested at the individual level – enhancing, specifying with much more accuracy or even modifying the mission of the company – to all stakeholders, in particular to the local body and the so-called third sector (nonprofit organizations) as well. Similarly, this pathway triggers an active dialogue, which takes place not only between companies and stakeholders but also among the stakeholders themselves. We are referring particularly to local public bodies, such as regions, provinces and municipalities, and nonprofit organizations, which can intervene, cooperating in areas where resources are scarce, due to the need to pursue binding objectives, both accompanying companies and sharing skills.

The progressive streamlining and the collocation of the state's functions – due to the difficulty of obtaining significant results in certain areas in spite of efforts made, or, also, to bear in mind it is necessary not to intervene in an emerging conflict of certain values at least until a certain minimum level[27] – offer new scenarios of socioethical financial activities which can be developed by different entities that discover cofinalities, namely convergence aspects, as for the resources to be allocated and objectives to be pursued. Thus in a wider prospect and keeping in mind the unifying element of pursuing the common good,[28] enlightened by pervasive culture and participating citizenship, both for companies and individuals, it is possible to predict a greater interaction among all actors which not only proves useful for companies for the above-mentioned reasons (political–democratic, individual–moral and ethical–behavioral trivalence), but it starts a new way of thinking: ethical–responsible strategic philosophy. A philosophy that – passing from the vision to the implementation – on the one hand unites all, and on the other, obtains the individual's active participation, even involvement at an emotional level in sharing/partaking of choices, in daily behavior, allowing not only a more rational allocation of the country's total resources but also sound investments on the social level; also, it corrects imbalances contributing to social instability.

In our opinion, the common good does not regard only distributional equity among individuals who compose the whole community but regards, moreover, the main conception of social justice that the individual has within himself/herself. A conception that is comprised of complex relations and interrelations of equivalence of the different forms of respects and the modalities which pursue such forms,[29] figuratively represented in the field of spirituality's four-leaved clover of observed contexts.

Conclusion

Finance with its SRI, to be consistent, has to change its conceptual framework from maximization (quantitative/efficient dimension) to optimization (qualitative/efficacious dimension) in order to solve the ethical dilemma which originates from the ambivalence of man "being like a subject of a community" part of the community[30] and "being like an individual" part of the whole community (collectivity).

In the development of the conceptual model, an individual's opinion is considered more reliable (emerging perception) – as it acts at a critical level of moral thought, in comparison with an analysis led in the group (existing perception[31]) – as it is regarded as conclusive in order to reach self-balance in the field of the prefigured spiritual four-leaved clover of respect. It is inspired to be ethical and moral, which at the same time gives it a greater democratic nature and, therefore, greater social stability related to the reduction of potential conflicts. The ambivalence or rather the divergence tends to coincide in a nondefinable hypothetical point – the result of a target in a bristly learning path – when the ethical, cultural and social maturity/growth of the groups is such as to reduce or remove the ethical dysfunction: the distortions between personal advantages/disadvantages and common advantages/disadvantages and the modalities in which they manifest themselves.

Finance and SRI should take into consideration the real interests of the whole community, shown individually by its components, which, identifying themselves as who they are – not as people but as areas of interest – and what weight the stakeholders should have, they allow refining and renegotiation with the represented interests (stakeholders) in the company. That is without debasing, but revitalizing, finance's trust, mission, prosperity and development that professionally interpret the social phenomena even more, with a view toward pragmatic and continuous improvement.

In other words, such a path could transform risks into opportunities or notwithstanding reduce uncertainty by narrowing the gap between public and private spheres. In that way only will the contract between the organization and its stakeholders be considered legitimate, democratic, social, fair and efficient. It would seem an authentic pacific "revolution" which even other business forms cannot avoid, namely, public and nonprofit forms, which appear involved all the same, even if in their original diversity, by the effects (responsibility) that their behaviors provoke on the collectivity (society). Such processes of change, widening the common cofinalized space, put forward new scenarios of involvement especially among the three classical sectors (profit, nonprofit and public).[32]

Hence, we propose levels of pondered dynamic balances no longer in bordering systems but in interacting systems (network) in which – in a *continuum* that contains levels and different forms of "competition" and "collaboration," and that has as extreme points "wild competition" and "concerted cooperation" – we increasingly tend to orient ourselves toward a confrontation respectful of the rules and toward a possible optimization. SRI must chase modalities for consent management, centered increasingly on persuasion and sharing, as results of participation. SRI must be based on existential investigation, on ethics and on the effects that behaviors show toward society, in which the main lever of possible success appears increasingly positioned in the beliefs and the active involvement of the whole community.

Notes

1. They are studies masterfully developed by Freeman (1984) and, later on, by other authors like Donaldson and Preston (1995), Mitchell et al. (1997), Stoney and Winstanley (2001), etc.
2. In our opinion, it is time to substitute the word "maximization" with the word "optimization" in decision-making in companies. The way of thinking in maximization is a little bit different in respect to optimization. Maximization easily excludes the other – the needs of others – optimization includes the opinion of others.
3. For the moment, we intend the term "community" to be a synonym of collectivity. Later on, such coincidence will be removed.
4. Everyone remembers how troubled the financial markets were during the scandals involving companies like Enron, Worldcom, Global Crossing, Parmalat, Nortel, etc.
5. The term "spirituality" does not mean "religiosity" even if it influences the reasons of equivalence, but a way of thinking and behaving through which personal balance is reached. On this point, see Korthals Altes (1999: 40).
6. The difficulties in reaching rational choices, according to certain utility measurements related to morals, are referred to by Gold (2004: 180): "Criticism ranges from the impossibility of assuming that human beings perform calculations to maximise their satisfaction to the gross difficulties in measuring utility itself." Etzioni (1986), for example, highlights the point that there are at least two different utilities relating to morality, duty and pleasure, which are in conflict with each other. Such utilities cannot be reduced to a single concept of preferences. The concept of preferences itself, moreover, is very difficult to accept in view of the numerous special relationships which people have with those closest to them.
7. See Hofstede (2004) for an examination of the extent to which the less powerful members of institutions and organizations expect and accept that power is distributed unequally.
8. We use the term "consent" in a wide sense, as sometimes, as we will see later on, it is an imposition that consequently it is not possible to refuse. As for the imposed consent, see Melé (2005: 293): "According to Weber,

bureaucracy is the rational and highly efficient response to large-scale social systems. It is characterised by a strong sense of authority, carefully outlined and with clearly-defined hierarchical lines and staff positions, established formal relationship, formal patterns of delegation, a high degree of centralisation, narrow spans of management, a high level of specialisation and departmentalisation by function."

9. On this point see Coda (1988: 221).

10. Perhaps we could think that, even with the stakeholder model, we are recreating contexts in which the governance is obtained through the creation of a decision-making majority that according to Hayek (1986: 383) "does not implement what the majority wants." Here the author refers to what is required by the majority of the collectivity, observed as a majoritarian set of individual expressions "but only what each group of the majority has to concede to the others for having their support in order to get what we wish."

11. It is well known that such a complex problem is based on different concepts as morality, ethics, theories of ethics and ethical dilemmas.

12. For this term, see *The American Heritage Dictionary of the English Language*, 4th edn, 2006, published by Houghton Mifflin.

13. Rusconi (1997: 46) states: "We have seen that the utilitarian has got the problem of establishing if it is possible to compare the advantages of one part with the disadvantages of the other; the deontologist has got the opposed problem, that is it can extend too much the concept of fundamental right ...." On the relevance of theories, Ferraris Franceschi (2002: 24) states that: "For economic studies goals, the most significant ethical theories can be united in two big groups: the deontological ethics (expression proposed by Bentham) to indicate, in an etymological sense, the ethics of the duty and the utilitarian ethics."

14. Concerning the definition of stakeholder, see Freeman (1984: 46): "A stakeholder in an organization is ... any group or individual who can affect, or is affected by, the achievement of the organization's objectives."

15. The explosion of mistrust and the requirement of ethical norms reached a climax when faced with the financial scandals.

16. The demarcation between profit enterprise and nonprofit enterprise depends on an adequate interpretation of the goals.

17. On this topic, see Kaptein and Wempe (1998), Kaptein (2004) and Arena (2006).

18. For an interpretation of the enterprise as a social entity Zadek (2004: 29) writes: "Corporate citizenship is about business taking into account their total impact on society and the natural environment. Successful companies in the New Economy will engage effectively with key stakeholders in the markets for goods and services, finance, labour and political patronage. Corporate citizenship implies a strategy that moves from short-term transactions towards relationships that seek to capture stakeholders' loyalty by ever more surgical interventions that align profitable opportunities with their social identities and underlying values."

19. By the way, the thought of Zsolnai (2003), who supports the need for rethinking the moral logic of capitalism centered on market fundamentalism, is clear: the invocation of the free market as a single efficientistic mechanism to obtain a rational allocation of resources.

20. We want to underline the indispensable pervasive value of ethics more than an integration.
21. We are going to try and reduce the difficulties to pursue what Apel (1977: 207) defines as planetary macro-ethics when he exposes the different fields of ethics: "if we distinguish between a micro-field (family, marriage, neighbourhood), a meso-field (the level of national policy), and a macro-field (the general fate of humanity), we can easily state that the currently effective moral rules with all the people are always concentrated in micro-fields." In our thought, the meso-field is that in which the enterprise unfolds its activity.
22. We believe that the triggering of such a process happens through the legitimization of greater interests within the enterprise, associated with socio-cultural changes of the collectivity. As for such deep ongoing changes, Arena (2006: 30) writes: "Civil society grows and widens also with the enterprise, that we defined as collectivity matured before sleeping awareness and required more transparent documents in order to evaluate ethical behaviours and social choices. Democracy widens and the collectivity wants to have a greater importance compared with the past. It would seem that the common space of these big sectors, non-profit making, public and private, is widening and that, even if there are some distinctive characters of differentiation but instrumental on the economic level, there is a macro-trend: a convergence process in the field of big choices on allocation of resources and results to be reached."
23. This conceptual framework could be seen as an attempt, if not to solve, at least to reduce, what has been defined as the "ethical paradox in management" (Bouckaert 2004: 54). For such a purpose, the author states that: "Ethics is at the same time a resource to enhance economic efficiency by reducing opportunism; on the other hand, it is a source of a new sophisticated opportunism and therefore a source of economic inefficiency." Bouckaert continues: "But a paradox is a puzzle that can be cleared up. We may solve the contradiction by making a distinction between ethics as moral commitment, which is always driven from within, and ethics as a management tool, which refers to a system of norms or procedures introduced by external incentives (sanctions, social pressure or economic incentives). By substituting moral commitment by ethics management through all kinds of external pressures and incentives, we undermine the moral commitment. The point is that we can only introduce ethics in business by combining intrinsic motivation (genuine moral commitment) with operational implementation." On criticisms of the multistakeholder approach centered on opportunism, also see Sternberg (1999) and Jensen (2001).
24. Crane and Matten (2004: 54) state that: "Thomas Donaldson and Lee Preston (1995) provide a convincing argument that there are in fact three forms of stakeholder theory: Normative stakeholder theory – this is a theory which attempts to provide a reason why corporations should take into account stakeholder interests. Descriptive stakeholder theory – this is a theory which attempts to ascertain whether (and how) corporations actually do take into account stakeholder interests. Instrumental stakeholder theory – this is a theory which attempts to answer the question of whether it is beneficial for the corporation to take into account stakeholder interest."
25. For example, see Sacconi (2005) and Hemmati et al. (2002).

26. The balancing ethical criterion, inspired by impartiality and efficiency, sees the social contract as an agreement in which a unanimous choice is ideally reached by the representatives of the stakeholders. That would be obtained through a strong motivation to participate and cooperate to reach an agreement according to the process of putting oneself (as a stakeholder), in turn, in each other's place. On the philosophical contractual approach and on the correspondence to the mathematical model of the contracting cooperative game, see Sacconi (2005).

27. On these aspects see Crane and Matten (2004: 55): "During the late 1980s and 1990s, we witnessed a growing tendency toward the privatization of many political functions and processes formerly assigned to government. There were two major reasons for this development: Government failure; Increasing power and influence of corporations."

28. On the orientation towards the common good, see Argandona (1998: 1093–102). Very illuminating is the recall of common good by Melé (2005: 300) who, inferring the principle of subsidiarity, quotes the Vatican Council II (1965), *Const. Gaudium et spes*, no. 26: "the sum total of social conditions which allow people, either as groups or as individuals, to reach their fulfilment more fully and more easily."

29. According to Rawls (2004: 24), "In general, we cannot determine a conception of justice only on the base of its distributive role, as this role could be useful in identifying the concept of justice. We have to take into consideration its wider implications: since also if justice, being the most important virtue of institutions, has got a certain priority, it is also true that, conditions being equal, a conception of justice is preferable to any others when its wider consequences are more desirable."

30. According to Zadek's opinion (2004: 221): "*After all, business behaviour and performance embodies, codifies and in many ways reinforces our own ambivalence as to how we trade off personal and collective interests, both now and into the future.*"

31. We are referring to the Kantian utilitarianism of Hare (1981). There are two perceptive levels of criteria: the level of intuition and the critical level of moral thought. The first level comprises the set of values which each individual brings along but is not able to solve the dilemmas; the second, instead, higher than the first, allows us to evaluate different conflicting intuitions and to judge them choosing the best one, according to an order of critical priority and not intuitively overriding priority.

32. They are topics focused on centrality of the individual and the environment, in which he/she lives, relates and works. It is crucial for example that the cofinality pursues the advance and the progress of humanity according to the principles of dignity and equity: the great challenge of the common topic of knowledge development.

References

Apel, K. O. (1977) "L'Apriori della comunità della comunicazione e i fondamenti dell'etica. Il problema d'una fondazione razionale dell'etica nell'epoca della scienza," *Comunità e comunicazione*. Rosenberg and Sellier, Turin.

Arena, P. (ed.) (2006) "The Contribution of Ethical Codes in the Development of CSR," in *Corporate Social Responsibility: Scientific Development and Implementation*, Aracne, Rome.

Argandona, A. (1998) "The Stakeholder Theory and the Common Good," *Journal of Business Ethics*, 17/9–10: 1093–102.

Bouckaert, L. (2004) *Spirituality and Economic Democracy*, ed. by L. Zsolnai. Kluwer Academic Publisher, Amsterdam, pp. 51–8.

Coda, V. (1988) *L'orientamento strategico dell'impres*. Utet, Turin.

Crane, A. and Matten, D. (2004) *Business Ethics, a European Perspective*. Oxford University Press, New York.

Donaldson, T. and Preston, L. E. (1995) "The Stakeholder Theory of the Corporation: Concepts, Evidence and Implications," *Academy of Management Review*, 20/1: 65–91.

Etzioni, A. (1986) "The Case for a Multiple-Utility Conception," *Economics and Philosophy*, 2: 159–83.

Fernández Fernández, J. L. (2004) *Finanzas y Ética, La Dimensión Moral de la Actividad Financiera y el Gobierno Corporativo*. UPCO, Madrid.

Ferraris Franceschi, R. (2002) "Etica ed Economicità," in Cavalieri, E. and Giappichelli, G. (eds) *Economia ed Etica aziendale*. G. Giappichelli editore, Turin, pp. 21–34.

Freeman, R. E. (1984) *Strategic Management: a Stakeholder Approach*. Pitman, Boston.

Gold, L. (2004) *The Sharing Economy: Solidarity Networks Transforming Globalisation*. Ashgate, Aldershot, Hampshire, UK.

Hajek, F. A. V. (1986) *Legge, legislazione e libertà*. Il Saggiatore, Milan.

Hare, R. M. (1981) *Il Pensiero Morale*. Il Mulino, Bologna.

Hemmati, M., Dodds, F., Enayati, J. and Mcharry, J. (2002) *Multi-Stakeholder Processes for Governance and Sustainability: Beyond Deadlock and Conflict*. Earthscan, London.

Hofstede, G. (2004) *Cultures and Organizations: Software of the Mind. Intercultural Cooperation and its Importance for Survival*. McGraw-Hill, New York.

Jensen, M. C. (2001) "Value Maximization, Stakeholder Theory, and the Corporate Objective Function," *Journal of Applied Corporate Finance*, 14/3: 8–21.

Kaptein, M. (2004) "Business Codes of Multinational Firms: What Do They Say?" *Journal of Business Ethics*, 50/1: 13–31.

Kaptein, M. and Wempe, J. (1998) "Twelve Gordian Knots When Developing an Organizational Code of Ethics," *Journal of Business Ethics*, 17/8: 853–69.

Korthals Altes, E. (1999) *Heart and Soul for Europe: an Essay on Spiritual Renewal*. Van Gorcum and Comp, Assen.

Melé, D. (2005) "Exploring the Principle of Subsidiarity in Organisational Forms," *Journal of Business Ethics*, 60/3: 293–305.

Mitchell, R. K., Agle, B. R. and Wood, D. J. (1997) "Toward a Theory of Stakeholder Identification and Salience: Defining the Principles of Who and What Really Counts," *Academy of Management Review*, 22/4: 853–86.

Rawls, J. (2004) *Una teoria della giustizia*. Feltrinelli, Milan.

Rusconi, G. (1997) *Etica e Impresa: Un'Analisi Economica Aziendale*. Clueb, Bologna.

Sacconi, L. (2005) "Verso un Modello allargato di Corporate Governance," *Guida Critica alla Responsabilità Sociale e al Governo d'Impresa*. Bancaria, Roma.

Sternberg, E. (1999) "The Stakeholder Concept: a Mistaken Doctrine," Foundation for Business Responsibility, Issue Paper No. 4. London.

Stoney, C. and Winstanley, D. (2001) "Stakeholding: Confusion or Utopia?: Mapping the Conceptual Terrain," *Journal of Management Studies*, 38/5: 603–25.

Zadek, S. (2004) *The Civil Corporation: the New Economy of Corporate Citizenship*. Earthscan, London.

Zsolnai, L. (2003) "L'etica e l'homo economicus," *Impresa and Stato*. Franco Angeli, Milan, 65/4.

4
Socially Responsible Investment: Global Convergence or Local Divergence?

Céline Louche

Introduction

The chapter conceptualizes the mechanisms that sustain the development of socially responsible investment (SRI). Empirical observations show that SRI has gained unprecedented momentum worldwide in recent years and has diffused on a global scale. The idea of SRI started several hundred years ago (Domini 2001). It was at that time a curiosity and a niche market phenomenon. No one would have ever expected SRI to grow beyond a marginal movement and cross national boundaries. Today, in 2008, SRI is embraced in most countries around the world – Europe, Asia, Latin America and Africa. The diffusion of SRI is characterized by the increase of SRI funds. Between 1995 and 2007, the number of SRI funds in the US has almost multiplied by five, from 55 to 260 (US SIF 2008) and by eight in Europe from 54 to 437 (SIRI Group 2002, 2007). Another feature of the development of SRI is the diversification of SRI-related products. SRI shifted from one single approach based on exclusion, also called "sin stocks," to multiple approaches offering different strategies able to satisfy a variety of growing demands.

Furthermore, a number of signs suggest that SRI is being mainstreamed through the development of SRI twin products. It consists in applying some specific aspects of SRI activity which does not necessarily mean labeling the product SRI as such. The most popular are the integration of environmental, social and governance (ESG) factors into mainstream financial investment products and the development of an engagement policy that is an active ownership and shareholders' right. This approach is being increasingly embraced by institutional investors especially in the UK and the Netherlands (Eurosif 2006). Another significant sign of mainstreaming is the launch in 2006 of the Principles for Responsible

Investment (PRI) by the United Nations. PRI signatories commit to adopt and implement considerations of ESG issues into investment decision-making and ownership practices. As of February 2008, the PRI had been subscribed to by some of the world's largest institutional investors, asset managers and related organizations totaling over USD 10 trillion under management.[1]

Despite the good news and high hopes, the development of SRI is raising some concerns about the huge diversity on what SRI exactly is and means, in terms of strategies and methods but also definition and criteria (Eurosif 2006). Recently, some studies have suggested that SRI varies greatly at local level (Gond and Boxenbaum 2004; Louche and Lydenberg 2006; Bengtsson 2007). Authors do not question the diffusion of SRI as such, but put forward that SRI is not as homogeneous and uniform as previous research and reports may have suggested. The growth and expansion of the SRI field raise the question of convergence versus divergence. In other words: how far is SRI traveling along a path of global convergence in practices and understanding, and conversely, to what extent is the influence of specific factors shaping SRI into a variety of forms and definitions?

The objective of the chapter is to address this question. It investigates which of the convergent or divergent mechanisms are at play in the development of SRI. The convergence mechanism posits that SRI is under a globalization process where practices and understanding are becoming increasingly similar across the world. SRI practitioners are left with limited discretion in terms of structuring and managing. For the defender of the convergence mechanism this process is key for SRI to remain and continue to be efficient and effective. The divergence mechanism, in contrast, argues that the development of SRI is embedded in the national context and can be diffused only in the extent to which it is adapted to fit the local specificity. As a consequence, SRI must be adapted according to the local context including rules, political systems, social norms, and economic development leading to a variety of SRI practices across nations. Although the two mechanisms may be seen as opposite and to some extent contradictory, I would like to argue that both are taking place. Indeed the very survival of SRI in the future may well depend on the interplay between convergence and divergence forces.

The chapter proceeds as follows. The first part introduces the field of SRI: definition, development and key actors. The next two parts develop the two mechanisms, that is global convergence and local divergence. For each of them, a theoretical framework and illustrative evidence are provided. The fourth part focuses on and discusses the interplay between the two mechanisms. Finally, the last part draws some conclusions and provides implications for further research.

4.1   Socially responsible investment

The definition of socially responsible investment has led to fervent debates and discussions (Cowton 1994, 1998; Sparkes 1995, 2001; Anderson et al. 1996). For the purpose of this chapter, SRI is defined as the constructing and managing of investment funds through the use of social, environmental and ethical considerations in addition to conventional financial criteria. This definition allows consideration of the broad SRI including both SRI and SRI twin products. We can distinguish between SRI as a product and as an activity. It is a product in the sense that shareholders buy, hold or dispose of corporations' shares based on social, environmental and ethical criteria (Boxenbaum and Gond 2005). Only companies that are evaluated as socially and environmentally responsible can be part of the investment universe. It is important to note that as of today there are no standards defining what is and what is not an SRI product, although there are some attempts like the Ethibel Label in Belgium for SRI funds.[2] It is an activity in the sense that financial experts dispose of a range of both formal arrangements and informal conventions and customs in order to exercise SRI and thereby judge the corporate social responsibility of firms. To exercise this activity, several tactics have been developed which can be used separately or simultaneously.

SRI activity consists of three main approaches: screening, engagement and divesting.[3] *Screening* refers to the use of criteria to select companies to be part of the investment universe. There are two broad categories of screens. Negative or exclusionary screening is usually related to controversial business areas such as human rights, weapons, corruption, and controversial projects. Companies involved in such activities are excluded from the investment universe. Positive screening, also called the best in class approach, refers to the selection of companies on the basis of positive criteria, such as good governance, environmental management, climate protection, stakeholder dialogue, community awareness and outreach. *Engagement* consists in the practice of monitoring corporate behavior and seeking changes through dialogue with companies or through the use of share ownership rights, such as filing shareholder resolutions. The more confrontational approach of engagement is called shareholder activism. Dominant in the US, this approach is very limited in Europe where engagement is favored. And *divesting* is the act of selling and disposing of shares from a portfolio. This tactic is often viewed as the last resort.

The origins of SRI date back to the eighteenth century in the US (Domini 2001). For hundreds of years, many religious investors have actively avoided investing in certain kinds of enterprises by applying the exclusionary approach. In the 1970s, the SRI movement was revitalized and took a new form. Shareholder activism and divesting became important strategies to protest against and exercise power toward companies. During this period, SRI began to attract a considerably larger group of American investors mainly due to concerns about South Africa and the Vietnam War. The first social investment fund, the Pax World Fund, was launched in 1970 by the Methodist clergy. Since then the SRI movement has grown dramatically. The 2007 US SIF report on SRI trends states that 11 percent of assets under management in the US, or $2.71 trillion, are involved in SRI, representing an increase of 324 percent since 1995 (US SIF 2008). In Europe, SRI is much more recent. It emerged in the 1980s but only took off at the end of the 1990s. The first SRI fund, Friends Provident Stewardship Unit Trust, was launched in the UK in 1984. In 2005, SRI assets under management had reached 1.033 trillion euro (Eurosif 2006). Although four countries dominated the European market, namely France, UK, Sweden and Belgium,[4] by 2007 most European countries were offering SRI products.

Not only were funds created but also organizations and platforms related to the activity of SRI such as social rating organizations, Social Investment Forum (SIF) networks and conferences. Social rating organizations like EIRIS (UK), Vigeo (France), the SIRI Group (international), KLD (US), SAM (Switzerland), are ESG and ethical information suppliers and in certain cases sustainable index providers. SIF are membership networks for sustainable and responsible financial services. Their members include all types of financial institutions. As of December 2007, there were 12 SIFs all over the world including one European SIF, the Eurosif. The creation of these new venues provides platforms where activity is discussed, diffused and shaped. Other factors including new regulations such as the SRI Pension Disclosure Regulation in the UK (2000) or the launch of sustainable indices such as the FTSE4Good (2001) and Dow Jones Sustainability Index (1999) have also significantly stimulated the growth of SRI.

From these facts and figures, it becomes clear that SRI has acquired a social interest that is a public awareness of its legitimate place and purpose in society. The SRI movement has managed not only to maintain itself over time, but also to grow. In Powell and DiMaggio's words

(DiMaggio and Powell 1983), SRI has become an organizational field that is a set of organizations that constitute a recognized area of institutional life. The remainder of the chapter explores which of the mechanisms, global convergence or local divergence, is shaping or likely to shape the development of SRI in the future.

4.2 Global convergence

The global convergence mechanism is based on the theoretical approach of new institutionalism (Meyer and Rowan 1977; DiMaggio and Powell 1983; Meyer 2000). This approach focuses on how homogenization of institutional environments across national boundaries takes place and how regulative, normative and cognitive processes lead to more and more standardized and rationalized practices across industries and national boundaries. Institutionalists argue that actions and practices are not context-free but are constrained by the environment (Scott 2001). To describe the process of homogenization DiMaggio and Powell (1983) refer to the concept of isomorphism, that is, the process through which various factors lead organizations to adopt similar structures, strategies and processes – and by extension management practices. As a result organizations, practices and strategies increasingly come to resemble one another. Isomorphism occurs through three mechanisms: coercive forces that stem from political influence and problems of legitimacy and occur through externally codified rules, norms or laws; mimetic changes that are responses to uncertainty and lead to direct imitation of competitors for example; and normative influences that result from professionalization through educational and professional authorities. These mechanisms are the result of the three processes mentioned above. They provide stability and meaning to social behavior and practices.

Homogenization does not happen at once but through a process. According to Tolbert and Zucker, institutionalization processes go through three stages: pre-, semi- and full institutionalization (Tolbert and Zucker 1996). Through this process, the field becomes highly structured and thus clear and defined. This leads to convergence toward normative practices, thereby lessening diversity and organizational forms within the field. As a result, organizations tend to become homogeneous. The global convergence suggests that national institutions are likely to be influenced by cross-national pressures and open to the emergence of a "world society" (Meyer et al. 1997). Following this perspective, if SRI is to stay and diffuse, it needs to progressively but ineluctably go through a process of homogenization and global isomorphism. As a consequence, it should become more and more uniform across all regions of the world. Standardization is a condition for the diffusion and stabilization of the activity. Indeed, defenders of global convergence may argue that if it fails to get institutionalized, SRI may well disappear or remain a marginal movement. Can we see any signs of convergence with the SRI field? In a study carried out on the Dutch SRI market, Louche (2004) shows that SRI is in a process of institutionalization. She investigated the development of SRI in the Netherlands between 1990 and 2003. Data confirm that many of the indicators of institutionalization, as defined by DiMaggio and Powell (1983) and Scott (1994), are met. The specific SRI field investigated reveals a certain degree of homogenization. Nonetheless Louche argues that it has not yet reached full institutionalization.

On the one hand, there is clearly an increase in interaction between organizations in the SRI field, although not equally among all actors. The analysis of the relationships between actors enables us to identify a clear structure in the field where rating organizations have taken a central and strategic role. A similar pattern is highlighted in France in the study of Boxenbaum and Gond (2005) where ARESE, the first French rating agency, has played a critical role in the construction of SRI in France. Secondly, there is an increase in the flow of information. Conferences related to SRI, like the Triple Bottom Line Investing conference (TBLI) in Europe and Asia or SRI in the Rockies in the US,[5] have increased and are attracting an increasing number of people, along with publications in periodicals, newspapers, and books. Boxenbaum and Gond (2005) confirm this tendency in the US, French and Quebec press[6] with a net increase as from 2000. At the same time SRI funds are becoming increasingly transparent. This has been especially stimulated with the launch of the Transparency Guidelines[7] initiated by the Dutch SIF in 2002 which has been signed by many SRI fund managers in the Netherlands but also Europe-wide. This document marks a first attempt at controlling what is or should be SRI activity. Thirdly, the activity of SRI is becoming increasingly standardized. The diffusion of SRI has been accompanied by a developing consensus about the different strategies to exercise the activity of SRI. Although there are differences in the use of the different strategies, actors in the field tend to agree on the categorization.

On the other hand, there is no sign of a mutual awareness by members of the field that they share a common meaning, there is no evolution of an increasingly clearer field boundary, and there is no agreement about the institutional logics that guide the activity. Empirical data show that SRI fund managers are rather evasive when defining their activity and product. They are not able to provide a common definition. One sign of this disagreement is the use of different names: "ethical investment," "sustainable investment," "responsible investment" or "SRI." Another characteristic is a lack of a common identity. Actors involved in the field, although they recognize that they are part of a common movement, still argue about their identity. Two main groups can be distinguished: values-based investors[8] and performance or [financial] value-oriented investors.[9] The first emphasizes the ethical dimension and the importance of creating social returns with SRI products, while the second is market oriented and focuses on the financial return. SRI has historically grown out of the first approach to develop increasingly toward the second approach during the last decade.

This development has been part of the mainstreaming of SRI with a refocus around ESG factors. Increasingly financial analysts – sell side and buy side – are integrating extra financial information into firms' analysis (see Goldman Sachs 2007; Aspen Institute 2008). A well-known example of such an initiative is the Enhanced Analytics Initiative (EAI).[10] The EAI was established in October 2004 by a group of institutional investors (including asset managers and pension funds) who believe that members and clients are best served when investors take into account extra-financial issues and intangibles into their mainstream (sell-side) research. Such issues typically include corporate governance, human capital management, value creation or destruction during mergers and acquisitions, or corporate performance on material environmental issues such as climate change. Interestingly, these financial analysts who use only one of the tactics of SRI activity do not talk about SRI. This division between values-based SRI and performance-oriented SRI highlights different motives among the SRI community (Jayne and Skerratt 2003; Schueth 2003; Clark and Hebb 2004) and reveals the existence of conflicting logics within the SRI field.

SRI is a maturing field. To a certain extent it has developed into a global movement with a global structure. We see a condensation of relationships and interactions between an increasing number of actors. We see a massive acceleration of global exchange through the creation of global networks, platforms and venues where all actors, regardless of their motivation and background, are meeting and exchanging ideas. We see some common models and reference frameworks emerging, such as the Principles of Responsible Investment,[11] the Aspen Institute Guiding Principles for Corporations and Investors[12] or even the Global Reporting Initiative[13] that serves as a standard in the definition of ESG indicators. We see a greater and expanded distribution of SRI products. It has diffused horizontally throughout the world (diffusion in space), and vertically within the financial community (mainstreaming). It has become a recognized and acknowledged activity (Deloitte 2002; CSR Europe, Deloitte et al. 2003; Taylor Nelson Sofres 2003; Ambachtsheer 2005). And as noted by Solomon et al. (2004), there is a strong desire within the SRI community to achieve a consensus on the practice and understanding of the activity.

However, the global standardization and homogenization of SRI have been criticized and questioned by both academic researchers and practitioners. The following section reviews the opposite mechanism and argues that SRI is highly influenced by the national context. As a result, SRI practices could not be standardized on a global scale, but indeed would remain highly diversified and heterogeneous.

4.3   Local divergence

Recent studies on SRI suggest that SRI differs from region to region and even from country to country (Sparkes 2001; Boxenbaum and Gond 2005; Eurosif 2006; Louche and Lydenberg 2006; Bengtsson 2007; Louche et al. forthcoming; Sakuma and Louche 2008). Although the authors do not reject the diffusion thesis, they show that the SRI field is embedded in national contexts and thereby tends to vary at the local level. For instance, Louche and Lydenberg (2006) provide a comparison between SRI in the US and Europe. The analysis in the two regions shows some similarities in terms of historical roots and shared purpose, but it above all highlights key differences in terms of definitions, actors involved, vocabulary and motivations, and strategies implemented. Similarly Sakuma and Louche (2008) compare SRI in Japan, Europe and the US. Here again, the authors find some similitude between the three regions, but they also note the specificity of the Japanese SRI market due to its national context such as the underdeveloped NGOs and the civil sector, the structure of the financial market, the role of the government, and the culture of quality management. Table 4.1 summarizes the main differences between the three regions.

According to Latour (1987), practices need to be adapted to fit new social contexts, which means reinterpretation or translation (Czarniawska and Sevón 1996; Czarniawska and Joerges 1998; Olson et al. 2003). Following Latour's reasoning, the diffusion of SRI within different countries leads to a certain adaptation at the local context (Latour 1987). The local divergence mechanism builds on the national business system (NBS) approach. In contrast to new institutional theory, the NBS approach focuses on the effect of the national level on organizations'

Table 4.1 Overview of the main differences between Japan, the US and Europe

	Japan	US	Europe
Historic roots		Religious background	
Motivation	A desire (1) to reinvigorate the Japanese financial sector after the bubble burst, and (2) to demonstrate Japanese management legitimacy	A desire to redefine the relationship between corporations and society	
Definition	Emphasis on financial objectives and investment impacts	Emphasis on personal values and social purpose	Emphasis on financial objectives and investment impacts
Actors	No active retail and institutional investors Independent SRI firms and financial-group-affiliated think tanks Companies Increasing government interest	Retail investors SRI firms independent of the mainstream financial community Little government involvement	Institutional investors Mainstream financial community promoting SRI activities Substantive government involvement
Vocabulary	Screening Ecoefficiency and ecofriendly Ethics compliance and integrity CSR Social contribution	Social responsibility Fairness and justice Access to capital Wealth creation Exclusionary and qualitative screens Shareholder activism	Sustainability Ecoefficiency and business case Triple Bottom Line investing Best-in-class investing Negative and positive screens Engagement
SRI strategies	Negative screens rejected Avoidance of companies with negative press coverage Nonconflictual and casting votes in the shareholders' meetings	Exclusionary screen crucially important Positive screens stress judgment Activism often public and through proxy resolutions	Negative screens not emphasized Positive screens stress quantitative measurements Engagement often through behind-the-scenes dialogue

Source: Adapted from Sakuma and Louche (2008) and Louche and Lydenberg (2006).

forms and practices (see Whitley 1999; Hall and Soskice 2001; Amable 2003). This perspective suggests that every country has a specific, historically grown institutional framework which shapes and constitutes what is called a "national business system" (Whitley 1997). The key argument is that despite ongoing processes of globalization in the sense of harmonization and standardization of management processes and structures, NBSs still remain distinct. As a consequence, the specific institutional configuration of a given country strongly affects corporate behaviors and strategies (Whitley 1998, 1999) and thereby business practices tend to vary from country to country.

Hall and Soskice (2001) identify two ideal types of NBSs based on corporate governance, education and training, intercompany relations and industrial relations variables. They categorize the economies in the US and the UK as the liberal market economies (LMEs) where coordination between the actors is organized by competitive market forces, while other economies, and in particular those like Germany, are added to the ideal model of coordinated market economies (CMEs) where coordination is centered on networks rather than on the market and competitiveness is embedded in strategic cooperation. A number of refined typologies of NBSs have developed in this literature since the opposition between continental and Anglo-American forms of capitalisms was introduced (Schmidt 2002; Amable 2003).

Although previous studies have mainly focused on the effect of NBSs on corporate economic performance (Hall and Gingerich 2004) and the adoption of management practices (Tempel and Walgenbach 2007), more recent research has used the NBS perspective to investigate CSR practices (Chappel et al. 2008; Matten and Moon 2008). Matten and Moon (2008) suggest that NBS characteristics strongly frame the national approach of what they call "implicit and explicit CSR."[14] Chappel et al. (2008) investigate the influence of institutional systems on stakeholder management and corporate responsibility across 22 countries. Based on the Amable (2003) typology, the analysis shows that the CSR pattern developed by companies is strongly influenced by the institutional context. This study not only confirms that CSR varies across countries but also explains why it varies. Results have direct implications for the SRI community, firstly on the way companies are evaluated and screened and secondly on the design itself of SRI products.

Based on this approach, it can be argued that NBSs create different "spaces" for SRI to develop and for local actors to adopt SRI practices and strategies that are the most relevant and suitable to their specific context. The translation process at the micro level – country or even more local level – needs to be adapted to fit the new social contexts. The success and legitimacy of SRI at the local level depend on the capacity of local actors to capture and encapsulate the specific dimensions of their context in the implementation of SRI. It is also what the sociology of translation has called the contextualization process (Latour 1996). This process requires transferred business practices to fit into the institutional order in the host society (Casper and Hancké 1999; Hall and Soskice 2001; Boxenbaum and Gond 2005). The practice of SRI needs to be framed in a way that makes sense and is consistent with the values and interests of the local actors.

4.4 Discussion

The two previous sections have presented two different mechanisms based on different theoretical perspectives (see Figure 4.1):

- global convergence: this mechanism is based on new institutional theory and emphasizes the global diffusion and homogenization of SRI practices;
- local divergence: this mechanism is based on the business systems approach and focuses on the influence of the national context and the local embeddedness of SRI leading to a variety of practices.

Is SRI moving towards convergence or divergence? This is not an easy question as the field shows signs of both. As was explained in the second

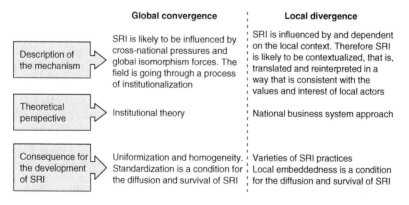

Figure 4.1 Overview of the global convergence and local divergence mechanisms

section, there are some clear signs of institutionalization. Diffusion is one of them. Indeed, SRI activity has spread and is acknowledged globally not only by the financial community but also the broader business community, the European Commission (European Commission 2001), and governments. We have seen an increase in terms of legislation with regard to ESG disclosure for pension funds such as in France, UK or Germany, but also with state-owned funds integrating SRI dimensions such as in Norway, Sweden, France or Switzerland. But section 4.3 pointed out that SRI products and practices vary greatly across the globe and even within a single country. The two mechanisms seem to be at play in shaping the SRI field. Therefore the answer to the convergence or divergence question cannot be straightforward and may best be tackled by analyzing the interplay between the two.

I would like to argue that global convergence and local divergence are both necessary for the development of SRI. Although they may be perceived as contradictory, they are not exclusive and on the contrary do feed each other. In other words, the homogenizing tendencies of SRI imply continued or even reinforced cultural heterogeneity. It refers to the concept of "glocalization" (Robertson 1995), that is, global localization. This neologism of globalization and localization has been modeled on the Japanese word *dochakuka*, which originally meant adapting farming techniques to one's own local conditions. According to Robertson, glocalization means "the creation of products or services intended for the global market, but customized to suit the local cultures." The interplay implies that SRI actors cannot only rely on what already exists. For legitimacy reasons, they need a global spread and recognition that allow them to reach a critical mass, not to remain a marginal and niche movement. But they have to create an "SRI" that is meaningful to them and the actors involved in their local context. It matches a world of growing SRI and diversity of practices. As a consequence, SRI remains ambiguous, chaotic and confusing since different practices and understanding exist side by side. Consequently, we are faced with a concept that becomes global in its diffusion but fragmented/diverging in its practices.

4.4.1   Preserve ambiguity and popularity

On the one hand global convergence provides a valuable basis to reduce conflict by producing frameworks that can be espoused by everyone. It offers the basis to establish social ties and a common identity within and among the SRI field, an identity that can also be recognized by actors outside the field. It creates consensus within the SRI field and enhances the likelihood of survival and dissemination of the SRI label. On the other, local divergence recognizes the existence of multiple viewpoints which in turn create ambiguity. It acknowledges that SRI has more than one meaning and by extension more than one practice. Ambiguity is an important attribute allowing various interpretations and actions and thereby local acceptance. Ambiguity can also help to create alliances between parties with different and sometimes divergent interests as long as it allows generality so as to encompass various situations.

4.4.2   Stimulate creativity and innovation

A number of actors in the SRI field, from both the academic and business community, welcome and encourage standardization. There are a lot of advantages related to standardization. It enables better coordination, facilitates interaction, enhances compatibility and makes communication easier. "The knowledge or expectation that others are following certain standards makes it unnecessary to spend time and resources gathering detailed information about the likely behaviors of others" (Brunsson and Olsen 1998). It can be argued that standardization makes it easier for the SRI community as well as for the companies that are screened and evaluated. It reduces the number of possibilities and questions that need to be considered. However, full standardization raises many questions which make it improbable too.

First, is the SRI activity mature enough to be standardized? SRI is obviously a new and still emerging activity. Although it has diffused all over the world, definitions and understandings are still widely and fiercely discussed (Cowton 1994, 1998; Sparkes 1995, 2001). As SRI is very much dependent on the CSR concept, it seems a difficult and maybe risky exercise to try to standardize it before CSR has even reached this stage. Similarly to SRI, there are some attempts to universalize the concept of CSR – for example the upcoming ISO 26000 for CSR – but its implementation remains very context dependent.

Second, is standardization the most suitable development for the objective defended by the SRI community and does it serve the demand? One of the objectives claimed by the SRI community is to stimulate corporate social responsibility. It is doing so by being critical toward firms' behavior, engaging with companies and, quantifying and benchmarking CSR performance of firms. Through the standardization process, SRI runs the risk of focusing on conformity and thereby losing its capacity to be critical. Moreover, we increasingly see the development of customized SRI products. They do not necessarily vary according to the cultural context but rather to the type of client – whether they are more values based or performance oriented, whether they are individual or institutional.

And third, is standardization the way to stimulate creativity and innovation? It has indeed been argued that sustainability can only be reached through new partners of consumption and production requiring in-depth changes where innovation and creativity are key components (Roome 2006). Innovation means new products, services and technologies as well as new organizational and institutional systems, structures and new business models. By standardizing SRI practices, CSR may exert the "wrong" pressures on corporations, namely compliance which in turn may sterilize discussion and debate instead of stimulating creativity and innovation.

4.4.3   Create an interface to rally different groups

Building from the previous arguments developed above, I would like to suggest considering SRI as a boundary institution inspired by Star and Griesemer (1989). This perspective encompasses the idea that ambiguity facilitates the translation of various interests and that generalization or standardization is to a certain extent necessary for a concept to diffuse. Star and Griesemer (1989) define boundary objects as

> objects which are both plastic enough to adapt to local needs and the constraints of the several parties employing them, yet robust enough to maintain a common identity... They have different meanings in different social worlds but their structure is common enough to more than one world to make them recognizable, a means of translation. (Star and Griesemer 1989)

As a boundary institution, SRI becomes first a common point of reference of conversation for actors in the field (people can all agree they are talking about SRI). However, actors do not have necessarily to talk about the same thing. They may attach different meanings to SRI. Second, SRI becomes plastic enough to adapt to changing needs (boundary objects are working arrangements, adjusted as needed; they are not imposed by one community, nor by outside standards) and satisfy different concerns simultaneously. And third, it can be construed as the interface where the activities of different groups coincide. It is indeed not defined and constrained by one particular group, but is managed actively by several groups or actors. Understanding SRI as a boundary institution helps understand the development of the movement as a coevolution between the two mechanisms developed in the previous sections, that is global convergence and local divergence. The SRI field can then be characterized as ambiguous and plastic and not unequivocal and stable. Although SRI has become global, the different groups and/or actors are not necessarily ascribing an identical meaning to it just as its significance has varied over time.

Conclusion

This chapter has examined the development of SRI and more especially the mechanisms supporting its development. Two paths have been identified: global convergence and local divergence. Based on two distinctive theoretical approaches, respectively institutional theory and the national business system approach, the mechanisms foresee two very different schemes for the future of SRI. In the global convergence scenario, SRI is expected to become increasingly homogeneous and uniform, while in the local divergence scenario, SRI practices are expected to vary and differ according to local contexts. Rather than rejecting the institutionalist perspective in favor of the other, or vice versa, it seems most likely that both mechanisms are and will continue to coexist. It has been argued that they are both of importance in legitimizing and sustaining SRI over time. As a result, the development of SRI is best analyzed and understood through the analysis of the interplay between the two mechanisms where convergence and divergence are in constant and continuous interplay.

A way to integrate the two mechanisms is to consider SRI as a boundary institution. This perspective allows a global diffusion and, to a certain extent, a consensus with regard to SRI activity. Through institutional forces – normative, coercive and mimetic – a universalistic rhetoric is being created around the activity under which actors can meet, discuss and exchange. The institutional process enables the field and actors involved to shape a common identity as well as establish a common vocabulary. These characteristics are very important for SRI to be recognized by outsiders and to keep expanding in terms of assets under management and geographic spreading. But at the same time, SRI as a boundary institution allows and recognizes that local contexts create distinctive spaces for SRI to develop and for local actors to reinterpret SRI practices and strategies. Similarly to CSR, SRI needs to be considered and adapted to the local context as it addresses issues that are embedded in values and norms. Contextualization enables us to translate SRI into practices that are aligned with local institutions and standards. Finally SRI as a boundary institution allows: (1) maintenance of a certain degree of ambiguity that renders possible various interpretations and at the same time reduces potential conflicts; (2) stimulation of creativity and innovation within the SRI field but also and above all with regard to CSR; and (3) enhancement of collaborative work between different groups that may have different interests. SRI separates and unites at the same time: it is both plastic enough to adapt to local needs and robust enough to maintain a common identity, which is crucial for the diffusion and recognition of the field.

To conclude, the chapter is an attempt to contribute to and bring forward the debate on the development and future of SRI. By conceptualizing the different mechanisms at play, it provides an approach to analyze SRI and bridges the current theoretical lack in understanding its diffusion and variations. However, more research is necessary on the mechanisms that sustain the diffusion of SRI practices. It is expected that the interplay between divergence and convergence will vary in time and space. It would be interesting to study the evolution of the interplay over time. The analysis could certainly gain from a quantitative research to investigate the different factors at play. It would also be useful to refine the mechanisms. SRI practices are not only explained by the national and institutional context. Variables such as type of financial institution (mainstream financial institution or niche player), the type of product (retail funds, pension funds, and others), the type of investor (values based or performance oriented), or the size of SRI funds may well contribute to explaining the degree of convergence or divergence. Another aspect that needs to be addressed is the link with CSR. Indeed SRI cannot be viewed separately from CSR. It would be valuable to examine how the two fields coevolve.

Moreover, SRI practitioners could benefit from the proposed conceptualization, as it provides a support to explain and justify differences and similarities in terms of SRI approaches. It reinforces the importance of establishing a common rhetoric but not necessarily common practices. It therefore emphasizes the potential opportunities for practitioners to be creative and innovative. And finally, it brings new insights into the future development of SRI and conditions for growth.

Notes

1. Principles for Responsible Investment website, www.unpri.org, 20 March 2008.
2. For more information: www.ethibel.org/subs_e/2_label/main.html.

3. Note that a fourth SRI strategy is often identified under SRI activity, namely community investment (see Kinder et al. 1994). It consists of direct capital from investors and lenders to communities that are underserved by traditional financial services institutions. The idea is using investment to assist local people or businesses to benefit local communities. This SRI strategy, although present in the European context, is much more developed in the US market. In this essay community investing is not considered as part of the SRI field.

4. France, UK, Sweden and Belgium account for about 63 percent of the funds available in Europe.

5. The Triple Bottom Line Investing conference was held for the first time in 1999 in Rotterdam, The Netherlands, and the eleventh conference was organized in 2008. Since 2005, the TBLI takes place every year in Europe and in Asia. The first SRI in the Rockies was launched in 1989. In 2008 it is running its nineteenth conference. These are just examples among many (see www.eurosif.org for more SRI-related events).

6. The newspapers that have been analyzed are: *The New York Times* (US), *Le Monde* (France) and *La Presse* (Quebec).

7. Transparency guidelines available at: www.eurosif.org.

8. Values-based investors are best defined as "integrating personal values and societal concerns with investment decisions [...] With SRI you can put your money to work to build a better tomorrow..." US Social Investment Forum (www.socialinvest.org).

9. "Companies most likely to be growing consistently over the next few decades are those promoting or benefiting from sustainable development. This approach is radically different from traditional ethical investment [values based investing]. Instead of focusing on negative criteria and then applying financial analysis to a restricted universe, the focus is on making a direct link between sustainable development and long-term returns" (Morley Fund Management).

10. Enhanced Analytics Initiative "is an international collaboration between asset owners and asset managers aimed at encouraging better investment research, in particular research that takes account of the impact of extra-financial issues on long-term investment. The Initiative currently represents total assets under management of €1.8 trillion," www.enhancedanalytics.com.

11. www.unpri.org.

12. Available at www.aspeninstitute.org.

13. www.globalreporting.org.

14. "By Explicit CSR we refer to corporate policies to assume responsibility for the interests of the society. Explicit CSR would normally consist of voluntary, self-interest driven policies, programs and strategies by corporations addressing issues perceived as being part of their social responsibility by the company and/or its stakeholders. By Implicit CSR we understand the entirety of a country's formal and informal institutions assigning corporations an agreed share of responsibility for society's interests and concerns. Implicit CSR normally consists of values, norms and rules which result in (mostly mandatory but also customary) requirements for corporations to address issues

stakeholders consider a proper obligation upon corporate actors" (Matten and Moon 2008).

References

Amable, B. (2003) *The Diversity of Modern Capitalism*. Oxford University Press, Oxford.

Ambachtsheer, J. (2005) *SRI: What Do Investment Managers Think?* Mercer Investment Consulting, Belgium.

Anderson, D., Frost, G., Hogson, P. E., Minogue, K., O'Hear, A., and Scruton, R. (1996) *What Has "Ethical Investment" to Do with Ethic?* The Social Affairs Unit, London.

Aspen Institute (2008) "Long-Term Value Creation: Guiding Principles for Corporations and Investors," http://www.aspeninstitute.org.

Bengtsson, E. (2007) "A History of Scandinavian Socially Responsible Investing," *Journal of Business Ethics*, 16/3 (November): 155–68.

Boxenbaum, E. and Gond, J.-P. (2006) Micro-Strategies of Contextualization: Cross-National Transfer of Socially Responsible Investment, DRUID Summer Conference 2006.

Brunsson, N. and Olsen, J.P. (1998) "Organization Theory: Thirty Years of Dismantling and Then?" in Brunsson, N. and Olsen, J.P. (eds) *Organizing Organizations*, Copenhagen Business School Press, Copenhagen.

Casper, S. and Hancké, B. (1999) "Global Quality Norms within National Production Regimes: ISO 9000 Standards in the French and German Car Industries," *Organization Studies*, 20/6: 961–85.

Chappel, W., Gond, J.-P. et al. (2008) The Influence of Institutional Varieties of Capitalism on Corporate Stakeholder Responsibility, Annual Meeting of the Academy of Management, Anaheim, Calif.

Clark, G.L. and Hebb, T. (2004) "Pension Fund Corporate Engagement," *Industrial Relations*, 59/1: 142–71.

Cowton, C. (1994) "The Development of Ethical Investment Products," in Prindl, A.R. and and Prodhan, B. (eds) *Ethical Conflicts in Finance*, Blackwell, Oxford.

Cowton, C. (1998) "Socially Responsible Investment," in Chadwick, R. (ed.) *Encyclopaedia of Applied Ethics*, Academic Press, San Diego.

CSR Europe, Deloitte and Euronext (2003) *Investing in Responsible Business: the 2003 Survey of European Fund Managers, Financial*. London.

Czarniawska, B. and Joerges, B. (1998) "Winds of Organizational Change: How Ideas Translate into Objects and Actions," in Brunsson, N. and Olsen, J.P. (eds) *Organizing Organizations*, Copenhagen Business School Press, Copenhagen.

Czarniawska, B. and Sevón, G. (eds) (1996) *Translating Organizational Change*. Walter de Gruyter, New York.

Deloitte (2002) *Socially Responsible Investment Survey 2002*. London.

DiMaggio, P.J. and Powell, W.W. (1983) "The Iron Cage Revisited: Institutional Isomorphism and Collective Rationality in Organizational Field," *American Sociological Review*, 48/2: 147–60.

Domini, A.L. (2001) *Socially Responsible Investing: Making a Difference in Making Money*. Dearborn Trade, Chicago.

European Commission (2001) *Promoting a European Framework for Corporate Social Responsibility*. Green Paper, European Commission, Brussels.

Eurosif (2006) *European SRI Study*. Paris.

Goldman Sachs (2007) "GS Sustain." http://www.unglobalcompact.org/docs/summit2007/gs_esg_embargoed_until030707pdf.pdf.

Gond, J.-P. and Boxenbaum, E. (2004) "Importing 'Socially Responsible Investment' in France and Quebec: Work of Contextualization across Varieties of Capitalism," EGOS Conference, Ljubljana.

Hall, P.A. and Gingerich, D.W. (2004) "Varieties of Capitalism and Institutional Complementarities in the Macroeconomy: an Empirical Analysis," Max Planck Institute for the Study of Societies, MPIfG discussion paper 04/5.

Hall, P.A. and Soskice, D. (2001) "An Introduction to Varieties of Capitalism," in Hall, P.A. and Soskice, D. (eds) *Varieties of Capitalism: the Institutional Foundations of Comparative Advantage*, Oxford University Press, New York, pp. 1–68.

Jayne, M.R. and Skerratt, G. (2003) "Socially Responsible Investment in the UK – Criteria that are Used to Evaluate Suitability," *Corporate Social Responsibility and Environmental Management*, 10/1: 1–11.

Kinder, P., Lydenberg, S.D. et al. (1994) *Investing for Good, Making Money While Being Socially Responsible*. Harper Business, New York.

Latour, B. (1987) *La science en action*. Gallimard, Paris.

Latour, B. (1996) *Aramis, or the Love of Technology*. Harvard University Press, Cambridge, Mass.

Louche, C. (2004) "Ethical Investment: Processes and Mechanisms of Institutionalisation in the Netherlands, 1990–2002." PhD dissertation, Erasmus University Rotterdam. Optima Grafische Communicatie, Rotterdam.

Louche, C. and Lydenberg, S. (2006) "Socially Responsible Investment: Difference between Europe and United States," Working Paper, Vlerick Leuven Gent Management School.

Louche, C., Markowtiz, L. et al. (forthcoming) "How Social Movements Generate New, Profit Driven Organizational Forms: Exploring Socially Responsible Investment Changes across Time and Space."

Matten, D. and Moon, J. (2008) "'Implicit' and 'Explicit' CSR: a Conceptual Framework for Comparative Understanding of Corporate Social Responsibility," *Academy of Management Review*, 33/2.

Meyer, J.W. (2000) "Globalization: Sources and Effects on National States and Societies," *International Sociology*, 15/2: 233–49.

Meyer, J.W., Boli, J., Thomas, G.M., and Ramirez, F.O. (1997) "World Society and the Nation-State," *American Journal of Sociology*, 103/1: 144–292.

Meyer, J.W. and Rowan, B. (1977) "The Effects of Education as an Institution," *American Journal of Sociology*, 87: 53–77.

Olson, N.R., Ventresca, M.J. et al. (2003) "How Institutions Emerge: Mechanisms in the Origins and Elaboration of Emerging Environmental Management Codes Field," Working Paper, School of Geography and the Environment, University of Oxford.

Robertson, R. (1995) "Globalisation: Time-Space and Homogeneity-Heterogeneity," in Featherstone, M., Lash, S. and Robertson, R. (eds) *Global Modernities*, Sage Publications, London.

Roome, N. J. (2006) "Competitiveness, Corporate Responsibility and Innovation." Presentation to the EU Conference on Competitiveness, Corporate Responsibility and Innovation under the Finnish Presidency, Brussels.

Sakuma, K. and Louche, C. (2008) "Socially Responsible Investment in Japan: Its Mechanism and Drivers," *Journal of Business Ethics*, forthcoming.

Schmidt, V. (2002) *The Futures of European Capitalism*. Oxford University Press, Oxford.

Schueth, S. (2003) "Socially Responsible Investing in the United States," *Journal of Business Ethics*, 43/3: 189–94.

Scott, W. R. (1994) "Conceptualizing Organisational Fields: Linking Organizations and Societal Systems," in Derlien, H.-U. (ed.), *Systemrationalitaet und Partialinteresse: Festschrift für Renate Mayntz*. Nomos Verlagsgesellschaft, Baden-Baden, Germany.

Scott, W.R. (2001) *Institutions and Organizations*. Sage Publications, Thousand Oaks, Calif.

SIRI Group (2002) *Green, Social and Ethical Funds in Europe 2002*. SiRi Group/Avanzi.

SIRI Group (2007) *Green, Social and Ethical Funds in Europe – 2007 Review*. SiRi Group/Avanzi, Milan.

Solomon, A., Solomon, J., and Suto, M. (2004) "Can the UK Experience Provide Lessons for the Evolution of SRI in Japan?" *Corporate Governance: an International Review*, 12/4: 552–66.

Sparkes, R. (1995) *The Ethical Investor*. HarperCollins, London.

Sparkes, R. (2001) "Ethical Investment: Whose Ethics, Which Investment?" *Business Ethics: a European Review*, 10/3: 194–205.

Star, S.L. and Griesemer, J.R. (1989) "Institutional Ecology, 'Translations', and Boundary Objects: Amateurs and Professionals in Berkeley's Museum of Vertebrate Zoology, 1907–1939," *Social Studies of Science*, 19: 387–420.

Taylor Nelson Sofres (2003) *Investing in Responsible Business – the 2003 Survey of European Fund Managers, Financial Analysts and Investor Relations Officers*. CSR Europe, Deloitte, Euronext.

Tempel, A. and Walgenbach, P. (2007) "Global Standardization of Organizational Forms and Management Practices? What New Institutionalism and the Business-Systems Approach Can Learn from Each Other," *Journal of Management Studies*, 44/1: 1–24.

Tolbert, P.S. and Zucker, L.G. (1996) "The Institutionalisation of Institutional Theory," in *Handbook of Organisational Studies*, Sage Publications, London.

US SIF (2008) *2007 Report on Socially Responsible Investing Trends in US – Executive Summary*. US Social Investment Forum, Washington.

Whitley, R. (1997) "Business Systems," in Sorge, A. (ed.) *Organization*, Thomson Learning, London, pp. 178–86.

Whitley, R. (1998) "Internationalization and Varieties of Capitalism: the Limited Effect of Cross-National Coordination of Economic Activities on the Nature of the Business System," *Review of International Political Economy*, 5: 445–81.

Whitley, R. (1999) *Divergent Capitalisms: the Social Structuring of Change of Business Systems*. Oxford University Press, Oxford.

5
The Use of Shareholder Proposals to Address Corporate Human Rights Performance

Adam M. Kanzer[1]

> [M]ost of those fail dismally when they come up on the ballot. They never get anywhere near the majority.... a few people are very interested or agitated about it, but not the many.
> I would suggest that Nelson Mandela didn't think they failed.
> Exchange between Paul Atkins, Commissioner, Securities and Exchange Commission and Damon Silvers, Associate General Counsel, AFL-CIO at SEC Roundtable Discussion on Shareholder Proposals, 2007[2]

The preamble to the Universal Declaration of Human Rights (UDHR) commits "every individual and every organ of society" to keep the Declaration "constantly in mind" as a "common standard of achievement for all peoples and all nations." This essay considers the role of two such organs of society – investors and the Securities and Exchange Commission (SEC) – in furthering this common standard.

Investors have a responsibility to society to consider the social and environmental implications of their investment decisions. By using social and environmental criteria to select holdings, and by communicating with companies about these issues, socially responsible investors have built a tremendous demand for corporate social and environmental performance data. Corporations have responded with a proliferation of increasingly transparent sustainability reports. To borrow a phrase from Louis Brandeis, these commitments to regular public reporting can serve as a "continuous remedial measure" to address human rights abuses.

This essay focuses on the use of shareholder proposals in the United States, filed pursuant to Rule 14a-8 of the Securities and Exchange Act of 1934 (the Exchange Act).[3] Shareholder proposals have been the primary mechanism for placing human rights issues on the agenda of US corporations for nearly 40 years, and have served as a critical tool for initiating long-term productive dialogues with corporate management. Many of these dialogues have resulted in policy and behavioral changes and greater public transparency on a broad range of human rights issues.

Institutional investors – including mutual funds, investment advisers, and public and private pension funds – have a fiduciary duty to vote their proxies in the best interests of their clients or beneficiaries. Fiduciaries, therefore, have a legal obligation to carefully consider any and all human rights issues presented to them on corporate proxy statements. An increasing number of institutional investors view human rights and other social and environmental issues as "material" to their investment decisions, and are therefore willing to support shareholder proposals addressing these issues. This increasing institutional support helps to increase the leverage of the proposal, and to encourage corporate management to address the concerns raised by its proponents.

5.1 Background: the SEC's public interest mandate

There are no current statutes mandating that US corporations comply with international human rights standards.[4] There are also certain gaps between US law and international human rights norms that place corporate stakeholders at risk and subject corporations to a range of litigation, operational and reputational risks. Allegations of corporate human rights abuses continue to surface.[5]

Securities regulation in the United States is based on compelled disclosure of information by issuers in order to allow investors to make prudent decisions. This disclosure regime is based in part on the notion that investors have a duty to monitor the behavior of the companies they own and that compelled disclosure provides a means to correct corporate behavior if it strays from the public interest.

In 1913 *Harper's Magazine* published a series of articles by Louis Brandeis on the money trusts that helped inspire this approach to securities regulation. In "What Publicity Can Do," Brandeis made the case that "publicity is justly commended as a remedy for social and industrial diseases. Sunlight is said to be the best of disinfectants; electric light the most efficient policeman."[6] Brandeis' reasoning, now taken as self-evident, was that investors will make better decisions if they have relevant information and their informed decision-making will serve as a check on fraudulent behavior. "Require full disclosure to the investor of the amount of commissions and profits paid," Brandeis reasoned, "and not only will investors be put on their guard, but... [e]xcessive commissions – this form of unjustly acquired wealth – will in large part cease."[7]

Brandeis stressed that disclosure to *investors* advanced the *public* interest: "Compliance with this requirement should also be obligatory, and not something which the investor could waive. For *the whole public* is interested in putting an end to the bankers' exactions" (emphasis added).[8] The investor, therefore, can be said to be serving a quasi-regulatory function on behalf of the general public. The disclosure is not for the investor's sole use – it should not be "something which the investor could waive." When the SEC was formed in 1934, in the midst of the Great Depression, these words were very much in Congress's mind.

Describing the "necessity for regulation," section two of the Exchange Act declares that "[n]ational emergencies, which produce widespread unemployment and the dislocation of trade . . . and adversely affect the general welfare are precipitated, intensified, and prolonged by manipulation and sudden and unreasonable fluctuations of security prices and by excessive speculation on such exchanges and markets. . . ." In short, securities regulation in the US was instituted to address the broad social and economic harm caused by unregulated capital markets.

The SEC is empowered by Section 14(a) of the Exchange Act to require proxy disclosure "as necessary or appropriate in the public interest *or* for the protection of investor" (emphasis added). The "or" in this clause suggests an independent public interest mandate.[9] According to the Third Circuit Court of Appeals," [i]t was the intent of Congress to require fair opportunity for the operation of corporate suffrage. The control of great corporations by a very few persons was the abuse at which Congress struck in enacting Section 14(a)."[10]

One legal scholar has argued that "Congress may have intended disclosure generally under the federal securities laws to be used to enhance corporate social accountability."[11] The original public interest mission of the SEC, however, has often been conflated into an exclusive mission to serve investors and vindicate state law rights. This was most evident during recent "roundtable" hearings convened by the SEC to revisit the purpose of the proxy rules.[12]

5.2 The mechanics of the shareholder proposal rule

Rule 14a-8 permits shareholders to place proposals on the corporate proxy for all shareholders to vote on.[13] Any shareholder holding at least $2000 worth of stock in the company for at least one year as of the date of submission may file a proposal, limited to 500 words. The proponent must hold this amount through the date of the annual meeting where she must present the proposal or send a representative to do so. This low eligibility threshold has made the corporate proxy accessible to a wide range of corporate stakeholders who are not professional investors.

A proposal must receive at least a 3 percent vote the first year, a 6 percent vote the second year, and a 10 percent vote in each subsequent year to be resubmitted. These thresholds, which have been revisited from time to time, have helped to ensure that social and environmental issues that may not have wide support among investors have an opportunity to remain on the proxy and build support over time.

Companies regularly submit "no-action requests" to the SEC, asking that the Commission "take no action" if the company omits the proposal from its proxy. The company bears the burden of proving that the proposal is improper based on a series of 13 substantive grounds for exclusion set forth in the Rule.[14] These decisions are generally one sentence, without a rationale, informing the company whether SEC staff agrees or disagrees with the company's argument. The decision and the accompanying correspondence (including briefs from both sides) become a matter of public record.

Generally, the board of directors will provide a "statement in opposition" to appear in the proxy statement. In many cases, this is the first time the company has made any substantive remarks about the subject matter of the proposal. In a sense, therefore, the mere filing of a proposal results in some form of report from the company, even if that report is generally less than satisfactory.

The proponent is normally given time at the annual meeting to make a brief speech in support of the proposal. Although most investors will have voted their proxies by the time of the annual meeting, this is a unique opportunity to address the board of directors and senior management in person. In the early days of social-issue shareholder activism several high-profile corporate annual meetings were transformed into Town Hall-style debates on the issue at hand.[15]

Shareholders have also brought affected stakeholders to the annual meeting either to present their proposal or to speak from their experience. In 1996, for example, the Benedictine Sisters brought a group of Mexican workers to Alcoa's annual meeting to describe their experiences working for Alcoa-Fujikura, the company's Mexican subsidiary. The proposal itself did not survive the SEC no-action process. According to Sister Susan Mika:

> It was an eye-opener. The CEO, Paul O'Neill, met with the workers afterwards and asked for six weeks to investigate. He went to the

border himself. He raised wages (even though he told stockholders he would not), he fired the CEO of Alcoa-Fujikura... (the man supposed to keep him informed of what was happening in Mexico), he paid profit-sharing to the workers (even though workers had been told there was no profit – at the meeting, they learned that Alcoa had made $790 million). We have been meeting with the company officials every six to eight months since that time.[16] Twelve years later, these meetings still continue.

The vast majority of shareholder proposals filed in the United States are nonbinding, or advisory (sometimes referred to as "precatory"), meaning that the company is not required to take any action even if the proposal receives a majority vote.[17] Binding proposals seeking bylaw changes (to establish a board committee, for example) may also be filed, but these are less common. For example, Harrington Investments has filed binding shareholder proposals asking companies to create a human rights committee of the board.[18]

Social-issue proposals rarely garner a majority vote and it is therefore often reported that they have been "defeated" or "failed," as expressed in the quote from SEC Commissioner Atkins that opened this essay. This is a misconception. These proposals are not analogous to elections. Rule 14a-8 is "informational," and affords shareholders an opportunity to "sound out management views and to communicate with other shareholders on matters of major import...."[19] A vote on a nonbinding proposal of 51 percent is of no more significance than a vote of 49 percent – the proposal is still advisory, and the board has no obligation to adopt it. Rather, the vote on a nonbinding proposal can best be understood as a gauge of investor sentiment, and many corporations appear to view them in this light. The proposals that brought Reverend Leon Sullivan to the board of General Motors received less than 3 percent support.[20] Some companies have responded to large votes,[21] while others ignore majority votes. Sister Mika's experience with Alcoa clearly demonstrates that the vote, in some cases, may be irrelevant.

5.3 Ordinary business and the significant social policy exception

Among the 13 bases for exclusion, the most commonly applied to human rights proposals is Rule 14a-8(i)(7), the "ordinary business" exception. Through a combination of case law and SEC interpretation, a safe space has been carved out to permit certain social-issue proposals, including those pertaining to human rights, to appear on the corporate ballot even if they address what would ordinarily be considered an "ordinary business" matter that should not generally be subject to shareholder oversight. In order for a proposal to be excludable pursuant to Rule 14a-8(i)(7), the proposal must not only pertain to a matter of ordinary company business, it must also fail to raise a significant policy issue:

> Certain tasks are so fundamental to management's ability to run a company on a day-to-day basis that they could not, as a practical matter, be subject to direct shareholder oversight. Examples include the management of the workforce, such as the hiring, promotion, and termination of employees, decisions on production quality and quantity, and the retention of suppliers. However, proposals relating to such matters but focusing on sufficiently significant social policy issues (e.g., significant discrimination matters) generally would not be considered to be excludable, because the proposals would transcend the day-to-day business matters and raise policy issues so significant that it would be appropriate for a shareholder vote.[22]

As of 1970, proposals which were "motivated by general political and moral concerns" were explicitly excludable under SEC rules.[23] In *Medical Committee for Human Rights* v. *SEC*, the US Court of Appeals for the District of Columbia explained the basis for establishing a "significant social policy" exception to the ordinary business rule this way:

> In so far as the shareholder has contributed an asset of value to the corporate venture, in so far as he has handed over his goods and property and money for use and increase, he has not only the clear right, but more to the point, perhaps, he has the stringent duty to exercise control over that asset for which he must keep care, guard, guide, and in general be held seriously responsible. As much as one may surrender the immediate disposition of (his) goods, he can never shirk a supervisory and secondary duty (not just a right) to make sure these goods are used justly, morally and beneficially.[24]

Although arguably dicta, the court was echoing Brandeis' idea that investors have a key role to play in holding companies accountable. Just as Brandeis argued that investors should not be able to waive access to certain information because the general public benefits from the "continuous remedial measure" of disclosure, here investors are said to have a supervisory "duty" – not just a right – to ensure that their capital is used appropriately.

The Medical Committee court was considering a shareholder proposal at Dow Chemical seeking to end the company's production of napalm for the US government. Dow executives had justified their continued production of napalm in political terms, rather than business terms – the company was working to support the war effort in Vietnam. The court noted:

> We think that there is a clear and compelling distinction between management's legitimate need for freedom to apply its expertise in matters of day-to-day business judgment, and management's patently illegitimate claim of power to treat modern corporations with their vast resources as personal satrapies implementing personal political or moral predilections. It could scarcely be argued that management is more qualified or more entitled to make these kinds of decisions than the shareholders who are the true beneficial owners of the corporation; and it seems equally implausible that an application of the proxy rules which permitted such a result could be harmonized with the philosophy of corporate democracy which Congress embodied in section 14(a) of the Securities Exchange Act of 1934.[25]

Although it is rare for corporate management to cite a political rationale for continuing a controversial line of business, the court's reasoning holds true for human rights issues generally. These issues rise above the day-to-day business of the corporation, and fall outside the authority of corporate executives.

It is worth noting that the court did not say that shareholders, as owners, are in *the best* position to make these decisions with broad political and moral implications. Rather, the court said that there is no rationale to support the view that management is in a *better* position than shareholders. After all, shareholders have no greater legitimacy than management when exercising power over innocent third parties. Is it the shareholder's role as "owner" (considering the often neglected obligations of ownership) that conveys the authority to make these decisions, or is it the widely dispersed nature of the company's shareholder base that adds a patina of "democracy" to the process? There are at least two lessons in this case. First, shareholders take on certain responsibilities to society when they become owners of a corporation, and second, corporate management is not given exclusive authority to make decisions that may affect the fundamental human rights of third parties. The court does not venture an opinion as to who would be *ideally* situated to make these decisions.

The SEC has not been consistent over the years in applying the significant social policy exception. In particular, there is a fairly complex history of how SEC staff handled proposals relating to "employment matters" from the mid-1980s through the 1990s. Perhaps the most important was its decision to permit Cracker Barrel Old Country Stores[26] to omit a proposal seeking a nondiscrimination policy protecting gay and lesbian employees. The New York City Comptroller's Office filed the proposal after Cracker Barrel publicly announced it would no longer be hiring homosexuals. After a series of court cases, an ICCR/Social Investment Forum campaign and pressure from members of Congress, the SEC famously reversed course, announcing that it would be returning to a "case by case" determination of proposals relating to employment matters and would no longer apply a *per se* exclusion to these proposals.[27]

In its reversal of Cracker Barrel, the SEC noted that its decisions on these matters would be somewhat subjective and in fact, the SEC has not disclosed any set of criteria used to determine whether a proposal raises a "significant social policy" issue. Proponents raising novel issues have generally sought to demonstrate that the issue is controversial and relevant to the company. Although the SEC is given broad discretion under Section 14(a) of the Exchange Act to regulate the proxy in the public interest, SEC staff expresses no view as to the merits of the proposal being offered, only whether the proposal comports with Rule 14a-8 and is a proper matter to be brought before shareholders.

Since the reversal of Cracker Barrel, SEC staff has generally been consistent in ruling that shareholder proposals relating to human rights issues raise such significant social policy considerations that the ordinary business exception is inapplicable to them.[28]

Staff's recent letter in *Certain Fidelity Funds*[29] regarding a proposal relating to the mutual fund manager's investments in corporations doing business in Sudan is a particularly strong affirmation of the "significant social policy" exception. That proposal requested that Fidelity "institute oversight procedures to screen out investments in companies that, in the judgment of the Board, substantially contribute to genocide, patterns of extraordinary and egregious violations of human rights, or crimes against humanity." If there is anything that constitutes "ordinary business" for a mutual fund manager, it is the criteria used to select holdings for its funds. Nevertheless, staff rejected Fidelity's arguments, and the proposal went on to receive between 21 and 29 percent of the vote at six funds.[30]

5.4   A commitment to dialogue

Proponents use a variety of criteria, often in combination, to select companies to "target" with a proposal, including the company's record on the issue at hand and its importance to the company's business model, the size and influence of the company (a company may be targeted, for example, if it is a leader in its industry and may set an example for others to follow), the degree of risk the company faces as a result of its performance on the issue, and the company's record with respect to its peers. Experienced proponents have learned that success will generally depend on their ability to make the "business case" to the company and its shareholder base. These factors, including corporate culture, can also play an important role in how the company responds to a proposal.

The majority of human rights proposals have been filed over the past 36 years by members and affiliates of the Interfaith Center on Corporate Responsibility (ICCR).[31] Although proponents use a wide range of tactics to advance their goals, Domini and other asset managers affiliated with ICCR have largely adopted ICCR's methodology. The shareholder resolution is not viewed as an end in itself, but a tool to encourage management to enter into dialogue.

Many companies have been unwilling to engage in substantive dialogue until a proposal is filed. When these dialogues break down, or when management is no longer willing to move forward on the issue, Rule 14a-8 provides shareholders with a legal "foot in the door." The implicit (and occasionally explicit) threat of a resolution can be sufficient to keep these discussions on track.

Many proposals are withdrawn prior to the annual meeting because proponents have been able to reach agreement with management. In 2006, for example, roughly one-third of the social-issue proposals filed were withdrawn.[32] Productive dialogues are based on trust. Institutional shareholders are in a unique position to establish this level of trust for two primary reasons:

1. Long-term shareholders' interests are aligned with the company, an alignment that can be difficult or impossible for other stakeholders to communicate; and
2. A fiduciary would presumably be legally barred from taking action detrimental to the long-term value of the company.

5.5   What the process can achieve

The use of shareholder proposals to address human rights issues came of age during the apartheid era. Two shareholder proposals at General Motors set a process in motion that brought the Reverend Leon Sullivan to the board. He later developed the Sullivan Principles, which became a critical framework for guiding companies doing business in South Africa. Shareholder proposals were successfully used to convince numerous companies to adopt the Sullivan Principles, to report on their activities and, ultimately, to pull out of South Africa. Shareholder pressure generally, through divestment and active engagement, has been credited as significantly contributing to bringing the system of apartheid to an end.

The flexibility of the shareholder proposal rule has permitted shareholders to file proposals on a broad range of human rights issues, and to address emerging issues. This section provides only a few highlights to provide a sense of the breadth of these efforts, and their efficacy. There are many other significant achievements to relate.

5.5.1   ILO core conventions

Shareholders have engaged in numerous dialogues to encourage companies to adopt codes that incorporate the core conventions of the International Labor Organization and to develop credible systems to implement these standards for their global operations and supply chains. As the ILO conventions were intended to apply to governments, these discussions can involve extensive debate, interpretation and drafting. As a result of these dialogues, companies are increasingly accepting the authority of the ILO to set labor standards, and building systems to enforce them at their suppliers.

Shareholder proposals have prompted companies that are now considered leaders in this area, such as Gap and Mattel, to take their first steps toward independent monitoring of working conditions in their supply chains. Many other companies have agreed to adopt or amend codes of conduct for their supply chains in exchange for the withdrawal of shareholder resolutions. For example, following a series of resolution filings, a shareholder coalition led by Christian Brothers Investment Services pursued a two-year collaborative dialogue with Sears to revise the company's supplier code of conduct and accompanying handbook. The process, which involved a line-by-line review of the company's code and manual against the ILO conventions, resulted in a revised manual that includes key requirements for each code provision, indicators of noncompliance and examples of best practice.[33]

Shareholder proposals preceded what is now a more than 10-year engagement with the Walt Disney Co. on global labor standards. This dialogue, which was eventually combined with a parallel dialogue with McDonald's, recently culminated in the completion of a multi-stakeholder pilot project to find more effective ways to sustain compliance with corporate codes of conduct. The project was tested at 10 factories in southern China.[34]

5.5.2 Public reporting on corporate human rights performance

In 2004, Gap Inc. released its first Social Responsibility Report, after two years of dialogue with shareholders. The company had initially resisted the idea of "quantifying" its performance in this area and a shareholder proposal served as an important negotiating tool.[35]

Gap's report, the first apparel company report to rate suppliers on their adherence to labor standards, drew praise from some of the company's toughest critics. The shareholder group[36] worked with Gap on its two subsequent reports, providing a statement in each. These reports tackled difficult challenges in enforcing global labor standards, including obstacles imposed by the company's own business model and purchasing practices.[37] Gap's initial report has also contributed to an informal standardization of reporting, with Nike and Hewlett-Packard using the format of a key chart in their reports.[38]

5.5.3 Nondiscrimination in the workplace

Shareholder proposals have been successfully used to address a range of discrimination issues, including the use of racist images in advertising, the addition of women and minorities to boards of directors, the disclosure of diversity data and religious discrimination in Northern Ireland.

The shareholder-driven campaign against sexual orientation discrimination has been particularly effective. In the absence of federal law, 430 Fortune 500 companies have adopted formal policies protecting their employees against discrimination based on sexual orientation.[39] This significant development is largely the result of years of shareholder proposals filed pursuant to Rule 14a-8. These dialogues have generally included the following components:

1. Informing the company of the significance of the issue, and identifying it as a "human rights" issue;

2. Discussing the ramifications of adopting a more inclusive policy, and the risks of not doing so, including legal risks and implications for employee morale, retention and recruiting;
3. Defining best practice in terms of policy implementation and communication.

5.5.4 Community impact of mining operations

In 1997, Newmont Mining Corp. endorsed a human rights proposal filed by Christian Brothers Investment Services and a coalition of faith-based investors seeking a report addressing community-based opposition to its operations in the US and around the world, resulting in a 92 percent vote. This was the first time a US mining company had called on its shareholders to vote for a social resolution.[40] An external independent advisory panel has been established to provide advice to the company on strengthening its environmental and social policies and practices.

In April 2008, the Public Service Alliance of Canada Staff Pension Fund, the Ethical Funds Company, and the First and Fourth Swedish National Pension Funds announced that they had convinced Canadian mining firm Goldcorp Inc. to conduct an independent Human Rights Impact Assessment in Guatemala in exchange for the withdrawal of a shareholder proposal.[41]

5.5.5 Corporate political accountability

US corporations are heavily engaged in the political process, contributing millions of dollars to support or oppose candidates, advance political agendas and even elect state judges that are perceived to be "business friendly." Most do so without sufficient oversight or disclosure.

Arguably, corporate political activity compromises a fundamental right enshrined in Article 21(3) of the UDHR: "the will of the people shall be the basis of the authority of government..." as well as other rights dependent upon universal suffrage. The International Chamber of Commerce and the Business and Industry Advisory Committee to the OECD recently acknowledged the potential link between corporate political activities and complicity in human rights violations committed by states, recommending that companies "remain politically neutral to avoid risks of accusations of complicit behavior."[42]

Since 2003, a shareholder campaign led by the Center for Political Accountability[43] has sought to bring greater accountability to corporate political spending through the adoption of codes of conduct, board oversight, and commitments to annual public disclosure of all political contributions, including payments to trade associations and other organizations. This campaign, although not described as a human rights campaign, is working to strengthen democratic systems in the United States that many believe have been undermined through extensive corporate political involvement. The campaign also seeks to address gaps in US law and corporate governance that do not require full disclosure of corporate political activity. To date, this campaign has convinced at least 43 large public companies to disclose their political contributions, including 27 percent of the SandP 100.[44]

Conclusion

> A trustee is held to something stricter than the morals of the market place.
> Chief Justice Benjamin Cardozo, New York Court of Appeals, 1928.[45]

During a series of recent roundtable discussions convened by the SEC to examine the proxy rules,[46] the elimination of nonbinding proposals was considered. During these discussions, and in the SEC releases that followed, very little was said about a fiduciary duty to rise above the "morals of the marketplace" or to monitor corporate behavior to affect a broader public purpose. The SEC's mandate to regulate in the public interest was lost in a discussion of the Commission's duty to vindicate shareholder rights under state law, market efficiencies, and shareholder value.

The Business Roundtable, an influential organization of leading CEOs, took the opportunity to ask the SEC to eliminate the "significant social policy" exception to the ordinary business rule, arguing that these proposals have "little to do with the economics of the company," a particularly difficult statement to reconcile with the numerous no-action requests submitted each year arguing that these proposals concern ordinary business matters. Xerox went so far as to say that the significant social policy exception "has encouraged the submission of shareholder proposals that have no discernable relation to company operations and creating shareholder value."[47] A handful of other major corporations – but only a handful – made similar requests.[48] The Commission even suggested that perhaps companies should be permitted to "opt out" of the shareholder proposal process altogether.

Fortunately, the morals of the marketplace themselves are changing. The SEC received an unprecedented number of public comments – more than 30,000 – with the vast majority opposing changes to Rule 14a-8, and supporting the right of shareholders to have a greater say in how directors are elected. Supportive comments were submitted by fiduciaries from around the world, despite the fact that shareholder resolutions are rarely used in non-US jurisdictions.[49] The SEC has tabled any changes to Rule 14a-8 for the time being.

It is beyond the scope of this essay to consider the history of the fiduciary "duty of loyalty" and the alleged tension between this duty and the pursuit of broader societal goals. It is clear that a fiduciary must vote proxies in the best interests of her clients or beneficiaries, and "best interest" is being defined more and more broadly, particularly for so-called "universal owners" that are invested in the entire market.[50]

As the link between social, environmental and financial performance becomes stronger, the scope of fiduciary duties are changing. The law firm of Freshfields Bruckhaus Deringer has made it clear that in every jurisdiction surveyed (United States, Europe, Japan, Canada and Australia), fiduciary duty arguably *requires* the consideration of environmental, social and governance factors when these factors may impact the long-term value of the portfolio.[51]

Rule 14a-8 and these legal duties work in tandem, forming an increasingly effective mechanism for holding US corporations accountable to international human rights norms.

Notes

1. This essay is based on a paper prepared at the request of Professor John Ruggie, the Special Representative of the United Nations Secretary-General on business and human rights. The author would like to thank Jonas Kron, Steven Lydenberg, Paul Neuhauser, and Vanessa Zimmerman for their comments and suggestions.
2. Unofficial transcript of the Roundtable Discussion on Proposals for Shareholders, Friday, May 25, 2007, p. 23, available at www.sec.gov/news/openmeetings/2007/openmtg_trans052507.pdf
3. A historical discussion of the evolution of Rule 14a-8 is beyond the scope of this essay, which focuses on the rule as currently formulated.
4. Fried, Frank, Harris, Shriver and Jacobson LLP, "Mandating Conduct by US Corporations: a Pro Bono Submission to the United Nations Secretary General's Special Representative for Business and Human Rights" (Oct. 29, 2007), Section III, paragraph 2, available at www.business-humanrights.org/Documents/Fried-Frank-Memo-Dec-2007.pdf
5. Human Rights Watch and Center for Human Rights and Global Justice, NYU School of Law, *On the Margins of Profit: Rights at Risk in the Global Economy*, 20/3(G) (February 2008), available at www.hrw.org/reports/2008/bhr0208
6. Louis D. Brandeis, *Other People's Money and How the Bankers Use It* (August M. Kelley, 1986. Originally published 1914), p. 92. The original article

is available at www.sechistorical.org/collection/papers/Pre1930/1913_12_20_
What_Publicity_Ca.pdf
7. Ibid., pp. 103–4.
8. Ibid., pp. 104–5.
9. On the public interest mandate of the SEC, and this particular insight, see Cynthia A. Williams, "The Securities and Exchange Commission and Corporate Social Transparency," *Harvard Law Review*, 112 (1999): 1197.
10. *SEC v. Transamerica Corp.*, 163 F.2d 511, 513 (3d. Cir. 1947).
11. *SEC and Corporate Social Transparency*, p. 1204.
12. www.sec.gov/spotlight/proxyprocess.htm
13. Rule 14a-8 is available at www.law.uc.edu/CCL/34ActRls/rule14a-8.html or www.sec.gov/rules/final/34-40018.htm. Additional guidance is available at www.sec.gov/interps/legal/cfslb14.htm, www.sec.gov/interps/legal/cfslb14b.htm and www.sec.gov/interps/legal/cfslb14c.htm
14. See Rule 14a-8(i)(1–13).
15. See, generally, David Vogel (1978) *Lobbying the Corporation: Citizen Challenges to Business Authority*. Basic Books, New York.
16. Carolyn Mathiasen, "Shareholder Proposal Success Stories, 1985–2000," *IRRC Corporate Social Issues Reporter* (November 2000), p. 13.
17. This is largely a reflection of state law. SEC Rule 14a-8(i)(1) allows companies to omit proposals that would be "improper under state law." In a note to this paragraph, the SEC explains "[d]epending on the subject matter, some proposals are not considered proper under state law if they would be binding on the company if approved by shareholders. In our experience, most proposals that are cast as recommendations or requests that the board of directors take specified action are proper under state law. Accordingly, we will assume that a proposal drafted as a recommendation or suggestion is proper unless the company demonstrates otherwise." For a more complete discussion of the legal basis of shareholder proposals, see Paul M. Neuhauser's letter to the SEC dated October 2, 2007, submitted on behalf of the ICCR, at www.sec.gov/comments/s7-16-07/s71607-476.pdf ("Precatory proposals are not the creation of Rule 14a-8. Rather they have independent existence under state law and derive from the common law of corporations."). The legal foundation of the shareholder proposal rule, and the SEC's ability to modify and/or eliminate it, were subjects of significant recent debate.
18. See Harrington Investments Press Release: "As Corporate Scandals Mount, Harrington Investments Advocates for Director Accountability in 2008" (March 22, 2008), available at www.harringtoninvestments.com/press/031108.html
19. *Amalgamated Clothing and Textile Workers Union* v. *Wal-Mart Stores*, 821 F. Supp. 877, 1993 U.S. Dist. LEXIS 5382, *12 (S.D.N.Y. 1993), quoting *Roosevelt* v. *E.I. Du Pont de Nemours and Co.*, 958 F.2d 416, 421 (D.C. Cir. 1992).
20. *Lobbying the Corporation*, p. 85.
21. In 2006, for example, Verizon agreed to annual political contributions disclosure after a proposal's support rose to 33 percent.
22. SEC Release 34-40018 (May 21, 1998).
23. James Peck purchased Greyhound shares in 1948 to raise the issue of integrating bus seating in the South at the annual meeting. This culminated in a

1951 federal court decision against Peck and in 1952 the SEC instituted new language prohibiting these types of proposals.

24. *Medical Committee for Human Rights* v. *SEC*, 432 F. 2d. 659, 680–681 (1970), vacated and dismissed as moot, 404 U.S. 402 (1972).
25. Ibid., p. 681.
26. *Cracker Barrel Old Country Stores, Inc.*, 1992 SEC No-Act. LEXIS 984 (Oct. 13, 1992).
27. See, generally, Romanek and Young's ShareholderProposals.com at § 20.01[A][1], *The Cracker Barrel Saga.*
28. There is at least one notable exception to this trend. Proposals that focus on wages being paid at supplier facilities (or elsewhere, with the exception of executive compensation) have continued to be excluded as "ordinary business." ICCR members seeking to address the question of sustainable living wages, for example, have been forced to recast their proposals to focus on other labor issues, despite the centrality of wages to the definition of "sweatshop." See Nordstrom, Inc., 2000 SEC No-Act. LEXIS 525, 526 (March 31, 2000) for Paul Neuhauser's argument exposing the inconsistencies in SEC staff's reasoning.
29. 2008 SEC No-Act. LEXIS 31 (January 22, 2008).
30. "Results of Voting on Genocide-Free Investing," available at www. investorsagainstgenocide.net/page10011382532 (visited on May 9, 2008).
31. ICCR is a member association of 275 faith-based institutional investors. ICCR also includes a broad range of "associate" members, including pension funds, foundations, hospital corporations, economic development funds, asset management companies, colleges, and unions. Each year ICCR members and associates sponsor over 200 shareholder resolutions on social and environmental issues. Domini is an associate member of ICCR, and this author currently serves as cochair of ICCR's contract-supplier working group. Each year, ICCR publishes the "The Proxy Resolutions Book," including the full text of each proposal filed by ICCR members and affiliates. For a status chart of current proposals, visit www.iccr.org/shareholder/proxy_book07/07statuschart.php
32. Mathiasen, C. and Welsh, H. (March 2007) *Social Policy Shareholder Resolutions in 2006: Issues, Votes and Views of Institutional Investors.* Social Issues Service, ISS.
33. For the investor press release, see www.cbisonline.com/page.asp?id=811 and to view the resulting code and manual, visit www.searsholdings.com/govern/code_vendor.htm
34. The Project Kaleidoscope Working Group included The Walt Disney Co., McDonald's, As You Sow Foundation, the Center for Reflection, Education and Action (CREA), Domini Social Investments, the Connecticut State Treasurer's Office, the General Board of Pension and Health Benefits of the United Methodist Church, ICCR, and the Missionary Oblates of Mary Immaculate. See www.domini.com/common/pdf/ProjectKaleidoscope.pdf
35. *The Gap, Inc.*, 2002 SEC No-Act. LEXIS 385, *40 (March 13, 2002). The proposal was withdrawn before SEC staff reached a decision.
36. As You Sow Foundation, Calvert Group, CREA, Domini Social Investments and ICCR.
37. www.gapinc.com/public/SocialResponsibility/sr_report.shtml

38. Compare p. 51 of Hewlett-Packard's 2005 Global Citizenship Report and p. 36 of Nike's Fiscal Year 2004 Corporate Responsibility Report to the chart on p. 14 of Gap's 2003 Social Responsibility Report.

39. www.hrc.org/Template.cfm?Section=Work_Life

40. Press release by Christian Brothers Investment Services, "91.6 Percent of Newmont Shareholders Support Resolution for Mining Company to Report on its Impacts on Local Communiites" (April 24, 2007), at www.cbisonline.com/page.asp?id=873

41. www.share.ca/files/Joint_release_on_Goldcorp_final_080424.pdf. The Canadian shareholder proposal rule is based on the US rule. For a helpful comparative analysis, see Aaron A. Dhir, "Realigning the Corporate Building Blocks: Shareholder Proposals as a Vehicle for Achieving Corporate Social and Human Rights Accountability," *American Business Law Journal*, 43 (Summer 2006): 365.

42. "Business and Human Rights: the Role of Business in Weak Governance Zones," submission to John Ruggie, the UN Special Representative to the Secretary General on business and human rights by ICC and BIAC, December 2006, paragraph 19, p. 6, available at www.reports-and-materials.org/Role-of-Business-in-Weak-Governance-Zones-Dec-2006.pdf

43. The campaign includes 26 institutional investors and allied groups. See www.politicalaccountability.net. The SEC has consistently held that lobbying activities constitute "ordinary business." This campaign, therefore, which uses the shareholder proposal as a primary tool, has avoided explicit requests for expenditures on lobbying activity.

44. See "Five New Companies Agree to Political Disclosure, Including Trade Association and c4 Payments: Number Hits 43 as 2008 Proxy Season Unfolds," www.politicalaccountability.net/files/CPApercent20-percent20presspercent20 releasepercent20-percent2043percent20-percent202-28-08.pdf

45. *Meinhard* v. *Salmon*, 164 N.E. 545, 546 (N.Y. 1928).

46. www.sec.gov/spotlight/proxyprocess.htm

47. Anne Mulcahy, the CEO of Xerox, is also Chair of the Business Roundtable Corporate Governance Taskforce, and the author of both letters, available at www.sec.gov/comments/s7-16-07/s71607.shtml

48. See, for example, letters from Apache, Caterpillar, and Burlington Northern Santa Fe Corporation (ibid.).

49. See, for example, letter to the SEC on behalf of 47 signatories from 10 countries, representing assets under management of approximately US$1.4 trillion, available at www.sec.gov/comments/s7-16-07/s71607-409.pdf

50. See Hawley, J. P. and Williams, A. T. (2000) *The Rise of Fiduciary Capitalism: How Institutional Investors Can Make Corporate America More Democratic.* University of Pennsylvania Press, Philadelphia.

51. Freshfields Bruckhaus Deringer, "A Legal Framework for the Integration of Environmental, Social and Governance Issues into Institutional Investment" (October 2005). For a cautionary view of the focus on "materiality," and the risk that it may lead to ignoring certain financially "immaterial" human rights issues, see Christoph Butz and Jean Laville, "Ethos Discussion Paper No. 2: Socially Responsible Investment: Avoiding the Financial Materiality Trap" (June 2007), available at www.ethosfund.ch/upload/publication/p180e_070702_No_Avoiding_the_Financial_Materiality_Trap_in_SRI.pdf

Part II
Adopting a Sustainable Perspective in Financial Institutions and Markets

6
Sustainable Banking: the Banco Real Model

Leo Johnson and Christel Scholten

Introduction and background

From the outset, with the acquisition of Banco Real in 1998, Banco Real's President, Fabio C. Barbosa, laid down a challenge – the organization needed to create a "new bank for a new society," integrating social, environmental and economic dimensions into all aspects of the business. Despite ranking tenth in 2006[1] in terms of GDP, Brazil, a country with a population of 184 million,[2] ranks seventieth[3] on the Human Development Index (HDI) and 116th[4] on the UN Gini Index, an income inequality metric. In terms of the environment, Brazil is losing significant amounts of its forests to deforestation each year and faces mounting issues around air, soil and water pollution. In Barbosa's words, "We need to influence capitalism to become more humane and inclusive." In 2000 Barbosa laid out a formal vision for the organization:

> The Brazilian market and society are evolving and require a new role for banks. Banks should act as facilitators of a society that is economically efficient, socially just, politically democratic and environmentally sustainable. We desire this change and aim to be one of the leaders of this transition in the market and in society.

The vision was there, compelling in its social and environmental logic. The task was implementation within the bank, and Banco Real faced a number of institutional challenges:

1. *Banking sector good practice*: while sustainability practices have become increasingly commonplace within leading commercial banks, with over 125 banks applying for the Financial Times 2008 Sustainable Banking Awards, back in 2000 to talk environmental and social issues

was outside banking norms. Two assumptions dominated best practice: first that banks did not pollute, second that environmental and social issues were a luxury good – a Western NGO concern and not the preoccupation of emerging markets. Put the two together, for a bank in Brazil to put sustainability as its core vision was not just a break with current practice. It could be seen as subversive – a potential violation of management's core duty to focus on making money for its shareholders.

2. *Competition within the Brazilian banking sector:* at the same time Banco Real's margin for error was particularly small. Brazil is a highly competitive financial market. In addition to the international banks, several high-quality national banks compete for market share and the best employees – among them Itaú, Bradesco, Banco do Brasil, Caixa Econômica Federal and Unibanco. Flawed or unsuccessful innovation in this competitive landscape would have a simple consequence – they would lose clients and market share.

3. *Size:* at the same time, Banco Real's size made the task of reorienting its offering around sustainability a challenging one. Banco Real is the third largest private bank in Brazil, with over 30,000 employees, 13 million clients, 2000 branches and banking service points, and approximately 1400 suppliers.

4. *Breadth of business lines:* in addition to this size, Banco Real has a diverse range of business lines, among them both wholesale and retail banking operations, asset management, private banking, microcredit and a consumer finance business. An integrated sustainability value proposition would have to make sense across this entire range of operations.

5. *Organizational complexity:* finally, there was the challenge of institutional history. Banco Real, at that point, was the product of the merger of four institutions, each with their own distinctive and diverse historic cultures. ABN AMRO Bank (a major Dutch bank active in Brazil since 1917), Banco Real (acquired by the ABN AMRO Group in 1998), and Bandepe and Sudameris (acquired since 1998 by Banco Real).

There are two classic approaches to implementing organizational change within an organization as complex as a merger-based bank. The first is fiat – the executive order: "I am telling you what we are going to do." The second is consultants – outsourced advisors providing an independent recommendation: "This is what independent advisors are confirming we need to do." Fabio Barbosa went for neither. Rather than hiring a consultancy to facilitate the process, the President led brainstorming sessions with groups of senior executives to discuss what the vision of a new bank for a new society meant in practice. It was "we are going to figure out ourselves what we need to do." And not just at the strategic/visioning level, but at the level of execution. For the Banco Real executives involved in these sessions, some of the dilemmas were immediately visible (Box 6.1).

Box 6.1   Initial dilemmas of implementation

- How do you require environmental compliance against a set of domestic and international competitors that may not be applying the same criteria, without risking losing clients?
- Do you cut clients when they fail to comply with environmental and social policies? Or do you get down into the trenches, and engage with substandard performers to bring them up to good practice?
- How, above all, even if you believe in it personally, do you reinforce the importance of sustainability internally without regulatory or nongovernmental pressure?

The triple bottom line, in short, sounds great. Is it possible though in practice, and in the emerging markets context of Brazil? Can a bank in fact reconcile the social, the environmental and the financial? Or is the gap between values and value unbridgeable? At the same time as Barbosa's vision led the bank to confront these initial dilemmas, signals were emerging from broader discussions with clients and client-facing staff; a shift was occurring in the market. A government sometimes hamstrung by inadequate resources to enforce regulation was being joined by new market forces. With increased connectivity, new stakeholders from NGOs to local communities to the media and export market customers were starting to act as informal environmental and social regulators on companies in Brazil. The effect, one that is still continuing, was what you could call the privatization of regulation – an evolution in accountability, with a new and complex set of informal regulators, offering a range of unpredictable and sometimes irreversible sanctions for nonperforming companies. These ranged from loss of export markets, to strikes and sabotage to land takeovers by the Movimento Sem Terra (Landless Peoples' Movement). The externalities of unsustainable practices were starting to be internalized onto the balance sheets of Brazilian business.

Clients were beginning to see environmental and social issues translate into risk to their operations, but they were also seeing opportunity. These risks and opportunities were evolving rapidly – from sustainable forestry companies winning market share with multinational retailers requiring certification, to textile companies reducing heating and water costs through energy efficiency, to oil and gas industry clients seeking capital from development banks and commercial banks with social and environmental requirements. The sectors and business lines were diverse, and the opportunities client-specific, but one role for the bank was emerging. Its approach to sustainability could not be based just around compliance – imposing the bank's risk management conditions – but around value added, providing solutions to clients that helped them transform the material risks they were beginning to face into opportunity, as well as managing the bank's own risk. Votorantim Celulose e Papel (VCP), a pulp and paper company, instantiated this possibility (Box 6.2).

Box 6.2   Case example: VCP

VCP, part of the Votorantim Group, and one of the largest pulp and paper producers in Latin America, identified an opportunity to expand production in the Brazilian state of Rio Grande do Sul, with the goal of setting up a state-of-the-art chlorine-free pulp and paper plant, processing eucalyptus to be harvested from local farmers. For VCP the project represented an opportunity to expand market share as a regional producer. For Rio Grande do Sul, the project represented a critical source of economic development.

The project nevertheless presented risks, including the threat of land takeovers by the Landless Peoples' Movement. In an innovative partnership between VCP and Banco Real, the Poupança Florestal Program was created, in which agricultural producers, members of the landless movement, received credit from Banco Real at lower rates to sustainably grow eucalyptus trees on a reserved part of their land. This partnership protects the forests, guarantees production for VCP and income for the members of the landless movement.

The core dilemma around sustainability, then, appeared to be an illusion. This was not forcing compliance on the client. Sustainability could be win–win. Clients, just like the bank, were facing sustainability issues from their stakeholders. The bank, if it did it right, could differentiate itself, gain business of enhanced asset quality, and achieve environmental and social impact by helping clients make it work. The mandate to differentiate the bank through sustainability value added was clear. The strategic benefit that could result to the bank was also becoming clear in principle: to grow the bank's business and to increase its value through attracting and retaining clients, increasing employee engagement and satisfaction and positioning itself as a leader in governance, ethics and sustainability. But how do you put that into practice? How do you develop and systematize sustainability products and services that can add value to the business of clients across a bank with 13 million clients? Where do you start in a country of continental dimensions? When asked during a facilitated discussion to reflect on the core values that underpinned the movement to roll out sustainability in the bank, Banco Real staff identified six essential principles,[5] summarized in Box 6.3.

Box 6.3   Essential principles of the movement

1. *Start from within.* The first step is to raise awareness with employees – not just emotional awareness of the problems of sustainability, but technical awareness of the potential solutions. What is created is a ripple effect. The emotional and technical awareness translates into engagement. This engagement translates into impact on the sustainability practices of the organization. The practices the organization adopts influence change in the market with clients, suppliers, partners and competitors, which then may have a wider impact on society and the environment.

2. *Integration of sustainability into the core business.* The key to innovation and creating traction with sustainability is to integrate sustainability into the core business – not just the core products and services, but the processes and policies that support them, underpinning sustainability as a core, not bolt on, operation of the bank.

3. *Windows of opportunity.* Banks are complex systems. Resistance to change is sometimes critical in defending these complex systems from disruptive change that may not ultimately support the business. Sustainability – challenging, as it does, some traditional banking assumptions – will encounter potential resistance within the traditional banking organization. At the same time, the fundamental shifts in the market supporting sustainability as a business approach will produce sustainability champions within clients, senior management teams and executives. Finding windows of opportunity, seeking out early adopters or building on existing initiatives, may reduce resistance, allowing the organization to generate the quick wins essential for convincing a broader target audience to adopt.

---

4. *The movement is not linear, and works by contamination.* There is no step-by-step approach to sustainability. There is no master plan. There is no off-the-shelf solution. Traditional planning approaches are not necessarily useful as the variables involved are people-dependent, diverse and complex. What is essential is to engage individuals one by one, reengaging and getting their feedback to confirm their individual commitment and validate the overall strategic direction. As the individuals become engaged, they become multipliers of the movement.

5. *Collective construction.* Implementing sustainability within a bank means delivering solutions that work for multiple stakeholders – from clients, to communities, to partners, suppliers and the government. These solutions cannot be developed or delivered in isolation. They depend on collaboration with others. Networks and partnerships with clients, suppliers, employees, the government and the wider society are crucial for solutions that will meet stakeholder needs and be embedded as best practice.

6. *There are various ways of implementing sustainability.* There is no strategic formula for implementing sustainability at the institutional level. Each organization has different issues and different starting points and therefore, sustainability will take on a different approach in each. Each organization must understand its needs, culture and identify the best approach to take.

6.1 Key success factors in implementing sustainability at Banco Real

In implementing these principles, a number of key success factors have emerged (Box 6.4). These ten factors will be examined in turn.

Box 6.4   Key success factors in the Banco Real story

1. Visionary leadership
2. Evolving the governance model
3. Integrating sustainability into the core business
4. Promoting client-focused innovation
5. Education and engagement for cultural change
6. Transferring ownership
7. Aligning the organization
8. Measuring progress
9. Engaging stakeholders
10. Shifting the system

6.1.1 Visionary leadership

In 2000, as a critical first step, Fabio Barbosa had articulated a vision for banks, "[...] as facilitators of a society that is economically efficient, socially just, politically democratic and environmentally sustainable." He elaborated this with a specific mission for the bank, one that was consistent with, and to some extent prefigured, the shift in the market toward a networked economy, with a web of stakeholders driving risk and reward for clients: "To satisfy the client, creating value for shareholders, employees and the community, maintaining the highest standards of ethics, and differentiating ourselves by the quality of our products, services and, most importantly, exemplary client servicing." This message, and his challenge – to create a new bank for a new society – has remained consistent, driven throughout the organization, across the Brazilian banking sector through Barbosa's role as President of Febraban (the Federation of Brazilian Banks), and has continued in initial discussions with Banco Santander.

6.1.2 Evolving the governance model

With a vision and mission established from the top, Barbosa then led the development of a governance structure to oversee implementation of this vision, with an explicit strategic objective to integrate sustainability into all strategies, products, processes, policies and relationships of the organization. This governance model, evolving over time, has played a key role in integrating sustainability into core businesses, with key milestones including the following:

- 2000 – The Bank of Value
- 2001 – Social Responsibility Department
- 2002 – Market, Management and Social Action committees
- 2003 – Education and Sustainable Development (ESD) Department
- 2006 – Sustainability Council

Box 6.5 provides an overview of this evolution in more detail.

Box 6.5 Milestones in the governance model

- *2000 – The Bank of Value*: as a first step in the implementation of the model, in 2000 the Bank of Value Committee was formed. This committee of senior leaders discussed detailed strategies for becoming "a new bank for a new society." Key ideas generated included specific initiatives around the environment, diversity and suppliers and task forces to create an ethical fund, microcredit business and risk policy.

- *2001 – Social Responsibility Department*: at the end of 2001, the Social Responsibility Department, reporting directly to the President, was set up to coordinate the integration of sustainable development into the organization with the clear intention that it would dissolve within the next few years to ensure this integration. Its mandate was not academic, but a combination of thought leadership, inspiration and the incubation and transfer of sustainability practices.
- *2002 – Market, Management and Social Action committees*: in 2002, three committees were set up, the Market, Management and Social Action committees, with the goal of providing decentralized forums for the emerging sustainability leaders within the bank to discuss and further develop ideas for the different streams of sustainable development. This approach produced an immediate series of results. The *Market Committee* began to elaborate a series of projects and ideas related to the core business from the ethical fund to microcredit to sustainability products. The *Management Committee* focused on internal management issues such as diversity, ecoefficiency and suppliers. The *Social Action Committee* discussed the social investment strategy and identified a range of specific projects to focus on and invest in.
- *2003 – Education and Sustainable Development (ESD) Department*: in 2003, in a pivotal decision, reflecting the key role of education in building engagement, the Social Responsibility Department temporarily merged with the training academy to form the Education and Sustainable Development (ESD) Department. After a period of three years, with sustainable development permeating the education model, the Training and Education Department returned to Human Resources and the Sustainable Development (SD) Department continued with its mandate, to integrate sustainable development in the organization. The Department currently consists of approximately 60 professionals.
- *2006 – Sustainability Council*: based on the progress in mainstreaming sustainability in the organization, in May 2006, Banco Real set up a Sustainability Council. The Council meets once a month and its membership includes 30 senior leaders from the majority of the departments of the organization and is chaired by the President. The objectives of the Sustainability Council include: (i) ensure the management of and accountability for sustainability including the development and management of the sustainability strategy; (ii) ensure the transition of responsibility for the integration of sustainability to the individual departments of the organization; and (iii) guarantee and monitor the sustainability performance of the organization.

6.1.3 Integrating sustainability into the core business

Critical to the success of the bank's mission was the conviction that sustainability was a core, not bolt-on, operation of a bank. Sustainability, in other words, did not and does not belong in a philanthropy department; it belongs in the business – harnessing the power of the main banking platform. The bank systematically identified opportunities to build the business within the core business, from the pioneering Ethical Fund to its social and environmental products and its microcredit operations.

6.1.4 Promoting client-focused innovation

Consistent with the vision of focusing on the client, a key success factor in making sustainability stick with the business was coming up with innovative sustainability products and services that were adapted to clients' core business needs, were profitable and were scalable. Critical to this innovation was to put together diverse teams, with a skills mix including client-facing staff, sustainability specialists, product specialists, legal experts, risk teams, marketing and where possible client representatives themselves.

6.1.5 Education and engagement for cultural change

Driven by the principle that engagement starts from within, and that implementing sustainability is ultimately therefore a cultural change process, Banco Real has from the outset invested significantly in employee training. Since 2002, the bank has provided programs on sustainability across all levels of the organization. The first large-scale program was run in 2002 in partnership with Friends of the Earth, training 1500 retail branch and relationship managers on social and environmental risk. Since then, the number of staff trained annually has increased substantially. In 2007 alone, 12,590 employees were trained on the topic of sustainability, with approximately 1.5 million hours of training sessions addressing different aspects of the Brazilian sustainability challenge.

One of the flagship programs in 2007 was the Development of Leaders in Sustainability Program, designed to develop leaders in sustainability in the retail branch network across Brazil. Participants in the program become a reference in sustainability in their region, not only for their teams but also for clients, suppliers and the wider community. The program consisted of 4 modules for a total of 52 hours in-class training. On completing each module, the 200 participants cascade the content to a further 2000 managers.

6.1.6   Transferring ownership

If sustainability is truly going to be integrated into the main banking platform, then the main banking platform has to own it. At the same time, the development of a cohesive set of sustainability products embedding international best practice will benefit from a core of specialists providing expertise, quality control support and coordination. Addressing this dual need was a core objective of the *Sustainable Development Department*, established with a mission to oversee the strategy for, and governance of, sustainable development in the organization and to support departments in the complex integration of sustainable development into their respective strategies, businesses, processes and policies.

The combination of structured building of capability of commitment, incubation of sustainability practices, followed by decentralization and ownership by the relevant business team under an institution-wide governance structure proved critical in gaining institutional buyin, and has generated a range of concrete results in terms of business development. The responsibility for sustainability no longer solely belongs to the Sustainable Development Department. Each department is responsible, and is held accountable by the Sustainability Council. Table 6.1 shows the results of this combined governance and support structure in the progressive incubation and mainstreaming of a series of sustainability initiatives.

Dispersed across the organization, there were as of 2008 over 400 employees dedicated part- or full-time to implementing sustainability in the bank. These consist of social and environmental risk managers, specialists in sustainability products, microcredit, carbon credits, SRI (Social Responsible Investment) funds, ecoefficiency, diversity, sustainability training and supplier management. The majority of departments of the organization now have a specific sustainability action plan. Each plan includes how the respective department aims to increase competitiveness through integrating sustainability into its core business, processes and policies, through the education and engagement of employees, and the engagement of clients, suppliers and other stakeholders. Plans for new products, innovations in processes, events to engage clients and suppliers and training and education for employees are also included. There are nevertheless a number of challenges remaining in terms of fully transferring from ownership to the business. One is to continue to align and integrate the sustainability plans and targets of each department into its regular business plans and targets. Another is to ensure further alignment between the overall sustainability targets and indicators and the corporate strategy.

Table 6.1 Establishment and transfer of sustainability initiatives

Initiative	Initial owner	Year	Transferred to/ set up in department	Year
Ethical Fund	Asset Management	2001	Asset Management	2001
Engagement with Suppliers	Social Responsibility/ESD	2001	Group Finance/Shared Services	2004/2008
Social and Environment Risk Policy	Working Group	2002	Risk Department	2002
Microcredit	Social Responsibility/ESD	2002	Risk Department/Retail Business Unit	2005/2008
Social and Environmental Products			Products Department	2003
Ecoefficiency	Working Group	2001	Infrastructure and Logistics	2006
Diversity	Working Group	2001	Human Resources	2003
Sustainability Report – content	Social Responsibility/ESD	2002	Brand Strategy and Corporate Communications Department	2006
Sustainability Indicators	Social Responsibility/ESD	2002	Group Finance	2006
Education and training	Social Responsibility/ESD	2003	Human Resources	2006
Sustainable Construction	Social Responsibility/ESD		Engineering Department	2006

6.1.7   Aligning the organization

For sustainability approaches to work, the organization needs to align its policies, processes and procedures to be consistent with and support the chosen strategy. To describe in detail the full range of organizational changes required and measures taken is beyond the scope of this chapter, but as a catalyst to induce broader systemic change, senior management incentives have proven critical in aligning interests. The performance management system of Banco Real management and senior management includes goals linked to the bank's performance in social, environmental and economic issues. The evolution of these indicators has a direct influence on the compensation of leaders. Crucially, these incentives contain both extrinsic and intrinsic elements.

In July 2007, the bank created the Sustainability and Innovation Recognition Program, which is aimed at identifying and awarding initiatives already implemented by employees and that have brought about a positive impact for sustainability. The program has quarterly award cycles. Amongst the projects awarded in 2007 is the "Othon Verde" Project, where Banco Real financed and advised on the implementation of sustainability principles for the Othon hotel chain in Brazil. The project generated a 47 percent reduction in water consumption and 25 percent in electric power consumption in the client's installations, implementation of waste separation activities and recycling, reduction in operating costs and an increase in the occupancy rate of the hotel.

6.1.8   Measuring progress

The Sustainability Council monitors the sustainability action plans for each department, overall sustainability indicators for the organization, performance of the competition in sustainability and debates and approves strategic projects. A list of the key sustainability performance indicators that are monitored is detailed in Box 6.6.[6]

Box 6.6   Performance indicators

Products and services

- Social and environmental products
- Business deals that address sustainability issues (social, environmental and economic)
- Ethical Fund
- Microcredit
- Carbon credit financing

Branding and client satisfaction

- Sustainable development brand attribute (comparison with peers)
- Brand attractiveness (comparison with peers)
- Client loyalty

Engagement

- Clients that received training or participated in forums on sustainability organized by Banco Real
- Suppliers that received training or participated in forums on sustainability organized by Banco Real

Recognition

- Mentions in the media on the bank and sustainability
- Awards

Risk

- Social and environmental risk analyses conducted

Internal ecology

- Water consumption
- Energy consumption
- Paper consumption
- Toner consumption
- CO_2 emissions and neutralization
- Recycling facilities (branches and administrative buildings)

Employees

- Employee engagement
- Employee turnover
- Employee lawsuits against Banco Real
- Employees trained in sustainable development
- Employee participation in Banco Real-sponsored volunteer activities

6.1.9 Engaging stakeholders

Stakeholder engagement has underpinned the bank's approach to sustainability from the outset, with employees, clients, suppliers, nonprofit organizations, external specialists and representatives of the community engaged as protagonists in a range of sustainability initiatives. In 2006, the organization set out to develop a position statement on stakeholder engagement:

> Together we can do things that we couldn't dream of doing on our own. Stakeholder Engagement is the bond that we aim to create with all who have a relationship with our organization, regardless of the role that individual plays: employee, supplier, shareholder, opinion-leader, citizen, client, etc. This bond will be stronger the greater the satisfaction of the individual with the relationship with the bank and the greater his/her identification with our values and with our dream of creating a better society, a better industry, a better bank.

The bank's position statement also recognized the linkage to the bank's core business, both in gaining and retaining clients: "*The greatest recognition we could expect from any of these relationships is the voluntary adhesion of an individual or organization in becoming our client. Relationships maintained through satisfaction of services provided and the sharing of common values and dreams ensure the success and continuity of these relationships and consequently, contribute to the generation of sustainable results.*" The satisfaction of the broader stakeholder group, in other words, was recognized as core to both the vision and the bank's direct business prospects.

To better understand the organization's relationships, a stakeholder map was developed using the criteria of value creation. The stakeholders are divided into four groups:

- those that contribute to the creation of value;
- those that regulate value;
- those that have interest in the creation of value;
- those that surround the creation of value.

The bank's approach has been to engage with these stakeholders, identifying their specific drivers or business needs, and specific initiatives that supported those goals or business needs while enhancing the triple bottom line returns. Table 6.2 gives illustrative examples.

6.1.10   Shifting the system

At the end of 2006, the organization's revised vision, mission and model were launched, updating them and aligning them with an emerging organizational belief – that people live, globally, in an increasingly interconnected society, that individuals are part of a web of diverse stakeholders, that there is a need to incorporate social, environmental and

Table 6.2 Examples of stakeholder engagement in Banco Real sustainability initiatives

Stakeholders	Nature of engagement	Example
Employees	• Participation in multidisciplinary groups • Participation in sustainability education programs • Internal communication • Participation in volunteer activities	• Ecoefficiency group • Sustainability workshop • Internal campaigns: What is sustainability to you? • Brazil School Project
Suppliers	• Participation in ongoing forums to discuss how to integrate sustainability in the business • Development of new products and/or services • Participation in volunteer activities	• Suppliers' Forum • Implementation of the use of recycled paper • Brazil School Project
Nonprofit organizations	• Product development • Support in education and training • Participation in social investment programs • Support with diversity initiatives	• Ethical Fund • Social and environmental risk training • Real Friend Program • Partnership to include and integrate staff with Down's syndrome
Clients	• Participation in external awareness campaigns • Use of social and environmental products • Participation in sustainability education programs • Participation in social investment programs	• Clients starring in external awareness campaigns • Clients using social and environmental financial products • Real Space for Sustainability Practices • Real Friend Program

economic aspects into all business decisions, and that employees should aim for the satisfaction of the individual, regardless of the relationship that person has with the organization – whether he or she is a client, supplier, part of the community, shareholder or employee.

The vision expanded in scope: "*A new bank for a new society. A society in evolution, increasingly better informed and aware, strives to integrate human and environmental to economic aspects in all of its decisions. We, as an organization and as individuals are change agents in this evolution.*" Linked to it, the formal mission, equally, was expanded: "*To be an organization renowned for providing outstanding financial services to our clients, achieving sustainable results and the satisfaction of individuals and organizations, who together with us contribute to the evolution of society.*" Consistent with the vision and mission, the new model, launched in 2006, had at its center the individual surrounded by a broader group of stakeholders including employees, clients, suppliers, shareholders, society and the environment (see Figure 6.1).

The evolution of the vision, mission and model marks a crucial further transition, perhaps more radical still than the first movement towards client focused sustainability offerings. While there are opportunities from delivering sustainability products and services to the client, there are broader opportunities and triple bottom line results from delivering sustainability to society as a whole. Not just that, but long-term financial results will not actually be possible without this societal approach. A bank is as successful as the society around it is healthy. As Fabio Barbosa has commented: "*The whole sustainability strategy is a win–win– win proposition, where shareholders, clients, employees and other stakeholders get good results*". This expanded vision, mission and model now drives Banco Real's engagement with an increasingly broad cross-section of the Brazilian economy, leveraging the bank's multiple points of intersection with society to create change beyond the bank's direct client base. Box 6.7 presents highlights.

Over the last eight years, Banco Real has gained significant experience in integrating sustainability into its business. Perhaps most importantly, Banco Real has achieved a demonstration effect, showing the triple bottom line returns that are possible in emerging market context and influencing the strategic visions and offerings of a range of leading domestic and international bankers. In December 2007, in response to growing demand by clients, suppliers and opinion leaders, Banco Real decided to open up its approaches and share them with the broader market to further the goal of societal change. With the launch of the "*Espaço Real de Práticas em Sustentabilidade (Práticas)*" or "Real Space for

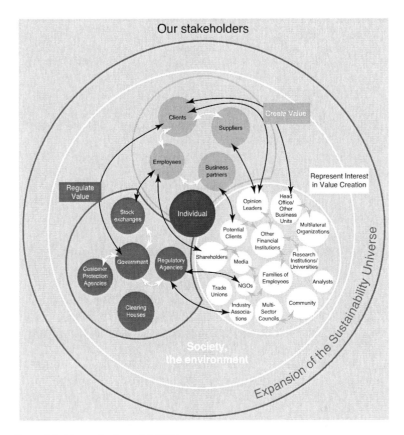

Figure 6.1 Banco Real model 2006

Box 6.7 Leveraging the bank's impact

Clients: Client Councils were set up, made up of clients from the different segments. Meetings are held periodically during which clients offer their feedback and ideas, contributing to strengthening the relationship with the organization. There are currently 10 groups spread out across several Brazilian cities, with a total of approximately 120 members. The organization also engages clients in sustainable development, raising awareness about the topic and exploring ways in which clients can adopt sustainability practices in their companies. This indirectly leads to increased business and increased client loyalty.

Suppliers: since 2001, the organization has increased engagement with its suppliers. Starting with a small group of 15 engaged suppliers in 2001, this number has grown to 164 in 2007; 458 have signed the organization's Value Partnership which includes a set of guidelines for the inclusion of social and environmental considerations into the suppliers' businesses. Many of these suppliers today are multipliers of sustainability practices in their respective industries. As a separate initiative, in 2006, the legal department engaged 100 law firms to incorporate sustainability issues within legal good practice.

Brokers: the treasury department also began to engage brokerage firms in 2006 to raise awareness of sustainability and influence the integration of sustainability criteria into their core business. The potential for influence is substantial as the brokerage firms engaged represent 80 percent of the capital market assets negotiated in Brazil. As a direct incentive, brokerage firms are ranked in terms of sustainability performance. Those that rank highest receive preference in providing services to the bank.

Insurers: in 2008, the bank coordinated with World Business Council a review of sustainbility risks and opportunities for the Brazilian insurance business. Core to the approach was the concept that insurers could play a win–win and value added role in helping clients mitigate sustainability risk rather than transferring risk to reinsurers, exiting markets, or increasing pricing.

Financial sector outreach: the bank has led a range of outreach initiatives with key target audiences within the Brazilian financial sector. These include the World Business Council's Chamber for the Financial Sector, FEBRABAN (The Federation of Brazilian Banks) and groups such as the Soy Roundtable.

Journalists: in 2008, the bank initiated a sustainability program for journalists to engage them more deeply in the topic. A series of workshops is being delivered throughout the year.

Employees and society: one of Banco Real's social investment initiatives, the Real Friend Program, involves the incubation of social projects focused on education and sustainable development. In 2007, 4614 clients and 17,472 employees participated in and donated to the Real Friend Program, where part of an individual's taxes can be destined to social projects. Also in 2007, the organization had 1959 volunteers working on the Brazil School Project, a project focused on education.

Sustainability Practices" the bank aims specifically to share the organization's experience in integrating sustainability with clients, suppliers and the wider public. Through online courses and forums, and in-class training programs, the "Real Space for Sustainability Practices" aims to support clients and suppliers in integrating sustainability into their business and raise awareness among individuals and organizations to *"shorten the distance towards a sustainable world."*

Box 6.8   Práticas: sharing with society

"Práticas" offers a series of online courses and in-class training programs on sustainability. The online courses available include a Sustainable Construction course, based on the bank's experience of building the first environmentally sustainably built bank branch in Brazil, a course on Human Rights based on the Universal Declaration and a Diversity course, based on the bank's experience with implementing a diversity program. Also available online include a virtual library, a database of Banco Real, client and supplier sustainability practices and sustainability discussion forums.

As for in-class training, Práticas offers a number of options including a monthly Open House for those interested in learning more about the Banco Real case, regular 1-day Sustainability Workshops, a Speaker Series and visits to the environmentally sustainably built bank branch. For Banco Real's clients and suppliers, a two-day course is offered to support companies in integrating sustainability into their business inspired by the bank's principles and practices. Regional workshops are also held to engage a wider group of clients and suppliers across Brazil.

Práticas aims to create an ever-growing network of companies, organizations and individuals committed to putting sustainability into practice and to raising the bar to *"shorten the distance towards a sustainable world."*

6.2   Sustainability in action: results for the bank to date

While it is difficult to quantify the aspects of performance directly due to sustainability, the bank appears to have derived significant benefit from its sustainability initiative. Key results include the following.

6.2.1   Group business results

Profit before tax: since the year 2000, Banco Real's net profit has increased from US$159 million to US$1.7 billion in 2007.

Revenues: revenues have also increased, from US$5.6 billion in 2002 to US$7.2 billion in 2007.

Credit volume: far from sustainability acting as a handbrake on deal flow, Banco Real's new sustainability offering and capacity to support clients in managing the risks of a borderline deal appears to have enhanced deal flows, with the volume of credit granted growing by 157 percent since 2001.

Assets: Banco Real assets totaled US$95.3 billion at September 30, 2007, with a growth of 73 percent in comparison with the same period last year.

Ratings: in 2007, Fitch Ratings increased Banco Real's long-term national rating from AA+ (bra) to AAA (bra), ranking it among the top Brazilian banks in risk rating. As a consequence, the long- and short-term ratings on a global scale were increased to BBB (long-term in foreign currency), BBB (long-term in domestic currency) and F3 (short-term).

Client growth: the number of clients that bank with the organization increased from 4.8 million in 2000 to 13.1 million in 2006. Fabio Barbosa comments: *"Business clients, both small and large companies, are now taking our stance into consideration and have either intensified their business or started doing business with us. Many have stated explicitly that they did this because of what we stand for."*

Client satisfaction: results from client satisfaction surveys by The Gallup Organization show that the number of clients that recommend the bank has grown from 34 percent in 2002 to 44 percent in 2006 and that client satisfaction has also increased during the same period from 68 to 74 percent.

Brand value: in a ranking of Brazilian brands by the Magazine *Isto É Dinheiro* in partnership with BrandAnalytics, Banco Real's brand ranked ninth, valued at US$384 million.

- The 119 percent increase of Banco Real's brand from 2005 to 2006 was the largest yearly increase among the 18 most valuable brand names listed. The magazine stated that the increased value of Banco Real's brand reflects the organization's consistent positioning in sustainability.
- *"Our brand has moved up from fifth to second place and has maintained this position since 2005 in terms of brand attractiveness and recognition. This means that when individuals are asked in a survey which bank they would open an account with, we rank second,"* says Fabio Barbosa.

- The gap between the bank that is the current leader in attractiveness and Banco Real is becoming smaller every year: 13 percent in 2004; 10 percent in 2005; 6 percent in 2006 and 3 percent in 2007.
- From 2003 to the last quarter of 2007, Banco Real's association with the sustainability concept evolved by 9 percent. With this, the Banco Real brand took on the number one position in sustainability among banks in Brazil, according to the brand image and communication survey conducted monthly by The Gallup Organization among the population served by banks.

Employees: core to the model has been to create a broad base of engaged employees committed to producing sustainable results.

- Employee satisfaction and engagement: in 2001 the employee satisfaction rate was 68 percent. By 2003 it was 77 percent. In 2006, the employee engagement rate was 91 percent and employee pride in working at Banco Real had grown to 98 percent. Almost 2000 employees are engaged in our corporate volunteering program and in 2007, over 17,000 employees (51 percent of staff) contributed to the *Amigo Real* Program, a social investment initiative. In the bank's last Engagement Survey, for 99 percent of staff, the bank acts in a responsible manner in relation to the environment and 97 percent stated that the organization acts responsibly within society and the community.
- Attraction of talent: the bank's sustainability profile has also strengthened the attractiveness of the bank in Brazil's labor market. In 2007, more than 20,800 young professionals signed up for the 20 openings offered by the bank's trainee program.

Credit risk management and asset quality: Banco Real was the first bank in the region to create a social and environmental risk process, aimed at reducing financial and reputational risk for the organization.

- Risk assessment: Banco Real analyzes the social and environmental risk of medium and large companies in 22 sectors of major impact, such as oil and gas, lumber extraction, agriculture, cattle raising and mining. Amongst items monitored are environmental licenses, disposal of solid waste, air pollution control, treatment of liquid waste, number of accidents, hygiene, occupational safety and health, signs of child or slave labor and outsourcing of dangerous and polluting processes.
- Risk mitigation: 3177 social and environmental risk analyses were conducted in 2006. The bank analyzes the corporate risk of clients

of all sizes. From small to large, the bank helps identify problems and ways to solve them. The offer of credit is conditioned to the adoption of good practices.

- Equator Principles implementation: since the adoption of the Equator Principles, 20 analyses have been conducted, of which 3 were rejected. In addition to enhancing asset quality, the bank's risk process has secured it lead arranger roles and fund manager roles for a range of socially and environmentally complex transactions.
- Predatory lending safeguards: Banco Real adopted the *Crédito Certo* (Right Credit) policy. Retail and corporate teams were trained to orient clients to seek types of loans that best contribute towards their enjoying a healthy financial existence, guaranteeing their satisfaction and that of the bank.
- Multilateral capital: because of its credibility and diligence with social and environmental issues, Banco Real gained long-term international capital, receiving a total of US$324 million from the International Finance Corporation (IFC) since 2004 for a pioneering social and environmental and corporate governance credit line.

Operational efficiency: the bank made an early commitment to practice what it preached, gaining revenue and skills that could be transferred to clients.

- Eco-efficiency initiatives: initiatives on the eco-efficiency front contribute to reducing costs and use of natural resources; 1027 branches have set up recycling facilities whereby the waste is collected by co-operatives. In addition, the organization was a pioneer in the mass use of recycled paper internally and was the first bank to produce cheque books with recycled paper. Efforts have been made to reduce paper usage, which currently is at approximately 75 kg per employee per year. The car fleet has been renewed, 1659 of which are now dual fuel systems (gasoline and ethanol). In terms of reduction in resource use, the organization reduced its energy consumption by 4 percent in 2004 with an additional reduction of 7 percent in 2005 and a further reduction of 4 percent in 2006 and 2007. The organization reduced water consumption by 9 percent in 2004 with an additional reduction of 3.4 percent in 2005 and a further reduction of 11 percent in 2006 and 2007.
- Efficiency savings: from 2003 to 2007, Banco Real achieved a financial gain of US$2.01 million through its main eco-efficiency processes, US$1.03 million was saved in electricity and US$426,000 in water expenses. US$353,000 was earned through recycling printer cartridges

and US$146,000 from the sale of recyclable waste materials. The income earned from recyclable materials is reverted into Banco Real's corporate volunteering program, *Escola Brasil* Project.

- CO_2 offsetting and reduction: as for carbon dioxide equivalent (CO_2e) emissions, an annual inventory is produced and plans are developed to reduce and adopt measures for compensation. A compensation program (*Floresta Real*) involves the plantation of over 126,000 trees to compensate for 100 percent of Banco Real's direct emissions.
- Certifications: in 2006, Banco Real received ISO 14000 certification for its administrative building in São Paulo and received a silver status certification by the Leadership in Energy and Environmental Design (LEED) Green Building Rating System for its first sustainably built branch.

6.2.2   Results in the core business lines

Banco Real's integration of sustainability into the business has led to the development of a range of innovative and profitable sustainability products and services for clients. Highlights include the following.

Ethical fund: Banco Real was the first bank in Latin America to launch an Ethical Fund. This fund was the world's best performer in Socially Responsible Investing (SRI) in 2004 and its portfolio grew from US$25.1 million in 2004 to US$434 million in 2007. Accumulated growth since its inception in 2001 to the end of 2007 was 504.5 percent while the accumulated growth of the São Paulo Stock Exchange Index (Ibovespa) during this same period was 418.2 percent.

Social and environmental products/Sustainable business deals: the organization also created new business and closed new deals with the new line of social and environmental products covering a range of corporate and retail needs from energy efficiency to disability to corporate governance to natural gas conversion. Credit that was extended for social and environmental projects for both consumer and corporate clients reached US$466 million in 2007. In an innovative partnership between Banco Real, Tetrapak, Klabin (a pulp and paper company) and Alcoa, Banco Real financed the implementation of a new technology developed by TSL Environmental Engineering that separates the aluminum, paper and plastic from Tetrapak containers. The separated material is used as raw material for the production processes of the partner companies.

Renewable energy: the organization is a pioneer in Brazil in investing in renewable technology and arranging carbon credit deals generating business and value. Up to 2006, the organization financed 20 small hydroelectric plants with a total generation capacity of 423 MW, four wind farms with a total generation capacity of 199 MW and two biodiesel plants. This contributed to the direct and indirect generation of 70,000 jobs, is a significant investment in infrastructure for the country and generates profit in fees for the bank. The organization also plays an important role in the development of the co-generation sector with biomass, associated with the production of ethanol and sugar. Expertise in socio-environmental risk has led the organization to be mandated to structure a large portion of this sector's projects in Brazil (see Box 6.9 below).

Box 6.9   Cerradinho Group

In 2007, Banco Real structured a project finance operation to enable the construction of an alcohol mill using a biomass energy co-generation system for the Cerradinho Group in the state of Goiás, in the Midwest of Brazil.

The plant will process 3.4 million tons of sugarcane and initially produce 300,000 m³ of fuel alcohol (anhydrate and hydrate) per year. The sugarcane baggase will be used for co-generation and, besides electric power to feed the mill, it will also supply 110 gigawatt-hour/year (equivalent to the consumption of a city with a population of 210,000 inhabitants) to the regional power grid, thus contributing to ease the supply deficit.

The mill will produce clean and renewable energy using local technology and, at the same time, will bring about social benefits, creating jobs in a region that is poor and lacks industries, dynamizing local development.

Carbon credits: Banco Real was the first financial institution to undertake carbon credit operations in Brazil and plays a leading role in this market in the country. Between 2006 and 2007, the organization intermediated the negotiation of more than 383,000 tons in carbon credits, at a value of US$8.04 million. The financing portfolio and anticipation of future carbon credit contracts amounted to US$24.75 million in the period.

Private equity: Banco Real's sustainability track record led it to be selected in 2004 to manage and administer the InfraBrasil – Equity Investment Fund, a Private Equity fund directed at qualified investors. Its purpose is to contribute to the development of the country's infrastructure through investments in areas such as logistics (highways, railways, ports, airports), telecommunications, gas transport and distribution, sanitation and energy, among others. InfraBrasil is one of the few sources of long-term domestic currency financing. In 2007, the fund invested in the construction of two small hydroelectric generation plants (PCHs) in the state of Rio Grande do Sul. In addition to being an alternative for serving isolated community populations, PCHs are a clean source of energy with low environmental impact.

Microcredit: Banco Real was also a pioneer in Brazilian microcredit. The number of clients grew from 579 in 2003 to 53,421 in 2007 with a total disbursed value of US$32 million in 26 communities. The break-even point was reached in November 2007 and at year-end Banco Real had the second largest microcredit operation in Brazil.

Sustainable construction: another innovative business initiative was the launch of *"Real Obra Sustentável"* in 2007. This initiative in the construction industry encourages the adoption of good social and environmental practices in real estate undertakings financed by Banco Real. To support clients, a best practice guide for sustainable construction was produced. Technical assessments are done and projects are monitored to ensure compliance with sustainability criteria.

Awards: Banco Real is beginning to receive recognition for its efforts in sustainability, contributing to the brand value and attractiveness of the organization to clients and other stakeholders. In 2007 alone, ABN AMRO received 35 awards for its performance in sustainable development. Box 6.10, below, highlights recent awards and recognition that the organization has received.

Box 6.10   Summary of sustainability awards for Banco Real

- Financial Times Sustainable Bank of the Year (2008), Financial Times Emerging Market Sustainable Bank of the Year (2008 and 2006), Financial Times Emerging Market Sustainable Bank of the Year in Latin America (2008)
- 100 Best Companies to Work For in Brazil (2006 and 2007 – Great Place to Work Institute and *Epoca* magazine)
- 100 Best Companies to Work For in Latin America (2004 to 2007 – Great Place to Work Institute and *Epoca* magazine)
- 150 Best Companies to Work For in Brazil (2002–2007 – *Exame* and *Você S.A.* magazines)
- One of 20 role model companies in sustainability in Brazil (Guia Exame de Sustentabilidade 2007)

- Prêmio ECO 2007 – awarded the Grand Prize for Management of Sustainability and in four other categories: Values, Transparency and Governance; Employees; Suppliers; and Government and Society
- 8th place among the Most Admired Companies in Brazil and 2nd place within the banking sector (2007 – *Carta Capital* magazine and the TNS InterScience Institute)
- World Business Awards (2006 – one of 10 companies awarded by the International Chamber of Commerce, UNEP and the Prince of Wales Business Leaders' Forum)
- Harvard Business School Case – Banco Real: Banking on Sustainability (2005)

Conclusion: beyond the role of a bank?

One question is often posed to Banco Real's leaders, and those of the multiple Brazilian banks engaging in pioneering sustainability initiatives – why Brazil? Why such an intensity of innovation around sustainability in the Brazilian financial sector? The answer is partly down to the leadership of the individuals in a highly developed and sophisticated banking system, but partly down to the scale and complexity of the social and environmental issues the country faces. Brazil's sustainability innovations, from its social technologies to its approaches to renewable energy, reflect the country's unique challenges and potential opportunities.

Is there replicability here? How unique is Brazil? Are the approaches adopted by Banco Real and other Brazilian banks of broader application? One hypothesis appears to be emerging. As patterns of immigration have changed, it has become clear that developed markets have un-banked and under-banked urban and rural poor who could benefit from access to affordable financing, and that conventional banking in a context of the 2007–2008 subprime crisis, is ill-equipped to deliver it. Developed markets, in other words, may have a number of lessons to learn from the emerging markets, among them using bottom of the pyramid approaches to dealing with the poor – technology transfer, but from South to North.

Equally, in emerging markets and to an increasing extent globally, a combination of social and environmental issues, from climate change to rising food prices to oil price spikes, threatens to roll back development progress. This is a trend that places sustainability concerns of the type that Brazil has confronted at the center of the economic and political agenda across an unexpectedly broad range of territories.

At a time of mounting need internationally, perhaps the most important result of Banco Real's initiatives is its potential for demonstration effect – for this type of initiative to be shared among leading banks and to become the norm. Banco Real, whose documented social, environmental and financial results earned it the award for 2008 Financial Times Sustainable Bank of the Year, is validating a different model of doing business. The model is clear. Addressing the needs of society – combating poverty, combating deforestation, combating health care deficits, helping agribusiness clients combat the impacts of climate change – these are not moral reflexes indulged in at the expense of the shareholder. They are the preconditions of a healthy portfolio. The conventional wisdom around the dilemma of sustainability can be shown to be false. Banks can deliver the triple bottom line, delivering returns for their shareholders and harnessing the main banking platform to act as transformational agents in society. *"Banco Real has passed the point of no return,"* comments Fabio Barbosa. *"There is no turning back and this drive will continue regardless of the actions of any individual. Every one of us can make a difference."*

Notes

1. World Bank 2006 GDP Ranking. Source: http://siteresources.worldbank.org/DATASTATISTICS/Resources
2. In 04/01/2007, there were 183,989,711 inhabitants in Brazil, according to population counting realized by IBGE (Brazilian Institute of Geography and Statistics). Source: www.ibge.gov.br
3. Human Development Index 2005. Source: http://hdr.undp.org
4. United Nations Development Program, *2007/2008 Human Development Report*. Source: http://hdrstats.undp.org/indicators
5. Source: facilitated discussions among Banco Real sustainability practitioners.
6. In addition to the indicators monitored by the Sustainability Council, since 2003, Banco Real has consistently reported on its progress on key indicators in its sustainability reports (see Bibliography for additional details).

References

Banco Real (2003) *Sustainability Report 2002/2003 – Banco Real, Human and Economic Values, Together*, São Paulo, September. www.bancoreal.com.br/sustentabilidade

Banco Real (2005) *Sustainability Report 2003/2004 – Banco Real, Human and Economic Values, Together*, São Paulo, May.

Banco Real (2007) *Sustainability Report 2005/2006 – Banco Real, A New Bank for a New Society*, São Paulo, April.

7
Insurers' Corporate Responsibility Policies: a Response to the Industry's Bad Image?

Henri-Claude de Bettignies, François Lépineux, and Cheon Kheong Tan

Introduction

The German sociologist Beck argues that a new frame of reference is needed to understand the world in which we have entered: that of a risk society on the global setting (Beck 1992, 1999). The alarming trend of environmental degradation, as well as the multiple advances of technological progress, bring about unprecedented risks and challenges; we thus need to learn how to address these new problems posed to our socio-economic system and to our culture, for instance by climate change and the mounting threats on ecosystems, or by the development of genetics or nanotechnologies. The advent of this "world risk society" with all its consequences provides new opportunities for insurance companies, which can find in this evolution new fields to apply their expertise, and strong motivations to develop innovative policies and practices that will contribute to restore the industry's tarnished reputation. This chapter will strive to answer three questions: why is the image of this industry so bad today? What are the corporate responsibility (CR) policies adopted by a group of pioneering companies? And is there a clear relationship between these two facts?

In its second part, the essay will thus present the results of an empirical research based on the study of a sample of nine companies, mainly European: Allianz, Aviva, AXA, ING Group, Insurance Australia Group (IAG), Lloyds TSB, Sompo Japan Insurance, State Farm Insurance, and Swiss Re. The methodology used for the constitution of this sample rests on a selection process based on several criteria:[1] (i) publication of detailed sustainability-related information in a dedicated report and/or on the company website; (ii) leading position of the company on its domestic market; (iii) presence of the company in the Dow Jones Sustainability

World Index; (iv) involvement of the company in business-led networks dealing with CSR- or sustainability-related issues such as the Global Compact, the WBCSD, CSR Europe, etc.; (v) participation in international working groups such as the UNEP Finance Initiative or the "Who Cares Wins" Initiative. Besides these company-related criteria, two other criteria have been added in order to increase diversity in the sample: (a) inclusion of three non-European companies (one in the US, two in Asia-Pacific); and (b) inclusion of a reinsurance company, as reinsurers play an important role in the industry. The data relating to the CR policies implemented by these companies has been collected from their Corporate (Social) Responsibility or Sustainability Reports, on their company websites, and through specialized international networks.

At first sight, one could estimate that the insurance sector enjoys a positive reputation in the public opinion, in so far as by its very existence, it brings multiple benefits to society. Through risk assessment and loss compensation, it ensures the smooth running of the economic system. The insurance mechanism is thus essential for individuals: it enables all of us as citizens to feel a relative sense of security in our everyday activities, and to lead our lives free from the fear of being left with nothing after a tragic event. It is also vital for companies: it releases entrepreneurial energies and allows economic agents to engage in risk-taking and develop their businesses without permanently having a sword of Damocles hanging over their head and feeling paralyzed by liabilities and their potential consequences. Moreover, the insurance industry generates positive effects at the macro level: it significantly contributes to wealth creation, and alleviates the need for regulation in a vast number of areas. In sum, this industry has taken such an important place in our modern lives that we can hardly imagine a developed society without insurance companies.

7.1 The insurance industry faced with its bad image problem

However, on closer inspection, it appears that the image of the insurance industry in the public opinion is not so good. In reality, it appears to be blurred, even bad. A number of reasons account for this negative perception: the opacity of the insurance business with its misrepresentation and misselling practices, the dissatisfaction about the insurance agents' reward system, and the problems associated with the respect of customers' privacy, are major determinants of the bad image conveyed by the industry. Moreover, its reputation has been further tarnished by corporate scandals such as the recent AIG affair.

7.1.1 Illegal activities and corporate scandals

Firstly, amid the spate of highly publicized accounting and corruption scandals that have been uncovered in several high-profile corporations around the world in recent years, the insurance business has not been spared. Some of the world's largest insurers and insurance brokers have been involved in illegal and unethical activities. The two main sectors of the insurance industry – the life insurance business, and the property and casualty insurance business – have received their fair share of criticism. These scandals have not only harmed the reputation of the companies involved, but also raised important issues of conduct toward investors, regulators and external auditors, and tarnished the whole industry's image.

Since late 2004, the American insurance industry has been shaken by the uncovering of a series of scandals of bid rigging and price fixing between insurance companies and brokers that provide property and casualty insurance. Eliot Spitzer, New York Attorney General, filed a civil suit against Marsh and McLennan, the world's largest insurance broker, for rigging bids and steering business that boosted its income at the expense of its clients' interests since at least the late 1990s. Aon Corporation and Willis North America, the country's second and third largest insurance brokers respectively, were also investigated for receiving contingent commissions from insurers. In addition, a number of former employees of major insurers such as AIG, ACE Ltd and Zurich American Insurance have been convicted of criminal offences.

In the UK, Equitable Life, the world's oldest mutual insurer, was unable to honor the payments of guaranteed annuity rate policies to hundreds of thousands of policyholders – including many retirees (Penrose 2004). Moreover, it was alleged that thousands of customers were missold mortgage endowment policies in the 1980s and 1990s (House of Commons Treasury Committee 2004; Financial Services Authority 2005; Financial Ombudsman Service 2005). Several insurance companies had been fined since 2000 by the Financial Services Authority (Abbey Life, Friends Provident, Legal and General, and Scottish Amicable, among others), and insurers had to compensate their customers for the losses incurred.

Problems with the insurance industry also appeared in Asia: even Singapore, a small country famous for its clean image, strong governance and heavy regulations, has not been spared. Controversies arose about life insurance policies with a "critical year"[2] feature aggressively marketed by American International Assurance (AIA), a subsidiary of AIG and one of the largest insurance companies operating in Singapore. As the actual return of the policies failed to meet earlier projections, AIA asked policyholders to continue paying premiums even after the "critical year" was reached. Moreover, several customers complained that they were misled into purchasing investment-linked insurance plans (ILPs), and expressed their dissatisfaction with the agents' service (Tan 2005). The fact that these episodes have happened on three different continents tends to reinforce the message that the negative image faced by the insurance industry is a global issue, not limited to a given country.

7.1.2 Misrepresentation and misselling practices

One of the sources of the negative image conveyed by the insurance sector resides in the perceived opacity of the language and procedures it has developed. Insurance professionals are viewed as specialists in financial techniques, who often use – and hide themselves behind – an unintelligible jargon. Contracts are usually fraught with a myriad of obscure clauses, which prove difficult to understand. More generally, the complexity of the market makes comparisons difficult for customers: due to the variability of available contracts, the insurance arena looks like a jungle, and customers often lack reliable elements to assess the offers of different companies. Moreover, in several instances, it is an obligation for customers – individuals or businesses – to subscribe to various policies (e.g. against fire, accidents, etc.) and they do not have the necessary knowledge to check that they are paying the right level of price for the coverage and service they receive.

It is no surprise then that the insurance industry has been the target of widespread criticism for its commercial practices, often characterized by misleading advertising, misrepresentation, and misselling – especially in the long-term savings and life insurance businesses. The marketing methods of insurance companies raise a number of ethical issues (Diacon and Ennew 1996). A frequent complaint against the insurance industry is that information about products presented in marketing, advertising or other sales materials is untruthful, misleading, or incomplete. For instance, insurers use bullish growth projections in the benefits illustrations of life insurance products to lure consumers to buy the policies, instead of highlighting the risky aspect of variable income, stock-based investments. Moreover, it happens frequently in insurance contracts that charges or exclusions of the coverage are hidden, or disclosed only in small print in advertisements, brochures or policy documents.

Besides, numerous complaints against the insurance industry concern agents who sell customers products that are unsuitable to them, in order to meet sales quotas and/or boost their earnings as these products give the agent higher commission: the policies are considered missold because they do not meet customers' needs. The above-mentioned mortgage endowment crisis in Britain is an illuminating example of customers misunderstanding the nature of the products or of the market variations, and hence, of misrepresentation and misselling practices in insurance. In sum, the frequency of dubious commercial methods is an indication of serious lapses in the insurers' monitoring of their agents' ethical conduct.

7.1.3 Issues linked to the insurance agents' reward system

The remuneration system of intermediaries for distributing investment products poses several problems that account for the bad reputation of the savings and life businesses, since it rests on heavily front-end loaded commission structures. Some critics believe that such a way of rewarding insurance agents is the underlying cause of unethical behavior as it often gives rise to a conflict between the agent's and the client's interests. The commission-based selling system would generate a bias to oversell, since this mode of remuneration of advisers can lead them to push a customer to purchase an investment product on the basis of the resulting payment it generates for them, irrespective of the best choice for the customer, who could alternatively prefer to reduce his/her debt or to hold savings in cash. Moreover, this system can also bring about a product bias, which occurs when the adviser has an incentive to recommend a particular investment product that does not necessarily meet the customer's needs, but that grants him a higher remuneration.

The structure of remunerations across products and providers is really confusing for customers, who often do not understand the rationale behind it. Whereas an initial cost is associated with the start of the advice process, ongoing commission (renewal and trail) is a current practice, the justification of which is not quite clear; it is hard to understand if trail commissions correspond to a deferred initial commission, or if they imply the provision of ongoing advice. The practice of "churning" customers' portfolios is also highly questionable. Churning refers to a sales method in which insurance agents persuade policyholders to terminate their existing policies after a short period of time and switch to new, similar ones for no valid reason; in the process, the insurance agent earns fresh commissions on the new policies sold.

In this regard, empirical research conducted by academics to study the influence of reward systems on financial sales agents' ethics has produced evidence that is mixed: whereas Kurland (1995) and Cupach and Carson (2002) found that the agents' compensation did not significantly affect the disclosure of product information and the product recommendations respectively, Howe et al. (1994) showed that customer-oriented sales agents engaged in less unethical behavior than their sales-oriented counterparts; and Schwepker and Good (1999) found that if salespeople believed they would suffer negative consequences for failing to achieve sales quota, they were more likely to behave unethically.

7.1.4 Problems associated with the respect of customers' privacy

The image of the insurance industry has also been dented by practices or initiatives that are seen to constitute an invasion of customers' privacy. In particular, concerns have been raised about insurers' practices of asking customers for detailed information about their health, especially genetic test information that is now made available thanks to technological advances. Insurers argue that if they do not have access to genetic test information, individuals who learn that their test results indicate an increased risk of serious diseases would purchase more insurance coverage at prices that are below an actuarially fair rate. As a result, the denial of access to the results of genetic tests for insurers may lead to adverse selection on the insurance market (Zick et al. 2000).

But in several countries, consumers have expressed strong objections to the use of genetic test information in insurance. Consumer groups contend that granting insurers access to genetic information will increase discrimination in life insurance premiums and discourage individuals from undergoing genetic testing that may benefit their health (Armstrong et al. 2003). According to a telephone poll conducted by Gallup in 2001 in the US, 74 percent of 494 adults, aged at least 18 years, interviewed felt that medical insurance companies should not have access to information about the genetic makeup of individuals when deciding about health care coverage for individuals (Carroll 2001). Similarly, a vast majority of consumers in the UK expressed a high level of discomfort with the use of genetic information in insurance (Human Genetics Commission 2001).

It seems that a balance needs to be found between customers' right to privacy and insurers' right to know the health condition of potential policyholders (Avila and Borna 1999). Recent studies have tackled this issue. On the contention that individuals with genetic disorders may be denied insurance when insurers have access to genetic test results, empirical evidence has been mixed. Lapham et al. (1996) surveyed 332 individuals in the US who had one or more family members with a genetic disorder, and 25 and 22 percent of the respondents believed that they or a family member had been refused life insurance and health insurance respectively as a result of the genetic condition in their family. On the other hand, Wingrove et al. (1996), Steinbart et al. (2001) and Armstrong et al. (2003) found no evidence of actual insurance denial from genetic testing. Moreover, studies that examined consumers' insurance purchase behavior after they had tested positive in genetic tests also gave mixed results (Zick et al. 2000; Armstrong et al. 2003).

For all these reasons – and some others (e.g. the offshoring trend that has extended, after call centers, to back-office and administrative functions, that has already massively transferred jobs to India and some other Asian countries, and that could continue to delocalize almost everything, with perhaps the exception of top management and some strategic functions. . .) – it is undeniable that the insurance industry conveys a bad image. The negative perception of the industry is reflected in various professional and academic studies. In annual surveys conducted by Gallup that investigated the American public's perception of the honesty and ethics of various professions, responses concerning insurance salesmen were very unfavorable (Moore 2001; Gallup 2003; Saad 2006). In addition, Cooper and Frank (2001, 2006) and Cooper et al. (2003), who had surveyed insurance professionals in the US, found that misrepresentation, misselling, conflict of interest and the lack of professional skills of insurance agents were perceived to be serious concerns that the industry should address.

At the same time, one can observe that some pioneering insurance companies – as well as other financial services organizations – increasingly tend to be concerned with responsibility issues. In his sustainability benchmarking study of European banks and financial services organizations, Weber (2005) identified five models for successful integration of sustainability into the banking business: (i) event-related integration of sustainability; (ii) sustainability as a new banking strategy; (iii) sustainability as a value driver; (iv) sustainability as a public mission; and (v) sustainability as a requirement of clients. The second part of the chapter will thus explore the corporate responsibility policies implemented recently by a group of nine pioneering companies.

7.2   CR policies implemented by pioneering companies

As we will see, these nine companies contribute to individual and collective welfare through their efforts to reduce and prevent risks; they strive to tackle environmental concerns, both internally and externally; they show a growing interest in socially responsible investment in its various forms; they are committed to reviewing their commercial practices; they keep enhancing their employees' competences and ethics; and eventually, some of them understand that they can act as a lever for change in society.

7.2.1 Fostering risk reduction and prevention

Beyond risk assessment and loss compensation, the insurance sector contributes to the reduction of risk in a number of domains. As regards individual subscribers, State Farm has developed safety and education initiatives at the national level in the US, such as "Project Ignition," which is a teen driver safety program. Through the "Safe Neighbors" program, it also helps ensure that children are buckled safely, intersections are safer, homes are stronger, and much more (State Farm Insurance 2006). Likewise, Sompo Japan works toward the reduction and prevention of traffic accidents, offering services based on the information it has collected and analyzed; a "Traffic Accident Blackspots Map" is available on its website (Sompo Japan Insurance 2005).

As regards insurance for businesses, insurers educate employers to view risk management as a useful concern that improves safety: they inspect hundreds of buildings every day, fund research to improve security standards (both against fire and crime), and audit company fleets to check the way commercial vehicles are maintained. IAG has devised a self-assessment tool, the "Risk Radar," which helps its business customers to improve their performance regarding the identification, assessment and monitoring of workplace hazards; it has also sponsored a "Cyclone Testing Station," which advises industry and governments on how to minimize damage caused by severe wind events; and with respect to the automobile industry, its Industry Research Center has been working with car manufacturers for almost 20 years to improve the repair costs and safety of vehicles (Insurance Australia Group 2005). Sompo Japan runs safe-driving campaigns in collaboration with its corporate customers (Sompo Japan Insurance 2005), and AXA Corporate Solutions Assurance provides specific training for drivers at interested client companies (AXA 2006). More generally, insurers exert continuous pressure on car manufacturers to influence vehicle design in a sense that improves security.

In addition, insurance companies are strongly involved in promoting public health. British companies are now placing the emphasis on the rehabilitation of individuals who have experienced an accident, and they are also concerned with patients at risk of developing chronic diseases (e.g. in the case of obesity). Sompo Japan offers lifestyle-related disease prevention services, as well as healthcare-related services (Sompo Japan Insurance 2005); and AXA has developed a "Health Coaching" program, tailored for customers willing to stop smoking or adopt a more balanced diet, and helping them preserve their health capital (AXA 2006).

7.2.2   Tackling the environmental concern

Although the environmental impact of insurance companies is much lower than that of many other multinationals, most of the insurers in our sample have chosen to take this issue seriously. Internally, they strive to minimize their ecological footprint, and have implemented environmental management systems, based on the conviction that good management in this area reduces business risks, cuts costs and improves efficiency. As an example, Swiss Re initiated a ten-year greenhouse neutral program in 2003: the company is committed to curb its CO_2 emissions by 15 percent and invests in the World Bank Carbon Fund to offset the remaining emissions (Swiss Reinsurance Company 2005). Likewise, ING's Global Environmental Statement outlines three areas where the company should be proactive: energy consumption, business travel, and paper consumption (ING Group 2006). Sompo Japan launched an energy-saving campaign in 1992 (Sompo Japan Insurance 2005); environmental management started at Allianz in 1995 (Allianz Group 2005); and Lloyds TSB has had a formal environmental policy since 1996 (Lloyds TSB 2006).

But of course, it is external challenges that insurance companies are – and will increasingly be – confronted with: the biosphere is deteriorating at a rapid pace, and a number of international organizations have already sounded the alarm on the seriousness of the global ecological crisis (Millennium Ecosystem Assessment 2005; United Nations Environment Program 2005). Economic losses due to natural disasters are doubling every ten years; should the current trends continue, they could reach almost US$150 billion per year in the next decade (UNEP Finance Initiative 2002). Therefore, new mechanisms are required to face the increase in extreme meteorological phenomena and their destructive effects (Clements-Hunt 2004).

Most companies in our sample are following closely the issue of climate change. ING has joined the Global Roundtable on Climate Change, which brings together senior executives from the private sector, governmental bodies and NGOs (ING Group 2006). Sompo Japan tackles global warming with two approaches: adaptation and mitigation (Sompo Japan Insurance 2005). For insurers and reinsurers alike, the necessity to face this issue represents both a risk of increasing loss potential, and an opportunity to create new types of cover, through innovative methodologies. For instance Swiss Re's environmental expertise, founded in its traditional lines of business, is now expanding into new areas: it plays a leading role in the development of insurance-linked securities (ILS) and weather derivatives (Swiss Reinsurance Company 2005, 2006).

7.2.3 Developing socially responsible investment

Insurance companies are financial institutions, and as such, they are involved in the management of significant financial investments. As institutional investors focused on the long term, they have a preference for companies that will deliver long-term value. Being themselves experts in risk analysis, they also take a growing interest in the way the businesses they invest in manage their own risks; increasingly, they play a more active role, investigating the reporting methods implemented by the boards of directors, and occasionally advising changes in corporate governance schemes. Several companies in our sample have adopted socially responsible investment (SRI) policies, which consist in the inclusion of nonfinancial criteria, such as sustainability, ethics or governance considerations, into the process of investment decision-making. A growing number of observers, financial analysts, and academics suggest that there is no fundamental contradiction between the promotion of social or environmental values, and the search for financial gain (Margolis and Walsh 2001; UNEP Finance Initiative 2004).

For instance, Swiss Re's SRI strategy is based on a positive screening approach: its sustainability portfolio is allocated in four main areas – alternative energy, water, waste management, and recycling (Swiss Reinsurance Company 2006). Allianz and its subsidiary companies – notably AGF and RCM – offer several funds designed according to ethical and ecological criteria; the total value of sustainable investments under management within the Allianz Group now amounts to more than €5 billion (Allianz Group 2006). And Sompo Japan is currently marketing two specialized funds: the Eco-fund "Beech Forest," and the SRI fund "Empowering Our Common Future," which invests in companies included in the Morningstar SRI Index (Sompo Japan Insurance 2005).

In another respect, Morley Fund Management, the Asset Management division of Aviva in the UK, has developed a shareholder activism policy: it engages with companies in which it has invested to raise social, environmental, ethical and governance issues with the management, and especially to advocate human rights (Aviva 2005, 2006). And Allianz, AXA, Sompo Japan and Swiss Re are actively involved in the Carbon

Disclosure Project (CDP) – a combined effort by the world's largest institutional investors to collect information on the climate change policies of the FT 500 largest companies in the world in terms of market capitalization[3] (Allianz Group 2006; AXA 2006; Sompo Japan Insurance 2005; Swiss Reinsurance Company 2005).

The ING Group represents a good example of a combination of various forms of screening, either positive or negative, and shareholder activism: it offers a range of sustainable investment opportunities that are marketed through its business units in Europe and Australia under various names, and has a global voting policy that promotes good corporate governance by exercising its voting rights in those companies in which it invests (ING Group 2005, 2006).

Another form of SRI consists in community investing, as exemplified by the well-known example of the Grameen Bank that has implemented a successful microcredit system in Bangladesh. As regards microinsurance for the economically deprived, Aviva has insured 450,000 people belonging to this category in India, almost exclusively poor women, thereby enabling them to commence productive activities (Aviva 2005). Likewise, Allianz Bajaj Life Insurance successfully introduced microinsurance life policies in India – more than 100,000 people have already been covered – and the Group is now exploring the potential for these products elsewhere in Asia, in collaboration with the United Nations Development Program and the German Society for Technical Cooperation (Allianz Group 2005, 2006).

7.2.4   Reviewing commercial practices

Legitimate concerns about misselling practices and problems linked to insurance agents' remuneration models, which cast an enduring slur on the industry's image, have led the British Treasury Select Committee to look into this pressing issue, and to recommend a clarification, simplification and standardization of the system, in order to reach a greater transparency and to restore customer confidence. It has expressed its position recently without ambiguity, recommending a change in the sales system of the long-term savings business, and a greater clarity on fees and commissions (House of Commons Treasury Committee 2004: 20, 26):

> In the Committee's view it seems likely that as long as most of the selling activity in the long-term savings industry is rewarded on a commission basis, many savers may remain suspicious that they are being sold a product for the wrong reasons. Shifting away from the current

commission based sales system common in much of the industry is likely to be a key component of any strategy to rebuild consumer confidence in the industry after the long catalogue of mis-selling scandals in recent years. [...] Full and open disclosure of fees and commissions in a manner that is readily comprehensible to savers and gives them a balanced view of the various options is a vital part of delivering an efficient market in financial advice and long-term savings products.

Another recent report for the Association of British Insurers also insists that initial and ongoing charges should be clearly distinguished and explained to subscribers, so as to ensure consumer-friendly selling practices (Charles River Associates 2005). These two reports provide very clear indications on how insurers could work to improve their selling practices and remuneration systems to reach greater transparency, especially – but not only – in the long-term savings business. The commission structure for any given product should provide advisers the incentive to give the right advice and to review product suitability and performance over time on behalf of the customer. There should be better disclosure of information about products in sales materials. Before consumers sign up for the products, they should be informed about all charges that would be incurred over time for the product, the projected returns that they would be getting, as well as the assumptions that the projections are based on. Some insurers in our sample have started to revise their commercial methods to be in line with these recommendations.

Moreover, policyholders should be able to see that channels are readily available for them to voice their dissatisfaction or file complaints, if this becomes necessary. As Jones et al. (2000) have commented, when customer dissatisfaction is an ongoing phenomenon, customers may remain due to high switching barriers, while engaging in negative word of mouth, which hurts the reputation of the company. Hence, good handling of complaints is an essential component of service quality. That is why Aviva, for instance, is committed to dealing with customers' complaints fairly and swiftly: its policyholders are informed that they have a right to complain internally and to seek recourse externally when necessary, and that their complaints will be handled efficiently and in a friendly manner. Every complaint is considered a business opportunity, since this kind of consumer feedback can help the company avoid future errors. Some companies of the sample also encourage policyholders to provide their feedback in several ways (via websites, research, one-on-one interviews, etc.) on products and service quality. These initiatives show that the insurers involved truly and sincerely value customers' views, and are eager to build long-term relationships with them.

Eventually, as regards the widespread concerns about privacy and confidentiality implications of the use of genetic information in insurance, several countries have imposed restrictions on the access to that kind of information for insurance underwriting (Knoppers et al. 2004). In the UK, in October 2001, the British government and ABI reached an agreement to institute a five-year moratorium on the use of genetic test results in assessing applications for insurance. In March 2005, the moratorium was extended by an extra five years to November 2011. It specifies that consumers can obtain up to £500,000 of life insurance, £300,000 of critical illness insurance and £30,000 annual benefit of income protection insurance, without having to disclose the results of any predictive genetic tests[4] that they have previously taken (Association of British Insurers 2005).

7.2.5   Enhancing employees' competences and ethics

Surveys conducted on insurance professionals have highlighted the existence of serious concerns regarding their competences. In two surveys of professionals working in the property and casualty insurance sector conducted in 1999 and 2005 respectively (Cooper and Frank 2001, 2006) and another survey of life insurance industry professionals conducted in 2003 (Cooper et al. 2003) in the US, the workers were asked to rate ethics-related issues on the extent to which each issue represented a major problem to those working in the respective sector. The property and casualty insurance sector surveys have revealed that the issues perceived as presenting the biggest ethical problems are the lack of knowledge or skills to competently perform one's duties, and the failure to identify the customer's needs and recommend products and services that meet those needs. Similar findings were obtained in the survey of life insurance professionals. These results clearly demonstrate that the lack of professional skills of insurance agents is a serious issue that the industry needs to address.

Therefore, it is essential for insurance companies to set high expectations in both the technical competence and ethical behavior of their agents. This involves adopting stringent requirements for the selection of affiliated sales agencies and individual agents. At the same time, there is a need to pay close attention to staff training, so as to make sure that the sales force is able to make the correct product recommendations to customers. This will minimize the incidence of misselling, in a context where financial institutions like insurance companies and banks are offering more sophisticated products in their bid to uphold their market share in an increasingly competitive environment. Hence, insurers – generally speaking – strive to make sure that their sales force has the technical skills to handle the enhanced complexity of such products, by stepping up on staff training. Improving – on a continuous basis – the competence and professional standards of their agents helps them win the public's trust and confidence. However, some companies in our sample realize that they need to extend their training programs beyond their home countries, and to spread them across all their international business units.

7.2.6 Acting as a lever for change in society

Additionally, and more importantly, insurance companies can act as a lever for change in society, should they be bold enough to engage in new avenues. Emerging risks resulting from technological developments, environmental problems and social inequalities entail considerable hazard potential for the insurance business, and are a cause of concern for society as a whole. As methodologies that are currently used by the insurance industry are not adapted to the mounting global ecological threat that is looming ahead, insurers can devise and implement new methodologies of risk assessment that integrate sustainability-related issues. They can manage new instruments in the field of carbon finance, and elaborate new product groups and new risk transfer markets to handle the renewable energy business. In another perspective, through their participation in international initiatives such as the Global Compact's "Who Cares Wins" Initiative developed in partnership between the United Nations and the world's largest investment companies – including AXA, Aviva or RCM (Allianz Group) – they seek to make the consideration of social, environmental and governance issues part of mainstream investment analysis and decision-making (Global Compact 2004).

The UNEP Finance Initiative is another major international network whose purpose is to create a forum where insurance companies, as well as interested banks and asset management companies, can exchange experiences, stimulate each other in pursuing sustainable development, and define best practices. Working groups have been set up to discuss and produce reports on a variety of subjects, including the impact of climate change, the development of renewable energies (UNEP Finance Initiative 2002), or the challenges associated with water scarcity. For instance, Aviva participates in the working groups on climate change, asset management, and general insurance (which is at an early stage);

and Swiss Re is another member of the working group on climate change. Eventually, the UNEP FI and the Global Compact have joined their efforts to elaborate a set of Principles for Responsible Investment (PRI), which have been endorsed by international funds worth US$4 trillion.[5]

Moreover, insurance companies can encourage the incorporation of CSR-related issues by all their stakeholders in general. Globally considered, they have repeated interactions with all economic sectors, with all kinds of organizations, and with all the citizens of the countries in which they operate, through the myriads of insurance contracts that are signed every year. Due to their central position in the economic system, they have the power to influence the mindsets and behaviors of virtually all actors in society. In particular, insurers can bring an essential contribution to raise the awareness of their suppliers on social, societal and environmental concerns, and to promote sound practices in the whole supply chain. For instance, Allianz established guidelines for environmental procurement in 2002 (Allianz Group 2005), and requirements regarding corporate responsibility issues are part of ING's contract templates (ING Group 2006). Similarly, Lloyds TSB has developed an extended supplier review process (Lloyds TSB 2006); Sompo Japan's purchase policy is based on its "Green Procurement" and "Socially Responsible Procurement" guidelines (Sompo Japan Insurance 2005); and IAG trains its preferred builders to become familiar with issues such as sustainability, energy efficiency, indoor air quality and waste minimization (Insurance Australia Group 2005).

7.3   Discussion

In the first part of this essay, we detailed the main factors that account for the public's negative perception of the insurance industry. In its second part, through an empirical research, we investigated the corporate responsibility approaches developed by a sample of nine insurance companies, mainly European. Now the following question deserves to be posed: is there a causal relationship between the industry's bad image and the adoption of CR policies by a group of pioneering companies? It seems that this is a complex question, to which no simple and unique answer can be brought. The CR policies recently implemented by these pioneering insurance companies can certainly be viewed as an attempt to improve their negative image, but also as a reflection of their willingness to address mounting challenges in a number of areas (e.g. environmental protection), to strengthen their competitive position, to influence other actors in society (e.g. regulators), or to develop their operations through the creation of new business models (as in the case of microinsurance in developing countries).

In all economic sectors, there is multicausality behind the current business leaders' interest in corporate (social) responsibility.[6] Several causes – not mutually exclusive – are observable: joining the bandwagon of a current fashion (the mimetism of "me too"), doing good to do well (instrumentalizing CR for improving the bottom line), improving the image (leveraging CR for enhancing reputation), just plain public relations efforts (the "cosmetic effect" for an impact internally and externally), a protective device against civil society's criticisms (fighting back in a hostile environment), a packaging of philanthropic activities (as a substitute for a real concern about the "common good") or a genuine concern for responsible behavior of the firm toward its many stakeholders (making explicit a vision and walking the talk, over a period of time) ... Some of those justifications explain the skepticism about the real value of CR and contribute to fuel the growing cynicism about it (and the "industry" it has produced). Obviously the strategic logic of engaging in CR activities varies according to industrial sectors: the tobacco industry has not much choice but to actively engage in such campaigns, while an organic food company may feel less the urge to do so than a chemical firm. Furthermore, within a given sector, different companies do have different positions, as exemplified by the choices made by the insurers of our sample.

We have seen that insurance companies lead to the adoption of higher security standards in several important areas such as car safety, that they conduct inspections in industrial establishments on a regular basis to reduce risks and prevent accidents, and that they are involved in research efforts for the prevention of fire and crime; they also promote public health through incentives for customers and investments in medical care and rehabilitation schemes. All these various initiatives undoubtedly contribute to the welfare of society. But insurance companies are interested in reducing risk and avoiding loss for profitability reasons in the first place: prevention is not only better but also cheaper than cure. Since insurers – often – bear most of the cost if a risk happens to become an actual event, they devote considerable efforts to minimize risks – and potential costs associated with them.

Similarly, the choice of insurance companies to adopt SRI policies is a matter of consistency between risk management and asset management: is it appropriate for an insurance company to invest in tobacco firms with a view to reaping high short-term benefits, knowing that at the same time these firms manufacture products that increase public health risks and will generate heavy compensations for the victims? Belth and Dorfman (1996) are right when they claim that insurance companies should divest their tobacco investments, not only on moral grounds, but also for good economic reasons. The acknowledgement of this simple reality has led some insurance companies to extend the logic of divesting from "bad" sectors, and instead, to invest in sustainable or socially responsible companies. These two examples of CR policies implemented by insurers suggest that their motivations are equally shared between instrumental and noninstrumental considerations: it is the combination of these two aspects that explains the logic of their commitment.

But identifying responsibility as an important dimension of their activities, and adopting a range of policies in this regard, is only a first stage for insurance companies. The challenge for them now – as well as for other multinational firms – is to live the responsibility dimension in their daily operations, to set the balance between their economic, social and environmental responsibilities, and to maintain a high ethical profile through all the aspects of their activities. Although they have made important advances in implementing CR policies, they now need to integrate the responsibility principle into their strategy, and to disseminate it, beyond their core business, throughout all their entities. Well-written CSR reports, dedicated websites, professionally managed PR exercises will, in that case, not be substitutes for a genuine incorporation of responsibility at all levels, but its illustration.

In this regard, insurers would gain by being more explicit on performance measurement, using indicators to assess their CR policies, and to compare their results from one year to another. For instance, Lloyds TSB and Allianz provide a number of aggregate quantitative indicators regarding social and environmental issues in their latest CR or Sustainability Reports, comparing data with previous years, and also present objectives for the next year (Lloyds TSB 2006; Allianz Group 2006). The publication of such objectives represents a very efficient means of progress at the company level, supports its commitment to continuous improvement over the years, and stimulates employees' efforts. Some of the reports issued by other companies in our sample such as ING (ING Group 2005, 2006) also rely on quantitative indicators; even though much of the CR approach is of qualitative nature, some elements can nevertheless be the subject of a quantitative analysis. Furthermore, several companies studied in this chapter have their reports certified by international audit firms – for instance KPMG has reviewed selected sustainability performance data reported by IAG (Insurance Australia Group 2006) – and provide external views expressed by independent stakeholders, which enhances the credibility of their statements.

Eventually, the centricity of the insurance industry within the economic system places it in an ideal position to raise the awareness of all its stakeholders regarding the common good issue. De Bettignies and Lépineux (forthcoming) have explored the three major determinants that are likely to induce multinational corporations to take the global common good into account: the deterioration of the biosphere, the rise of an antiglobalization sentiment, and the necessity to design new mechanisms of global governance. Because of the very nature of their activity and their financial might, insurance companies have a tremendous lever on socioeconomic change. By the huge investments they make, they exert an impact on corporate behavior. Through their education function, they influence the conduct of their customers and suppliers. Furthermore, in their efforts to lobby governments and regulatory agencies, they contribute to shape the rules of the game they play. If they can prove to their stakeholders that responsibility starts at the top and effectively percolates throughout the organization, so that they can serve the common good and not only their short-term financial interests, then an enduring change in the image of the industry will take place: the "image" of the insurance industry will be restored because the "reality" will have changed.

Conclusion

Over the past few years, insurance companies that constitute the sample studied seem to have gained a comprehensive understanding of responsibility issues. These companies have devoted significant resources to define clear approaches in this regard and to implement a range of CR policies; they are committed to developing processes and practices that change the way they carry on their operations across all their businesses. They are taking into consideration the interests of their various stakeholders: customers, shareholders, employees, business partners and society at large. Most of them strive to be good corporate citizens. The CR policies developed by these pioneering insurers are necessary to reach two fundamental objectives: their appropriation by every employee, and the internal consistency of the CR approach at the group level, across all management functions and lines of business. The attainment of these two closely intertwined objectives is essential to enable insurance companies to improve the image of the industry; it provides the keys for them to become fully responsible corporate citizens in every country where they operate.

For insurers, long-term success also depends on the existence of shared values inside and outside the company: the quality of service and relationships, a true sense of care, mutual trust, and integrity. Integrity is not only a matter of compliance with external rules and regulations, such as the Sarbanes Oxley Act, with general principles, such as those of the UN Global Compact or the OECD Guidelines for Multinational Enterprises, or with internal codes of conduct. It also involves implementing responsible sales practices, and adopting an attitude governed by fairness and openness toward all the company's stakeholders. A lack of integrity seriously damages a company's reputation, and insurers are especially sensitive to reputation risks, as their legitimacy as an enterprise rests on the trust their stakeholders have in them. In particular, customers' trust is driven by how easy the company is to deal with, its ability to offer products they understand, and whether it treats them fairly. As trust is vital to the insurance business and represents its main asset, transparent and ethical practices are needed to restore the reputation of the industry.

In all the transactions with its many stakeholders, if the industry can rebuild, maintain and enhance trust, then its genuine internalization of CR will have its optimum impact (internally and externally). This will only be possible if – at the management level – insurance companies walk the talk by the policies they define, the products they design, the methods they use to promote and sell them; by the way they manage and reward their employees; and by the level of transparency they practice. It will demand skills in managing change – now very visible in some parts of the industry: the investment made by Norwich Union Insurance (a subsidiary of Aviva) to change its culture through the "Leadership and Care" effort is a good example in this respect. If insurers – and reinsurers – can introduce new methodologies of risk assessment and management that foster environmental protection and contribute to social equity, the enduring change necessary will be on track. Moreover, the future of insurance will also gain from the development of prevention programs. Here again, the role of corporate leaders is fundamental. Insurers can play a decisive role in the education of the public regarding a number of important issues, and for the promotion of a safety culture. Future generations may then have the possibility to cope better with the riskier world they will inherit from us.

Notes

1. To be selected, insurance companies do not need to meet all the criteria listed; however, those that have eventually been chosen meet most of them, and in some cases, all of them.
2. The critical year is the point at which a policy has built up sufficient cash value to fund future premium payments and an annual interest cost. It was stated as the thirteenth year for a number of the policies sold.
3. The CDP currently brings together more than 200 institutional investors with more than US$30 trillion in assets. Reports published by the CDP and company responses are available on the website www.cdproject.net
4. If an individual takes a genetic test before he shows any symptoms, the test is known as a predictive genetic test. In contrast, if he takes a genetic test to confirm his condition after he has begun to show symptoms of the illness, the test is known as a diagnostic genetic test.
5. The full text of the Principles for Responsible Investment, as well as an updated list of the asset owner signatories, is available at http://www.unpri.org
6. Whereas some business leaders use the phrase corporate social responsibility (CSR) to characterize their approach, others prefer to focus on corporate responsibility (CR), corporate global responsibility (CGR), sustainability, triple bottom line (TBL), corporate citizenship – or other expressions. We will not enter here into this semantic debate; in order to remain coherent with the rest of the essay, we will keep referring to CR as an "umbrella term."

References

Allianz Group (2005) *Status Report 2005, Sustainability in the Allianz Group.*
Allianz Group (2006) *Status Report 2006, Sustainability in the Allianz Group.*
Armstrong, K. et al. (2003) "Life Insurance and Breast Cancer Risk Assessment: Adverse Selection, Genetic Testing Decisions, and Discrimination," *American Journal of Medical Genetics Part A*, 120A/3: 359–64.
Association of British Insurers (2005) *Concordat and Moratorium on Genetics and Insurance.*
Avila, S. and Borna, S. (1999) "Genetic Information: Consumers' Right to Privacy versus Insurance Companies' Right to Know a Public Opinion Survey," *Journal of Business Ethics*, 19/4: 355–62.
Aviva (2005) *Corporate Social Responsibility Report 2005.*
Aviva (2006) *Corporate Social Responsibility Report 2006.*
AXA (2006) *2005 Activity and Sustainable Development Report.*
Beck, U. (1992) *Risk Society: Towards a New Modernity.* Sage Publications.
Beck, U. (1999) *World Risk Society.* Polity Press.
Belth, J. and Dorfman, J. (1996) "Insurance Companies Should Divest their Tobacco Investments," *Business and Society Review*, 97: 26–31.
Carroll, J. (2001) "Most Americans Oppose Giving Genetic Information to Health Insurers and Employers," Gallup News Service, July 11, http://www.gallup.com
Charles River Associates (2005) *Study of Intermediary Remuneration. A Report for the Association of British Insurers.* London.

Clements-Hunt, P. (2004) "The Challenge of Sustainability for Financial Institutions," in Seiler-Hausmann, J.-D. et al. (eds), *Eco-Efficiency and Beyond. Towards the Sustainable Enterprise*, Greenleaf Publishing, Sheffield, UK, pp. 182–95.

Cooper, R. and Frank, G. (2001) "Key Ethical Issues Facing the Property and Casualty Insurance Industry: Has a Decade Made a Difference?" *CPCU Journal*, 54/2: 99–111.

Cooper, R. and Frank, G. (2006) "The Property and Casualty Insurance Industry's Ethical Environment: an Update," *CPCU eJournal*, 59/3: 1–12.

Cooper, R., Frank, G. and Williams, A. (2003) "The Life Insurance Industry's Ethical Environment: Has it Improved in the New Millennium?" *Journal of Financial Service Professionals*, 57/6: 38–50.

Cupach, W. and Carson, J. (2002) "The Influence of Compensation on Product Recommendations Made by Insurance Agents," *Journal of Business Ethics*, 40/2: 167–76.

De Bettignies, H.-C. and Lépineux, F. (forthcoming) "Can Multinational Corporations Afford to Ignore the Global Common Good?" *Business and Society Review*.

Diacon, S. and Ennew, C. (1996) "Ethical Issues in Insurance Marketing in the UK," *European Journal of Marketing*, 30/5: 67–80.

Financial Ombudsman Service (2005) *Annual Review and Report and Financial Statements: April 2004 to March 2005*.

Financial Services Authority (2005) *Mortgage Endowments: Shortfalls and Consumer Action*.

Gallup (2003) "Public Rates Nursing as Most Honest and Ethical Profession," Gallup News Service, December 1, http://www.gallup.com

Global Compact (2004) *Who Cares Wins: Connecting Financial Markets to a Changing World*. United Nations Global Compact Office, New York.

House of Commons Treasury Committee (2004) *Restoring Confidence in Long-Term Savings: Endowment Mortgages*. Fifth report of session 2003–2004.

Howe, V., Hoffman, D. and Hardigree, D. (1994) "The Relationship between Ethical and Customer-Oriented Service Provider Behaviors," *Journal of Business Ethics*, 13/7: 497–506.

Human Genetics Commission (2001) *Public Attitudes to Human Genetic Information*.

ING Group (2005) *Corporate Responsibility Report 2004*.

ING Group (2006) *Corporate Responsibility Report 2005*.

Insurance Australia Group (2005) *Sustainability Report 2005*.

Insurance Australia Group (2006) *Sustainability Report 2006*.

Jones, M., Mothersbaugh, D. and Beatty, S. (2000) "Switching Barriers and Repurchase Intentions in Services," *Journal of Retailing*, 76/2: 259–74.

Knoppers, B.M., Godard, B. and Joly, Y. (2004) "A Comparative International Overview," in Rothstein, M. (ed.) *Genetics and Life Insurance: Medical Underwriting and Social Policy*, MIT Press, Cambridge, pp. 173–94.

Kurland, N. (1995) "Ethics, Incentives, and Conflicts of Interest: a Practical Solution," *Journal of Business Ethics*, 14/6: 465–75.

Lapham, V., Kozma, C. and Weiss, J. (1996) "Genetic Discrimination: Perspectives of Consumers," *Science*, 274: 621–4.

Lloyds TSB (2006) *Corporate Responsibility Report 2005*.

Margolis, J. and Walsh, J. (2001) *People and Profits? The Search for a Link between a Company's Social and Financial Performance*. Lawrence Erlbaum, Mahwah, NJ.

Millennium Ecosystem Assessment (2005) *Synthesis Report*.

Moore, D. (2001) "Firefighters Top Gallup's 'Honesty and Ethics' List," *Gallup News Service*, December 5, http://www.gallup.com

Penrose, G. (2004) *Report of the Equitable Life Inquiry*. House of Commons, The Stationery Office, London.

Saad, L. (2006) "Nurses Top List of Most Honest and Ethical Professions," *Gallup News Service*, December 14, http://www.gallup.com

Schwepker Jr., C. and Good, D. (1999) "The Impact of Sales Quotas on Moral Judgment in the Financial Services Industry," *Journal of Services Marketing*, 13/1: 38–58.

Sompo Japan Insurance (2005) *Corporate Social Responsibility Report 2005*.

State Farm Insurance (2006) *2005 Year in Review*.

Steinbart, E. et al. (2001) "Impact of DNA Testing for Early-Onset Familial Alzheimer Disease and Frontotemporal Dementia," *Archives of Neurology*, 58/11: 1828–31.

Swiss Reinsurance Company (2005) *Sustainability Report 2004*.

Swiss Reinsurance Company (2006) *Sustainability Report 2005*.

Tan, L. (2005) "Some ILPs Not Suitable for Older Folk: Guidebook," *The Straits Times*, September 26, Singapore Press Holdings, Singapore.

UNEP Finance Initiative (2002) *The UNEP Sustainable Energy Finance Initiative*.

UNEP Finance Initiative (2004) *The Materiality of Social, Environmental and Corporate Governance Issues to Equity Pricing*.

United Nations Environment Program (2005) *2004 Annual Report*, UNEP.

Weber, O. (2005) "Sustainability Benchmarking of European Banks and Financial Service Organizations," *Corporate Social Responsibility and Environmental Management*, 12/2: 73–87.

Wingrove, K. et al. (1996) "Experiences and Attitudes Concerning Genetic Testing and Insurance in a Colorado Population: a Survey of Families Diagnosed with Fragile X Syndrome," *American Journal of Medical Genetics*, 64/2: 378–81.

Zick, C. et al. (2000) "Genetic Testing, Adverse Selection, and the Demand for Life Insurance," *American Journal of Medical Genetics*, 93/1: 29–39.

8

The Relative Valuation of Socially Responsible Firms: an Exploratory Study

Ali Fatemi, Iraj J. Fooladi, and David Wheeler

Introduction

Various aspects of "corporate social responsibility" (CSR) have recently captured the attention of researchers in the fields of economics and finance (Orlitzky et al. 2003; Statman 2005; Goss and Roberts 2006; Milevsky et al. 2006). This phenomenon follows more than a decade of research and dozens of studies published largely in the strategic management and business ethics literatures which have striven to explore the links between corporate social performance (variously defined) and corporate financial performance (Waddock and Graves 1997; Roman et al. 1999; Margolis and Walsh 2001; Orlitzky and Benjamin 2001). While one interpretation of these studies may be that the evidence for a causal, or even de facto link between social and financial performance remains elusive, another would be that the balance of evidence suggests that enhanced social performance may be a lagging indicator of effective management and therefore a leading indicator of future financial performance (Wheeler 2003). In their 2003 review of 52 studies internationally, Orlitzky and colleagues were somewhat unequivocal in judging the evidence as favoring social responsibility as a more likely benefit than impairment to investors.

All of these studies leave open the question of the purpose of the firm and ideological contestations of whether managers should deploy corporate resources toward social goals where likelihood of a financial return is moot. In the Anglophone corporate governance literature, the traditional view regards CSR as an activity that may or may not lead to the creation of value for society and the broader universe of stakeholders, but it is certainly not in the interests of investors and should therefore be discouraged if not outlawed. Strident commentaries advocating this

140

somewhat simplistic application of agency theory have long been associated with Milton Friedman and Michael Jensen (Friedman 1970; Jensen 2005; Jensen and Meckling 1976, 2005). An alternative proposition, expounded in corporate governance, strategic management and business ethics literatures is that of pragmatic "stakeholder theorists" such as Edward Freeman who contends that not only is it the right thing to do to take into account the impact of the firm on its various constituencies, but most importantly that it is only through the effective mobilization of the resources of the stakeholders that value is created both for the firm *and* its stakeholders (Freeman 1984; Freeman and McVea 2001; Freeman et al. 2004). This position separates Freeman from more normative stakeholder theorists who adopt a more critical stance toward the role of business in society.

John Roberts (2004) takes a similar approach to the pragmatic approach of Freeman (and even the later writings of Jensen where a case is made for an "enlightened value maximization" perspective). Consistent with European and Asian constructions of corporate governance and the purpose of the firm, he argues that "firms are institutions created to serve human needs." The more complex question, however, is whether the needs to be served are those of the shareholders alone, customers, employees, society at large, the government, the environment, or those of yet others. Roberts's assessment is that the answer might be reduced to that of Friedman, i.e. that the purpose of the firm is to serve shareholders and the maximization of their wealth, under a very restrictive set of assumptions. But he argues further that these assumptions do not hold in "the real world." Therefore, he concludes – like Freeman – that "it is necessary that all relevant interests are recognized and taken into account."

So it seems that a long-standing dichotomy may be beginning to heal. The traditional stockholder versus stakeholder debate that has raged in Anglophone jurisdictions for several decades may now be converging, with shareholder advocates coming to recognize that shareholder value may be directly impacted by stakeholder perspectives and so it may be wise to take the pragmatic view. Both sets of former views: corporate social responsibility as an "ethical" approach to corporate management that should transcend financial and other trade-offs versus the more traditional view that a manager's responsibility should be limited to the maximization of shareholders' wealth, imply that there is a conflict between the interests of the investors and CSR. However, the emerging perspective recognizes a potential "business case" for CSR (and especially "CSR reputation," given the increasingly socially constructed nature of value) and thus researchers are turning to investigate to what extent corporate financial objectives may be aligned with CSR objectives and indeed even enhanced by the practice of CSR.

In the finance literature, for example, Rubin and Barnea (2006) argue that the relationship between the firm value and CSR expenditures is a nonmonotonic function with a maximum point. At low levels of CSR expenditure, there is a positive relationship between these expenditures and firm's value. Beyond a certain level, the marginal cost of these expenditures will outweigh their benefits to shareholders. Thus, the value-maximizing approach calls for keeping these expenditures at the level where the nonmonotonic function is at its maximum level. However, they still argue that managers and corporate insiders may overdo CSR expenditures for their personal benefits at the expense of majority shareholders.

The nonmonotonic relationship between firm value and the level of CSR expenditures seems to be confirmed by Goss and Roberts who examine the issue of CSR from the perspective of a lender. They report that firms that exhibit a very low level, or no degree, of social responsibility are penalized by banks through a higher cost of borrowing. Specifically they report an average borrowing cost that is higher by 16 basis points for firms with little or no concerns for their social responsibility. Furthermore, by using the Granger Causality technique, they find that increases in earnings induce firms to undertake socially responsible investments but that these investments do not increase earnings. The premise of their work is that, beyond a certain level, socially responsible activities do not help the firm.

Statman (2005) compares the returns of the four indexes of socially responsible companies (the Domini 400 Social Index (DS 400 Index), the Calvert Social Index, the Citizens Index, and the US portion of the Dow Jones Sustainability Index) with that of the S&P 500 Index and finds that Socially Responsible Investment (SRI) indexes did better than the S&P 500 during the boom of the 1990s but lagged during the bust of the early 2000s. Further, he finds that the DS 400 performed better than the S&P 500 during the overall May 1990–April 2004 period but not in every subperiod.

Zakri Bello (2005) uses a sample of socially responsible stock mutual funds matched to randomly selected conventional funds of similar net assets to investigate differences in characteristics of assets held, portfolio diversification, and effects of diversification on investment performance. He reports that socially responsible funds do not differ significantly from conventional funds in terms of any of these attributes. Furthermore, he reports that the effect of diversification on investment performance does not differ across the two groups.

Becchetti et al. (2005) investigate whether the inclusion and permanence in the Domini Social Index affects corporate performance. They find that inclusion in the Domini Index is associated with a significant increase in total sales per employee but a reduction in return on equity. However, the lower returns on equity for the Domini firms seem to be accompanied by relatively lower conditional volatility and lower reaction to extreme shocks.

Milevsky et al. (2006) investigate whether the imposition of a constraint, on portfolio selection, to include only "socially responsible companies" has a negative effect on the performance of such companies. Using an optimization algorithm, they eliminate a group of "socially undesirable stocks" and replace them with comparable "socially responsible firms" and show that the difference in returns is "economically insignificant."

Given that the focus on the issue of social responsibility and its effect on corporate performance is a recent phenomenon, it is not surprising that many of the findings are inconclusive. This chapter aims to contribute to this debate by addressing the following questions:

1. Is it possible to impose a constraint (e.g. CSR) to a nonmonotonic function (e.g. profits function) that results in the attainment of a higher maximum point than what would be possible without such a constraint?
2. Can an investor form a portfolio of socially responsible firms and achieve a better performance than would investors who do not face such a constraint (and who have a broader selection base that includes CSR firms)?

To address the first question, we introduce a mathematical model wherein the constraint contains an argument that also affects the function. Within such a model, we show that the answer to the first question is in the affirmative. More specifically, we introduce a constraint into the firm's production function that results both in a higher cost per unit of product and also shifts the demand curve so that the net result is higher profits for the firm.

Addressing the second question has several dimensions. If socially responsible firms can produce better than average profits, they may be able to also provide better than average returns for their stockholders. Whether a portfolio of such firms can outperform similar portfolios that are formed without this constraint remains to be examined. Many managers claim that their stock-picking ability enables them to choose a subset of stocks from a well-diversified portfolio and form a smaller portfolio with a better return.[1] Assuming these claims are valid, a trade-off question arises as to what these managers give up in order to achieve a higher return. By holding a less than fully diversified (market) portfolio, the managers are exposed to some level of unsystematic risk. Whether a portfolio of socially responsible firms provides sufficient (if any) extra return to compensate for the added unsystematic risk remains an unanswered empirical question.

The issue of performance evaluation has dramatically evolved during the last quarter of a century. Given that portfolio performance can now be measured along various dimensions, it is not always easy to unequivocally rank various portfolios. Even when one considers only two such dimensions, risk and return, one may use different measures to judge among the various portfolios. More importantly, these measures are not always consistent in ranking portfolios. Nonetheless, the question of proper risk/return trade-off cannot be addressed without picking one such measure. Furthermore, if a portfolio outperforms the market on a consistent basis, it may also imply a persistent mispricing. This, in turn, contains implications for the Efficient Market Hypothesis (EMH). Therefore, any potential valuation benefits in becoming a socially responsible corporation may be captured quickly during a brief window of time. This calls for an examination of the effect of announcements that help clarify a firm's commitment, or lack thereof, to social responsibility.

As the first step in addressing some of these questions, in this study, we examine the characteristics of firms making up the DS 400 Index and compare them with that of a control group of firms not included in the DS 400. Using data over the 16-year period 1990–2005, we examine the degree of market risk and the total risk of firms making up the DS 400 and compare them with the degrees of market and total risks of a control portfolio outside the DS 400 index. We also compare their returns over the same time period. We find that while firms included in DS 400 Index have essentially the same market risk and return as the control group, their total risk is lower. This implies that a portfolio of socially responsible firms has a lower residual risk. It also implies that this portfolio may offer a better risk/return trade-off than the control portfolio. Furthermore, we compare the two groups on the basis of their ongoing valuations. More specifically, we compare the group of firms designated as socially responsible to their control group on the basis of their market-to-book ratio, excess equity/sales ratio, and their Tobin's Q.

We observe that socially responsible firms appear to enjoy the same valuation, and at the margin a more favorable one, when compared to their peers.

To investigate how the investors respond to signals regarding a firm's commitment to corporate social responsibility, we examine the market's reaction to announcements regarding the inclusion in or deletion from the DS 400 index. We find that the addition to (deletion from) a socially responsible index enhances (reduces) the appeal of the assets to the investor base.

The rest of this chapter is organized as follows. In section 8.1, we present a model to illustrate that, under some circumstances, the introduction of a constraint may enhance the corporate profits (maximum point of a nonmonotonic function). In sections 8.2–8.5, we explain the nature of our data, followed by our empirical results. Section 8.6 summarizes the paper and presents a conclusion regarding our findings.

8.1 Mathematical justification for CSR

To claim that a portfolio of socially responsible investments outperforms more broadly based portfolios is similar to claiming that the introduction of a constraint (limiting investments to socially responsible companies) to a nonmonotonic function will result in a higher maximum (a better performance) than the one that could be obtained in the absence of such constraints on the investment strategy (i.e. forming a portfolio from the universe of all securities). This may appear contrary to simple mathematical intuition. However, if the constraint also forces a shift in the objective function, it is possible to imagine cases where the resulting maximum is higher than the maximum obtained without such a constraint. In our attempt to apply this to corporate profitability and investment performance, we set out to investigate the following two questions:

1. Can a firm impose a constraint on its activities such that it becomes socially responsible and yet have a higher profitability than the rival firms who do not impose such constraints?
2. Can an investor form a portfolio of socially responsible firms and obtain better results than investors without such a constraint?

In addressing the first question, we design a simple example of a firm operating in a perfectly competitive market for its products. We assume that its production function exhibits "decreasing returns to scale" and can be described by $q = f(x_1, x_2) = A x_1^\alpha x_2^\beta$, where q denotes quantity of the output, x_1 and x_2 denote input variables, and $\alpha + \beta < 1$. The input variables, x_1 and x_2, can also be obtained in a perfectly competitive market at a price of r_1 and r_2, respectively. The profit function for this firm, therefore, is: $\pi = p f(x_1, x_2) - r_1 x_1 - r_2 x_2 - b$, where π denotes profits and b denotes the fixed cost. This profit function can be maximized with respect to x_1 and x_2.

The first-order condition for maximizing this profit function with respect to x_1 and x_2 is that we set the partial derivatives with respect to these inputs to zero:

$$\frac{\partial \pi}{\partial x_1} = p f_1 - r_1 = 0 \quad \text{and} \quad \frac{\partial \pi}{\partial x_2} = p f_2 - r_2 = 0 \tag{1}$$

The second-order condition for maximization requires that the production function is strictly quasi-concave. This means that in our production function the principal minors of the relevant Hessian determinants alternate in sign:

$$\frac{\partial^2 \pi}{\partial x_1^2} = p f_{11} < 0 \quad \text{and} \quad \frac{\partial^2 \pi}{\partial x_2^2} = p f_{22} < 0 \tag{2}$$

and

$$\begin{vmatrix} \dfrac{\partial^2 \pi}{\partial x_1^2} & \dfrac{\partial^2 \pi}{\partial x_1 \partial x_2} \\ \dfrac{\partial^2 \pi}{\partial x_2 \partial x_1} & \dfrac{\partial^2 \pi}{\partial x_2^2} \end{vmatrix} = p^2 \begin{vmatrix} f_{11} & f_{12} \\ f_{21} & f_{22} \end{vmatrix} > 0 \tag{3}$$

Condition (2) ensures that profit is decreasing with respect to further use of either x_1 or x_2 (given that $p > 0$ marginal product of both inputs are decreasing), and condition (3) ensures that profit is decreasing with respect to further use of *both* x_1 and x_2.

Maximizing this profit function with respect to x_1 and x_2 results in determining an optimum level of input utilization (x_1^* and x_2^*), output quantity (q^*), and the profit level (π^*). Assume, now, that there is an alternative production technique that uses a more environmental friendly input, x_3, (say green fertilizer) which has the same marginal productivity as x_1 but is more expensive. If the manager substitutes x_3 for x_1, its production cost will increase. Under ordinary circumstances, introducing this (self-imposed or otherwise) constraint will reduce the profit level. However, if as a result of introducing this constraint (going green) the demand curve for the product shifts rightward and the product is sold at a higher price p^* ($p^* > p$), the optimizing procedure could result in a higher profits level π^{**} ($\pi^{**} > \pi^*$).[2]

This simple example illustrates that firms may have the ability to impose constraints on themselves to be socially responsible and still make higher profits than their otherwise "nonconstrained" peer firms. Higher profits, if sustained, will result in a higher valuation of these firms as well. The example may be extended to much more complicated cases in many directions. One can introduce a constraint that shares an argument with the price function (more applicable to markets other than perfectly competitive markets). One can also introduce the time element into the model so that it can reflect characteristics of market trends and the advantage of being an "early bird" firm. The example can also be extended to a more realistic uncertain framework, where many of the variables in the firm's objective function are probabilistic. Also, one can introduce the element of risk management and long-term sustainability. In that framework, it may be possible to show that socially responsible managed firms are less likely to face lawsuits or customer boycotts and may enjoy a lower cost of capital and a higher valuation, *ceteris paribus*.

In all these cases, one can show that the answer to the first question presented in this section (i.e. whether a firm that imposes a constraint on itself to be socially responsible can experience a higher level of profits), may be in the affirmative. Our second question can be addressed in many ways. If socially responsible firms are able to produce better than average profits, they may also be able to provide better than average returns for their stockholders. However, whether or not this implies that a portfolio of socially responsible firms can outperform a portfolio constructed without such a constraint rests on the answer to a few questions including whether such portfolios have higher residual risks than other portfolios. Therefore, we must address the issue of risk/return trade-off.

8.2   Data

We obtained the names and the CUSIP numbers of the firms in the Domini 400 Social Index for 1990, and all subsequent additions and deletions to the index during the course of the following 15 years (1991–2005) from KLD Research & Analytics. Based on this information, we developed the "dynamic" list of Domini 400 firms for a 16-year period (1990–2005) covered by our study. In order to ensure that we compare the

Table 8.1 Definition of characteristics used to create the control group firms

Variable	Definition
Market to book	The fiscal year-end close price/((total assets – total liabilities)/#shares)
ROA	Net income/total assets
ROE	Net income/stockholder's equity
ROS	EBIT/sales
Leverage ratio	(Long-term debt + current liabilities)/total assets
CapEx to sales	Capital expenditures/sales
R&D to sales	Research and development expenditures/sales
Advertising to sales	Advertising expenditures/sales
Excess equity to sales	(Market value of equity – book value of equity)/sales
Tobin's Q	Market value of assets/total assets

Note: Control firms are screened out of the universe of publicly traded firms that are (1) in the same line of business (two-digit SIC code) as the Domini firms and (2) are the closest in size (market cap.) to the Domini firms as possible.

performance of firms considered as having a socially responsible portfolio with a relevant benchmark, we form a portfolio of control firms from the companies traded in NYSE and AMEX with characteristics that match those of the Domini 400 firms. This control portfolio is formed by screening firms out of the universe of publicly traded companies that are (1) in the same line of business (have the same two-digit SIC code) and (2) are the closest in size (market capitalization) to the Domini firms.[3]

We then compare the performance of the two portfolios on the basis of several characteristics. These characteristics and their definitions are listed in Table 8.1. Table 8.2 illustrates the details of these selected characteristics; market-to-book values (MV/BV), return on assets (ROA), return on equity (ROE), return on sales (EBIT/sales), leverage ratio, capital expenditures to sales ratio, R&D expenditures to sales, advertising to sales, excess equity to sales[4] and Tobin's Q. All balance sheet and income statement data were extracted from COMPUSTAT, and the data items related to prices and returns are obtained from the CRSP tapes. The means and standard deviations of the underlying variables for the two portfolios are presented in panels (i) through (x).

8.3 Empirical results

Our discussion of the empirical results is divided into two parts: we first discuss the valuation and risk return characteristics of the two groups.

Table 8.2 Comparison of firms included in the Domini Index with their control group with regard to:

i. Market-to-book ratio

Year	Mean of Domini companies	Mean of control companies	Standard deviation of Domini companies	Standard deviation of control companies	t-value	Pr > |t|
1990	1.0550638	0.9513670	0.9250071	0.9335211	1.69	0.0927
1991	0.8964885	0.7954807	0.8180624	0.8393508	2.16	0.0313
1992	1.1815660	1.2028052	1.3968726	1.7176394	0.08	0.9380
1993	1.1750595	1.2839703	1.1898937	1.5407070	−1.02	0.3062
1994	1.1089877	1.3601867	0.9304682	2.4199247	−1.84	0.0670
1995	0.9876253	1.0020734	0.8738460	1.1345612	0.06	0.9533
1996	1.0923785	1.4329814	1.0898711	2.1982894	−2.59	0.0099
1997	1.1808613	1.3229807	1.1082267	1.4560499	−1.34	0.1822
1998	1.3602025	1.2543764	1.1900774	1.2478261	0.85	0.3955
1999	1.4804359	1.5064421	1.5442897	2.1392374	−0.71	0.4803
2000	1.8357651	2.5182584	3.5147504	4.6933028	−2.35	0.0191
2001	1.5813634	1.9467298	2.1110166	3.0948840	−2.28	0.0233
2002	1.4309256	1.5537581	1.3740055	1.7497751	−1.07	0.2835
2003	1.0573805	0.9630336	0.9717072	1.1089068	1.43	0.1537
2004	1.2955015	1.2606577	1.1383645	1.2761321	0.49	0.6275
2005	1.3673209	1.4706542	1.2705945	1.7594411	−0.29	0.7696
1990–2005	1.2546177	1.3651121	1.5058442	2.0947096	−3.32	0.0009

ii. ROA

Year	Mean of Domini companies	Mean of control companies	Standard deviation of Domini companies	Standard deviation of control companies	t-value	Pr > |t|
1990	0.0567792	0.0452249	0.0676256	0.0824743	2.22	0.0269
1991	0.0497819	0.0441951	0.0686619	0.0873086	1.31	0.1906
1992	0.0425857	0.0226986	0.0756419	0.1298993	2.68	0.0078
1993	0.0437789	0.0284256	0.0816462	0.1436798	1.87	0.0621
1994	0.0563317	0.0590054	0.0706573	0.1856074	−0.60	0.5521
1995	0.0533388	0.0446479	0.0731512	0.0967610	1.31	0.1916
1996	0.0514819	0.0423047	0.0852920	0.1115491	1.39	0.1654
1997	0.0503245	0.0496262	0.0839312	0.0805931	−0.01	0.9948
1998	0.0451680	0.0390048	0.1128787	0.0942605	0.38	0.7038
1999	0.0633048	0.0372997	0.0642071	0.1578737	2.75	0.0063
2000	0.0595084	−0.0087795	0.0726321	0.2842129	4.64	<0.0001
2001	0.0282247	−0.0405650	0.1284949	0.4189544	3.30	0.0011
2002	0.0243001	−0.0126959	0.1319392	0.2337214	2.92	0.0038
2003	0.0449174	0.0358508	0.0785744	0.1117968	1.59	0.1116
2004	0.0547148	0.0529787	0.0702853	0.0931454	0.47	0.6392
2005	0.0643477	0.0520309	0.0636922	0.1058483	1.72	0.0867
1990–2005	0.0492044	0.0304464	0.0863236	0.1782224	7.57	<0.0001

Table 8.2   Continued

iii. ROE

Year	Mean of Domini companies	Mean of control companies	Standard deviation of Domini companies	Standard deviation of control companies	t-value	Pr > |t|
1990	0.1180840	0.1078263	0.1613116	1.2006047	0.19	0.8482
1991	0.0779940	0.1056119	0.4162830	0.8128213	−0.57	0.5677
1992	0.0722372	0.0062757	0.2709574	0.9300122	1.32	0.1886
1993	0.6726616	0.0141155	11.1868248	1.0492090	1.15	0.2489
1994	0.1567074	0.1113235	0.2732779	1.3676843	−0.99	0.3238
1995	0.2393071	0.0510813	2.3056882	0.9318670	1.42	0.1553
1996	0.0798862	0.1569967	0.9135009	6.2433710	−0.24	0.8123
1997	0.0711252	0.1204384	1.0083757	0.3341395	−0.96	0.3400
1998	0.1397219	−0.0892932	0.4903028	2.2521418	1.83	0.0682
1999	0.1695202	0.4742966	0.2876090	5.9794146	−0.97	0.3321
2000	0.1905915	0.0068453	0.7225693	1.2674081	2.47	0.0139
2001	0.0573099	−0.1578607	0.4848529	2.8767153	1.45	0.1471
2002	0.1223019	0.0467256	1.0147027	1.2217247	1.04	0.2984
2003	0.0387169	0.2814981	1.5626202	3.3276972	−1.23	0.2186
2004	0.1349291	0.0579121	0.3526366	1.5849063	0.96	0.3372
2005	0.1877736	0.3027186	0.4529380	2.7590164	−0.68	0.4992
1990–2005	0.1581958	0.0984420	2.9562073	2.7116458	1.11	0.2690

iv. ROS

Year	Mean of Domini companies	Mean of control companies	Standard deviation of Domini companies	Standard deviation of control companies	t-value	Pr > |t|
1990	0.1290961	0.1959347	0.1140479	1.4977689	−0.86	0.3909
1991	0.1228549	0.1184918	0.1162219	0.1734370	−0.19	0.8495
1992	0.1282426	0.0701523	0.1201439	0.7042087	1.61	0.1077
1993	0.1346777	0.0293660	0.1330672	1.1702127	1.68	0.0936
1994	0.1394018	0.1266737	0.1242017	0.2134118	0.53	0.5939
1995	0.1406118	0.1374294	0.1192244	0.1643787	0.05	0.9564
1996	0.1364664	0.1252148	0.1258790	0.2588664	0.35	0.7296
1997	0.1413446	0.1401890	0.1254844	0.1586200	−0.31	0.7551
1998	0.1285905	−0.7113294	0.1530055	12.5914620	1.27	0.2059
1999	0.1438535	0.0761246	0.1300256	0.6715664	1.95	0.0523
2000	0.1503284	−0.9837710	0.1403495	11.6552519	1.86	0.0633
2001	0.1214678	−0.1496340	0.1490841	2.2201142	2.40	0.0167
2002	0.1360028	−0.1277045	0.1545850	3.3980559	1.52	0.1298
2003	0.1481995	0.1174672	0.1549193	0.2838364	2.07	0.0394
2004	0.1627728	−0.0951232	0.1474960	5.0601968	1.01	0.3137
2005	0.1715339	0.1385120	0.1452973	0.2133736	2.48	0.0136
1990–2005	0.1396791	−0.0497770	0.1357805	4.6065870	3.12	0.0018

Table 8.2   Continued

v. Leverage ratio

Year	Mean of Domini companies	Mean of control companies	Standard deviation of Domini companies	Standard deviation of control companies	t-value	Pr > |t|
1990	0.1799361	0.2027913	0.1624310	0.2128397	−1.42	0.1564
1991	0.1748604	0.2062450	0.1579371	0.2043200	−2.19	0.0289
1992	0.1720135	0.1939950	0.1553919	0.1905987	−1.94	0.0534
1993	0.1624754	0.1903127	0.1497896	0.1915715	−2.61	0.0093
1994	0.1640801	0.1897212	0.1487931	0.1772559	−2.03	0.0430
1995	0.1738371	0.2006649	0.1433845	0.1918733	−2.65	0.0084
1996	0.1752138	0.1958746	0.1390135	0.1828380	−1.80	0.0728
1997	0.1821699	0.1964653	0.1433371	0.1935798	−1.59	0.1117
1998	0.1975904	0.2274640	0.1589492	0.2022309	−2.37	0.0182
1999	0.1937145	0.2324062	0.1560145	0.2327719	−2.32	0.0208
2000	0.1870325	0.1952085	0.1458593	0.1917146	−0.41	0.6798
2001	0.1943040	0.2061705	0.1496916	0.1848758	−1.08	0.2820
2002	0.1883448	0.2071667	0.1496928	0.1864304	−2.20	0.0283
2003	0.1817000	0.2111835	0.1433301	0.1850453	−2.59	0.0100
2004	0.1723097	0.1887696	0.1438825	0.1756754	−1.69	0.0926
2005	0.1693626	0.1777884	0.1495274	0.1624098	−1.25	0.2105
1990–2005	0.1792028	0.2012255	0.1500809	0.1921711	−7.57	<0.0001

vi. Capital expenditures as a fraction of sales

Year	Mean of Domini companies	Mean of control companies	Standard deviation of Domini companies	Standard deviation of control companies	t-value	Pr > |t|
1990	0.0022373	0.0031618	0.0063269	0.0128007	−1.65	0.1001
1991	0.0020321	0.0018578	0.0053892	0.0059642	−0.07	0.9451
1992	0.0018032	0.0027453	0.0052140	0.0225265	−0.85	0.3971
1993	0.0014878	0.0050937	0.0048408	0.0528781	−1.29	0.1973
1994	0.0013705	0.0031275	0.0044655	0.0198975	−1.61	0.1081
1995	0.0016959	0.0028212	0.0059063	0.0140454	−0.82	0.4128
1996	0.0015514	0.0026024	0.0052710	0.0154820	−0.98	0.3282
1997	0.0012453	0.0028023	0.0036531	0.0191515	−1.50	0.1350
1998	0.0014636	0.0023701	0.0050912	0.0111442	−1.25	0.2123
1999	0.0017086	0.0020975	0.0082086	0.0138495	−0.21	0.8319
2000	0.0012530	0.0015644	0.0049089	0.0053692	−0.94	0.3480
2001	0.0011730	0.0011746	0.0047395	0.0045060	0.28	0.7788
2002	0.00086817	0.0011584	0.0034541	0.0049406	−0.76	0.4473
2003	0.000900864	0.000625653	0.0032840	0.0018560	1.80	0.0731
2004	0.000741708	0.000875159	0.0023547	0.0039685	−0.28	0.7827
2005	0.000838216	0.000865310	0.0026263	0.0030322	−0.45	0.6496
1990–2005	0.0013987	0.0021710	0.0049451	0.0179246	−3.01	0.0027

Table 8.2　Continued

vii. R&D expenditures as a fraction of sales

Year	Mean of Domini companies	Mean of control companies	Standard deviation of Domini companies	Standard deviation of control companies	t-value	Pr > |t|
1990	0.0363623	−0.0224112	0.0446126	0.7963084	0.85	0.3953
1991	0.0378657	0.0553305	0.0474715	0.1673509	−1.56	0.1224
1992	0.0374062	0.1507194	0.0453975	0.8897385	−2.24	0.0267
1993	0.0396960	0.2076874	0.0504335	1.4559757	−1.46	0.1465
1994	0.0417611	0.0611944	0.0538319	0.1784361	−1.68	0.0965
1995	0.0394125	0.0393686	0.0559828	0.0605494	−0.84	0.4040
1996	0.0420017	0.0785051	0.0590544	0.2194600	−2.01	0.0470
1997	0.0444206	0.0514355	0.0581471	0.0772410	−0.90	0.3712
1998	0.0473657	0.7355578	0.0656847	6.1943712	−1.47	0.1447
1999	0.0452931	0.1330099	0.0554354	0.8081076	−1.33	0.1867
2000	0.0490560	0.6033199	0.0598326	3.2644814	−2.07	0.0396
2001	0.0562275	0.3760892	0.0747084	2.1508784	−2.05	0.0419
2002	0.0674774	0.4335634	0.1364374	3.7246768	−1.44	0.1510
2003	0.0652001	0.0976660	0.1273770	0.2504406	−1.71	0.0889
2004	0.0553545	0.4047717	0.0700479	4.8744062	−1.05	0.2951
2005	0.0528915	0.0878164	0.0696327	0.2066479	−1.87	0.0630
1990–2005	0.0482943	0.2299407	0.0747175	2.5123112	−3.65	0.0003

viii. Advertising expenditures as a fraction of sales

Year	Mean of Domini companies	Mean of control companies	Standard deviation of Domini companies	Standard deviation of control companies	t-value	Pr > |t|
1990	0.0491489	0.0344041	0.0123080	0.0346677	0.85	0.3961
1991	0.0373271	0.0374314	0.0422706	0.0510584	−0.51	0.6120
1992	0.0374777	0.0381527	0.0426763	0.0421093	−0.18	0.8594
1993	0.0395657	0.0368040	0.0458605	0.0371144	0.69	0.4950
1994	0.0461068	0.0383336	0.0472554	0.0395945	−0.51	0.6114
1995	0.0488156	0.0495636	0.0478002	0.0618200	−0.48	0.6377
1996	0.0444628	0.0484924	0.0421910	0.0524085	−0.88	0.3831
1997	0.0440815	0.0469252	0.0415934	0.0551912	−0.93	0.3590
1998	0.0443364	0.0432697	0.0427730	0.0557862	0.74	0.4646
1999	0.0421189	0.0426413	0.0431152	0.0552240	−0.21	0.8384
2000	0.0378048	0.0457937	0.0429219	0.0645905	0.56	0.5797
2001	0.0332276	0.0338326	0.0387458	0.0420445	0.18	0.8558
2002	0.0312814	0.0286268	0.0348390	0.0335634	0.87	0.3852
2003	0.0329809	0.0296984	0.0403353	0.0404882	2.26	0.0267
2004	0.0317050	0.0287434	0.0396368	0.0384245	1.69	0.0940
2005	0.0296557	0.0303129	0.0364705	0.0467266	0.22	0.8275
1990–2005	0.0378146	0.0366680	0.0420655	0.0464347	1.04	0.3008

Table 8.2   Continued

ix. Excess equity value as a fraction of sales

Year	Mean of Domini companies	Mean of control companies	Standard deviation of Domini companies	Standard deviation of control companies	t-value	Pr > |t|
1990	0.5743226	0.6463566	1.0002277	2.5019440	−0.42	0.6723
1991	0.8298486	0.9394652	1.2401624	2.4037178	−0.66	0.5066
1992	0.8390163	1.8943805	1.1751653	9.1611416	−2.14	0.0329
1993	0.8864858	1.7800252	1.0754772	5.1323977	−3.29	0.0011
1994	0.7069791	1.1343205	0.8138042	2.3967822	−3.04	0.0025
1995	0.8621377	1.2399026	1.0472798	3.2462792	−2.03	0.0435
1996	0.9218585	1.7218837	1.0621322	4.3399676	−3.76	0.0002
1997	1.2107265	1.5336302	1.2799403	1.9754305	−3.01	0.0028
1998	1.3031333	22.2852023	1.6859118	360.1262909	−1.11	0.2671
1999	1.4833432	2.7451662	2.4518360	10.4820254	−2.23	0.0265
2000	1.6756690	19.9389083	2.8709277	175.5535314	−1.99	0.0472
2001	1.3997880	3.5741973	2.0344779	15.8702954	−2.66	0.0081
2002	1.0871109	1.0860144	1.6107477	2.1478503	0.08	0.9334
2003	1.5383952	1.5989698	2.2769644	2.8204826	−0.35	0.7279
2004	1.4804402	6.5639614	1.9828094	97.7825944	−1.02	0.3081
2005	1.3921243	1.6634032	1.8516634	2.5423392	−2.27	0.0237
1990–2005	1.1352345	4.3737899	1.7243592	102.5606279	−2.41	0.0158

x. Tobin's Q

Year	Mean of Domini companies	Mean of control companies	Standard deviation of Domini companies	Standard deviation of control companies	t-value	Pr > |t|
1990	0.0390880	1.4435291	0.0440725	1.6937635	0.30	0.7652
1991	1.2764824	1.1121993	0.9904867	1.2610521	1.56	0.1200
1992	1.6941371	1.8453856	1.7560525	2.9241417	−0.71	0.4753
1993	1.7455472	1.8383659	2.0109864	2.0087501	−0.70	0.4846
1994	1.6052566	1.8685855	1.3087864	2.2662488	−1.54	0.1257
1995	1.4145908	1.4617101	1.0804928	1.4487128	−0.19	0.8527
1996	1.6376914	2.1809537	1.5000133	3.6268269	−2.37	0.0185
1997	1.7687284	1.9451970	1.5917510	1.9265145	−0.89	0.3759
1998	2.0773980	1.9097394	1.8601131	1.6594065	1.72	0.0874
1999	2.3397777	2.3615257	2.6430480	2.8835983	−0.35	0.7232
2000	3.1111393	4.8101329	6.1513127	9.4328724	−2.92	0.0037
2001	2.6324126	3.3706063	3.4115840	5.2008387	−3.02	0.0027
2002	2.4721500	2.6607250	2. 5001377	2.9363442	−1.05	0.2929
2003	1.8117175	1.6289213	1.6432689	1.8102481	1.36	0.1734
2004	2.2411830	2.1344736	1.8173218	1.7727351	0.47	0.6365
2005	2.4227985	2.5632964	2.1153128	2.8341121	−0.46	0.6450
1990–2005	1.9896731	2.2048966	2.4861286	3.5770211	−3.93	<0.0001

We then discuss the valuation consequence (in terms of abnormal return) of being added to or deleted from the Domini 400 Index.

8.3.1 Risk/return characteristics of the two groups

For each of the characteristics listed in Table 8.1, we test the null hypothesis that the difference between the means of the two groups is statistically indiscernible. An examination of the *t*-statistics for the pooled time series cross-sectional data over the 1990–2005 period indicates that the two groups are significantly different than one another with regard to all but two measures: return on equity and the ratio of advertising to sales. These results are reported in the last row of each of the panels (i) through (x) of Table 8.2.[5] According to these results, Domini firms have a lower market-to-book ratio, higher return on assets, higher return on sales, lower leverage, lower capital expenditures per dollar of sales, lower R&D expenditures per dollar of sales, a lower ratio of excess equity value per dollar of sales, and lower Tobin's Q ratios.

Interestingly, most of these differences disappear once we consider only the cross-sectional tests. More specifically, when we examine the *t*-statistics for the comparison of the two groups for each of the years 1990 through 2005 (reported in the first 16 rows of each panel of Table 8.2) we often cannot reject the null hypotheses of no difference between the means of the measures for the two groups. The two groups are sometimes significantly different on the basis of a given measure of comparison in one year, but not so the next and certainly not uniformly different across all periods.[6] However, the null hypotheses of no differences across the two groups are rejected most frequently for two measures, the degree of leverage and the ratio of excess value of equity to sales. Therefore, it appears that we can safely state that, on the basis of these test results, socially responsible firms (represented by those included in the Domini Index) use less leverage in their capital structure and also suffer from a lower level of valuation of their equity per dollar of sales. However, tests of significance of differences across the two groups with regard to two other measures of relative valuation, i.e. the market-to-book ratio and the Tobin's Q ratio, cast a shadow of doubt with regard to any inferences for the valuation of socially responsible firms. First consider the market-to-book ratio: out of the 16 periods considered, the null hypothesis of no differences across the means of the market-to-book ratios of the two groups is rejected, once in favor of the socially responsible firms and three times against them. Therefore, on this basis, we can safely set aside the explanation that socially responsible firms suffer from a lower level

Table 8.3 Comparison of the total risk (standard deviation of returns) of firms included in the Domini Index with those of the control group

Year	Mean of Domini companies	Mean of control companies	Standard deviation of Domini companies	Standard deviation of control companies	t-value	Pr > |t|
1990	0.0210786	0.0263288	0.0051509	0.0072011	−16.22	<0.0001
1991	0.0215634	0.0239623	0.0038543	0.0038705	−11.21	<0.0001
1992	0.0208363	0.0236993	0.0036531	0.0032172	−11.87	<0.0001
1993	0.0196376	0.0248952	0.0025033	0.0066279	−11.93	<0.0001
1994	0.0189513	0.0225098	0.0027024	0.0031787	−17.09	<0.0001
1995	0.0190395	0.0230278	0.0041494	0.0050950	−10.30	<0.0001
1996	0.0195261	0.0241707	0.0032259	0.0040634	−16.70	<0.0001
1997	0.0203458	0.0243559	0.0040546	0.0046030	−13.38	<0.0001
1998	0.0250177	0.0288743	0.0067615	0.0083245	−11.19	<0.0001
1999	0.0270240	0.0310610	0.0045851	0.0056395	−13.03	<0.0001
2000	0.0332584	0.0458608	0.0059895	0.0110450	−22.91	<0.0001
2001	0.0279075	0.0369719	0.0074403	0.0102728	−20.89	<0.0001
2002	0.0268655	0.0339471	0.0068719	0.0093574	−16.16	<0.0001
2003	0.0195346	0.0210819	0.0039720	0.0044419	−6.29	<0.0001
2004	0.0167832	0.0195436	0.0033152	0.0040306	−12.46	<0.0001
2005	0.0157646	0.0189407	0.0034859	0.0045004	−11.35	<0.0001

of valuation. This is reinforced by an examination of the results with regard to the Tobin's Q ratios. Out of the 16 periods considered, the null hypotheses of no differences between the means of the two groups are rejected only for the 1996, 2000 and 2001 periods. For all other periods, the means are statistically identical. Therefore, it appears that the lower ratio of excess value of equity to sales for our socially responsible firms may be driven by other factors. The lower levels of leverage employed by these firms may be considered one such factor.

We also compare the total risk (standard deviation of returns) of firms in the two groups. Table 8.3 reports the means and standard deviations of total risk calculated for each group for each year. As these results illustrate, total risk of the firms included in the Domini 400 group is lower than that of the control group in each and every year. The differences are statistically significant at less than 1 percent confidence level for all 16 years. Therefore, we can safely conclude that socially responsible firms, represented by those included in the Domini 400, have significantly lower degrees of total riskiness and are, therefore, less risky when held as individual assets.

Table 8.4   Comparison of betas of firms included in the Domini Index with that of the control group

Year	Mean of Domini companies	Mean of control companies	Standard deviation of Domini companies	Standard deviation of control companies	t-value	Pr > |t|
1990	1.0619951	0.8691810	0.4598639	0.5275240	6.03	<0.0001
1991	1.0136125	0.8541262	0.4490522	0.5230134	5.16	<0.0001
1992	1.0429253	0.9631679	0.5497720	0.6824146	2.12	0.0345
1993	0.9768522	0.9979216	0.5591633	0.6407043	−0.58	0.5632
1994	0.9618448	0.9944624	0.4531555	0.5416259	−0.97	0.3324
1995	0.9001040	0.9757674	0.6241551	0.7507515	−1.68	0.0931
1996	0.8875869	0.8974699	0.4067326	0.5389230	−0.33	0.7405
1997	0.8263969	0.7745547	0.4097112	0.4411178	2.00	0.0465
1998	0.9014177	0.9324106	0.3820609	0.4852344	−1.15	0.2508
1999	0.6604891	0.6147772	0.4412224	0.5095890	1.77	0.0779
2000	0.6453086	0.9218340	0.5197232	0.8347534	−7.51	<0.0001
2001	0.8886698	1.0569948	0.6021466	0.8899527	−4.23	<0.0001
2002	0.9790852	1.0395474	0.4202900	0.5463407	−2.14	0.0333
2003	1.0324505	1.0178383	0.4192433	0.4727041	0.56	0.5756
2004	1.1215086	1.1692195	0.4730536	0.5367160	−1.69	0.0909
2005	1.1142402	1.1235272	0.4357667	0.4725329	−0.37	0.7087

We next proceed to investigate the differences across the two groups with regard to the degree of market riskiness (i.e. differences in the riskiness of the two groups when they are held within well-diversified portfolios). Table 8.4 reports the means and the standard deviations of the betas of the two groups for each of the 16 years (1990–2005) covered in our analysis. An examination of these results suggests that the betas of the Domini 400 firms are neither lower, nor higher, on a uniform basis. To be precise, the betas of the Domini firms are significantly higher than those of their control groups for four years (these are concentrated in the early periods of comparison: 1990, 1991, 1992, and 1997). However, they appear to be significantly less risky than their counterparts in three other periods (2000, 2001, and 2002). We conclude, therefore, that firms classified as socially responsible have the same degree of market risk as those not classified as such. By extension, we can also conclude that these firms have significantly less unique risk than their counterparts.[7]

The lower unique risk of the DS 400 may be evidence that the socially responsible firms offer products and/or services that are perceived to be less controversial, less risky, and safer (both from the perspective of the consumer and the society at large). If so, it follows that these firms will

Table 8.5 Comparison of daily returns to the shareholders of firms included in the Domini Index with those of the control group

Year	Mean of Domini companies	Mean of control companies	Standard deviation of Domini companies	Standard deviation of control companies	t-value	Pr > |t|
1990	−0.000384011	−0.000680299	0.0098212	0.0087392	1.51	0.1331
1991	0.0015254	0.0015386	0.0084635	0.0075076	−0.08	0.9347
1992	0.000716597	0.000599698	0.0061315	0.0059958	0.87	0.3845
1993	0.000630591	0.000638938	0.0050973	0.0055996	−0.06	0.9531
1994	0.000074033	−0.000127242	0.0057347	0.0061723	1.52	0.1301
1995	0.0010258	0.000844718	0.0044357	0.0051084	1.27	0.2050
1996	0.000796371	0.000695814	0.0062510	0.0066054	0.67	0.5009
1997	0.0012191	0.000867270	0.0084580	0.0081665	2.26	0.0244
1998	0.000651556	0.000189541	0.0113361	0.0122967	2.45	0.0149
1999	0.000421180	0.000423597	0.0078981	0.0076918	−0.02	0.9872
2000	0.000624201	−0.000090136	0.0115543	0.0152936	1.43	0.1525
2001	0.000653275	0.000274835	0.0128540	0.0152757	1.29	0.1970
2002	−0.000300369	−0.000708698	0.0154772	0.0167044	1.94	0.0531
2003	0.0014245	0.0015487	0.0105802	0.0105644	−1.11	0.2689
2004	0.000691481	0.000782110	0.0081043	0.0085612	−0.80	0.4272
2005	0.000334040	0.000253980	0.0073989	0.0075715	0.86	0.3912

have a lower degree of unique risk. This can be attributed, for example, to the steady demand from a loyal customer base, lower probability of consumer boycotts, fewer environmental challenges and lawsuits, and a less hostile but more committed and energized employee base.

Next, we compare the two groups on the basis of the daily returns provided to their shareholders. Results, as reported in Table 8.5, indicated that for 11 out of 16 years of study, Domini firms outperform their counterparts. However, only for two years (1997 and 1998) are the differences statistically significant (with probability value of less than 3 percent). For the remaining nine years, the differences are not statistically discernible at 5 percent level. In none of the 16 years covered by our analysis did Domini firms significantly underperform their counterparts.

Therefore, it appears that our socially responsible firms, at a minimum, provide the same return on equity as their counterparts outside the index. Indeed, a case can be made, albeit a weak one, that they dominate their peers along this dimension. Further, they are not dominated by their peers on the basis of their betas, and dominate them on the basis of their degree of unique risk. Therefore, the conclusion can be drawn that the socially responsible firms, represented by those firms

Table 8.6   Comparison of alphas of firms included in the Domini Index with that of the control group

Year	Mean of Domini companies	Mean of control companies	Standard deviation of Domini companies	Standard deviation of control companies	t-value	Pr > |t|
1990	−0.000161294	−0.000433609	0.0013153	0.0018549	2.35	0.0195
1991	0.000338980	0.000564614	0.0012814	0.0015508	−2.42	0.0160
1992	0.000353339	0.000236862	0.0011027	0.0014670	1.31	0.1926
1993	0.000196133	0.000201899	0.0011330	0.0013090	−0.07	0.9445
1994	0.000099504	−0.000075017	0.0010425	0.0013697	2.19	0.0292
1995	−0.000060565	−0.000296773	0.0013402	0.0017775	2.21	0.0280
1996	0.000104258	0.000020664	0.0010668	0.0014936	0.90	0.3673
1997	0.000331851	0.000040295	0.0011878	0.0015400	3.09	0.0022
1998	−0.000059527	−0.000568910	0.0017202	0.0017709	4.28	<0.0001
1999	−0.000165184	−0.000072410	0.0017188	0.0019629	−0.79	0.4314
2000	0.000858826	0.000222565	0.0020116	0.0031545	3.51	0.0005
2001	0.000988523	0.000682894	0.0016916	0.0018266	2.63	0.0090
2002	0.000492957	0.000080537	0.0012316	0.0022158	3.24	0.0013
2003	0.000198750	0.000340083	0.000946380	0.0011853	−1.88	0.0605
2004	0.000118611	0.000181332	0.000940511	0.0011570	−0.85	0.3968
2005	−1.214428E−6	−0.000093417	0.000949844	0.0014377	1.15	0.2528

in the Domini 400, provide a better risk/return profile than the control group. Bear in mind that firms in the Domini 400 Index generate superior performance on the basis of ROA. This superior performance diminishes when it comes to ROE due to significantly lower leverage.

To further examine whether these Domini firms provide for better investment vehicles than their peers, we also study the differences across the two groups with regard to their alphas. These results, reported in Table 8.6, indicate that our socially responsible firms have significantly higher alphas in eight of the 16 periods considered. The reverse holds true only for one period (1991). Therefore, we can safely conclude that socially responsible firms provide the investors with alphas superior to those of their peers.

As a final test of the viability of socially responsible firms as investment vehicles, we compare the two groups on the basis of their Sharpe ratios. These results are reported in Table 8.7. A quick overview of these results leads one to the observation that in all but two of the periods analyzed, the Sharpe ratios of Domini firms have been larger than those of their peers, and for four of these years (1995, 1997, 1998, and, marginally,

Table 8.7 Comparison of Sharpe ratios of firms included in the Domini Index with those of the control group

Year	Mean of Domini companies	Mean of control companies	Standard deviation of Domini companies	Standard deviation of control companies	t-value	Pr > |t|
1990	−0.0383460	−0.0447261	0.4254044	0.3009570	0.56	0.5748
1991	0.0398944	0.0394569	0.3695271	0.2906636	0.05	0.9595
1992	0.0195549	0.0151147	0.2847784	0.2431931	0.65	0.5169
1993	0.0286264	0.0219512	0.2498115	0.2194477	1.02	0.3100
1994	−0.0035527	−0.0154342	0.2927974	0.2642784	1.74	0.0829
1995	0.0429830	0.0286359	0.2280668	0.2160777	2.06	0.0407
1996	0.0279946	0.0197922	0.3162629	0.2641690	1.09	0.2782
1997	0.0581994	0.0241790	0.3729233	0.3141639	3.76	0.0002
1998	0.0153081	−0.0065991	0.4054931	0.3694084	2.92	0.0038
1999	−0.0033481	−0.0025843	0.3009335	0.2586840	−0.12	0.9019
2000	0.0033059	−0.0156079	0.3250107	0.3037869	1.89	0.0598
2001	0.0070443	−0.0057861	0.4113711	0.3553444	1.56	0.1193
2002	−0.0269123	−0.0363750	0.5184519	0.4465960	1.06	0.2893
2003	0.0670152	0.0665891	0.5116310	0.4780404	0.06	0.9524
2004	0.0337083	0.0344402	0.4880312	0.4290184	−0.09	0.9318
2005	0.0205186	0.0136002	0.4521347	0.3970140	0.83	0.4078

2000) the differences are statistically significant. Combined with the results on the comparison of the alphas, these results suggest that, if one is to draw any conclusions regarding the relative merits of the two groups as investment vehicles, it would be that the socially responsible firms are at least on a par and quite possibly superior to their peers.

In summary, the results of our examination in this section seem to provide evidence (albeit not statistically significant on a uniform basis) that socially responsible orientation does not come at a cost to the shareholders. On the contrary, it appears that these firms provide their investors with risk/return opportunities that are at least equal to, and at times superior to, those provided by their peers. To further examine this hypothesis, we next investigate the market's reaction to the announcement of deletion from or addition to the Domini 400 Index.

8.3.2 Market reaction to announcements of additions to/deletions from the index

As previously described, we obtained a listing of all additions to and deletions from the Domini Index from KLD Research and Analytics.

As a matter of policy, KLD drops a firm from its index once it makes a determination that it has violated one of its indicators of social responsibility. Although the information regarding these violations may be widely available to markets for some time prior to KLD's announcement of a deletion, the announcement itself sends an unambiguous signal about KLD's assessment of violations. Therefore, one may hypothesize that this constitutes a signal to those monitoring KLD's pronouncements. As such, it may cause the participants in the marketplace to revise their valuation of the firm through a process of "social reconstruction" of value. Once a firm has been targeted for deletion from the index it is replaced with a firm deemed socially responsible. Here, too, the activities of firms targeted for addition to the index may be fully transparent to the markets at large. However, a case can be made that a decision by KLD to add the firm to its index sends an unambiguous signal regarding its socially responsible behavior. Therefore, once again, there may be attendant (socially constructed) valuation consequences for these firms.

To evaluate the market's response to KLD's announcements we perform two event studies for which the event date is defined as the first date on which KLD makes its decisions public. In one we will examine valuation consequences to those firms that are added to the index, and in the other those accrued to firms slated for deletion. The methodology utilized is the standard event study technique.

8.4   The model

We employ the traditional market model, Equation (4), to determine the expected (required) rate of return of all stocks as a linear function of market rate of return. For each group, we run the following regression:

$$R_{it} = a_i + b_i R_{mt} + u_{it} \tag{4}$$

where
R_{it} = Return on stock i in period t
a_i = Intercept term for stock i
b_i = Slope term for security i (an estimate of betas)
R_{mt} = Return on the market index (S&P 500) in period t
u_{it} = Error term on security i in period t.

The statistical package used for this purpose is the Eventus Package. To obtain regression coefficients a_i and b_i for each company, we used a 255-day estimation period, ending at 30 days before the day for which we calculate abnormal return (from day −290 to day −35, from day −289 to day −34, and so forth). Using these regression estimates, we examine the abnormal returns of all firms during the 10-trading-day period surrounding the announcement day (day −5 to day +5, where day 0 is the announcement date) for firms in each group separately. The abnormal return for security i at time t is estimated as follows:

$$\hat{e}_{it} = R_{it} - \hat{a}_i - \hat{b}_i R_{mt}, \tag{5}$$

where $\hat{e}_{it}$ is the estimate of the abnormal return for security i at time t, and $\hat{a}_i$ and $\hat{b}_i$ are the least squares estimates of a_i and b_i, respectively. Because the event day is not the same for all firms, the chance for cross-sectional correlation of the abnormal returns is very low. For each day, we calculate the average abnormal return (AR_t) across all firms. We also calculate the cumulative average return at time t, CAR_t, as the sum of average returns from the day −5 up to the time in which we are interested, as shown below:

$$CAR_t = \sum_{i=-5}^{t} AR_i, \quad \text{for } t = -5, -4, \ldots, 5 \tag{6}$$

We measure the impact of announcements by examining AR_t and CAR_t around the announcement date (day 0). If the announcement has a positive (negative) impact on the firm, we expect to observe a significantly positive (negative) cumulative abnormal return during the event window (−5 to +5).

8.5 The results

The results of our these tests, summarized in Tables 8.8 and 8.9, suggest that firms that are added to the Domini Index experience a positive revaluation by the market. On the contrary, firms that are no longer deemed socially responsible and are dropped from the Domini Index experience a negative revaluation by the market. More specifically, we find a statistically significant positive abnormal return of 0.43 percent on the day of the announcement of the inclusion a firm in the index (Table 8.8). The three-day cumulative abnormal return surrounding the announcement (−1, 0, +1) is also statistically significant at 0.67 percent. The CAR during the event window are shown in Figure 8.1 for firms that are added to the index.

Firms that are deleted from the index experience an average abnormal return of −0.44 percent on the day that the announcement of a deletion

Table 8.8 Abnormal and cumulative abnormal returns experienced by the shareholders of firms added to the Domini Index

Event	AR (%)	CAR(%)	Patell Z	Generalized Z
−5	0.28	0.28	1.297$	−0.194
−4	0.16	0.44	1.473$	0.396
−3	−0.17	0.27	−0.477	−0.587
−2	0.25	0.52	2.294*	1.575$
−1	0.14	0.66	1.511$	1.575$
0	0.43	1.09	4.342***	2.902**
1	0.10	1.19	0.514	−0.068
2	0.31	1.50	2.135*	1.22
3	0.08	1.58	0.481	1.121
4	0.11	1.69	1.06	0.13
5	0.09	1.78	0.409	0.13

The symbols $,*,**, and *** denote statistical significance at the 0.10, 0.05, 0.01 and 0.001 levels, respectively, using a 1-tail test.

Table 8.9 Abnormal and cumulative abnormal returns experienced by the shareholders of firms deleted from the Domini Index

Event	AR (%)	CAR(%)	Patell Z	Generalized Z
−5	0.19	0.19	1.950*	0.391
−4	−0.10	0.09	0.648	0.391
−3	−0.22	−0.13	−0.503	0.292
−2	−0.08	−0.21	1.206	2.559**
−1	−0.36	−0.57	−2.060*	−0.2
0	−0.44	−1.01	−0.748	1.226
1	−0.42	−1.43	−1.22	0.776
2	−0.18	−1.61	0.316	−0.397
3	0.90	−0.71	3.428***	0.348
4	0.67	−0.04	3.793***	1.340$
5	0.12	0.08	1.937*	−0.775

The symbols $,*,**, and *** denote statistical significance at the 0.10, 0.05, 0.01 and 0.001 levels, respectively, using a 1-tail test.

is made public. However, although this is not statistically significant, the preceding day's return of −0.36 percent is statistically significant, as is the cumulative three-day abnormal returns of −1.22 percent (Table 8.9). The *CAR* during the event window are shown in Figure 8.2 for firms that are deleted from the index.

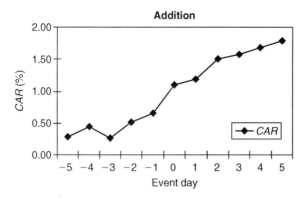

Figure 8.1 CAR during the event window for the firms that are added to the index

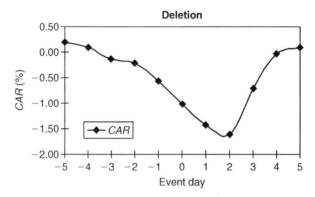

Figure 8.2 CAR during the event window for the firms that are deleted from the index

In both cases (addition to and deletion from the index) there is a significant (positive for the addition and negative for the deletion) abnormal return on day −2, which we attribute to "leakage of information." These results suggest that the market attaches a significant value to signals confirming a firm's socially responsible activities or a confirmation of its failure on such measures. Once a firm is classified as a socially responsible entity, the market rewards it with an upward reestimation of its value. Firms classified as "not socially responsible" will experience a negative market reevaluation.

8.6   Summary and conclusion

In this chapter we provide a model to illustrate that imposing a constraint in a nonmonotonic function could lead to a higher maximum point if the constraint has the ability to also shift the objective function. Applying this concept to the issue of corporate profitability, we argue that imposing a "social responsibility" constraint could lead to increased profitability of the firm. We support this argument by introducing an optimization model and a numerical example. In an empirical attempt to test this argument, we compare the characteristics of firms making up the DS 400 Index with that of a control group of firms not included in the DS 400. We find that socially responsible firms are, at a minimum, at par with their peer companies on the basis of return on equity (their return on assets is superior) and betas, but dominate their peers on the basis of their degree of unique risk. Our analysis also indicates that a socially responsible orientation does not come at a cost to shareholders. On the contrary, it appears that these firms provide their investors with risk/return opportunities that are at least equal to, and at times superior to, those provided by their peers. Further, we find strong evidence indicating that socially responsible firms employ significantly less leverage in their capital structure.

Using 16-year data (1990–2005), we examine announcements of addition to/deletion from DS 400 Index and their impact on the companies that are added or deleted. Our results indicate that firms that are added to (deleted from) the DS 400 Index experience a positive (negative) abnormal return upon the announcement. For firms that are added to the index, the three-day cumulative abnormal return surrounding the announcement (-1, 0, $+1$) is positive (0.67 percent) and statistically significant. In contrast, those firms that are deleted from the index experience a negative cumulative three-day abnormal return, in the magnitude of -1.22 percent, which is also statistically significant. This observation adds further weight to observations made elsewhere that it may be *reputation* for CSR, or good corporate governance, that really matters to firm valuation regardless of the actual performance characteristics involved (Orlitzky et al. 2003; Wheeler and Davies 2007).

Appendix

To expand on our discussion of section 8.1 with a specific example, consider a farmer who is operating in perfectly competitive markets for inputs and outputs. Its production function can be displayed by $q = f(x_1, x_2) = 10x_1^{.25}x_2^{.5}$. Its output is sold for \$20/unit. The input variables, x_1 (fertilizer) and x_2 (labor), can be obtained at a price of \$1.5 (per 100 g of fertilizer) and \$8 (per hour of labor), respectively. The profit function for this firm is $\pi = pq - C = \$20(10x_1^{.25}x_2^{.5}) - \$1.5x_1 - \$8x_2 - \$10,000$, where the \$10,000 is the fixed cost (say rent for the land). Maximizing this profit function with respect to x_1 and x_2 results in $x_1 = 173,611$ units of fertilizer and $x_2 = 65,104$ labor hours as the optimum combination of inputs. This combination will provide the farmer with \$250,416 profit.

Now suppose there is an alternative production technique that uses a more environmental friendly input, x_3, (say green fertilizer) which has the same marginal productivity as x_1 but is 33 percent more expensive, \$2 per 100 g. If this farmer (or another firm with the same characteristics) uses this input instead of x_1, the optimizing process will result in hiring 97,656 units of x_3 and 48,828 units of x_2, which in turn will result in \$185,312 profit.

Obviously, introducing the constraint to "go green" has reduced the profit for the firm. But what if, as a result of going green (producing organic food, for example) the demand curve for the product is shifted so that the product now could be sold at a 10 percent higher price (\$22)? In that case, by following the same optimizing procedure the firm should hire 142,978 units of x_3 and 71,489 units of x_2, which will result in \$275,957 profit, a \$25,541 extra profit over the competitor firm that uses the "cheap and dirty technique."

Notes

1. Whether a portfolio of socially responsible firms could be one of these smaller portfolios or not is essentially an empirical question.
2. A numerical example is presented in the Appendix to illustrate this point.
3. Given that KLD has an apparent emphasis on the largest publicly traded firms our control firms are, invariably, smaller in size than Domini firms.
4. The excess equity to sales ratio is a measure of valuation, capturing possible differential valuation effects. It differs from Tobin's Q in that it captures the effect on equity value, as opposed to the overall value of the firm. See, for example, Bodnar et al. (1997).
5. As expected, and discussed under note 3, the two groups are different with regard to size. When the two groups are compared on the basis of their capitalization figures, the null hypotheses of no differences in the means of the two groups are uniformly rejected for all time series and cross-sectional time series tests.

6. Our examination of these differences over time does not reveal a discernible pattern of association of significance in differences of means, or lack thereof, with any particular set of macro developments or market cycles.
7. Therefore, they may be ideal candidates for intending to hold less than fully diversified portfolios.

References

Becchetti, L., Di Giacomo, S. and Pinnacchio, D. (2005) "Corporate Social Responsibility and Corporate Performance: Evidence from a Panel of US Listed Companies," CEIS Working Paper No. 7, SSRN Working Paper Series, Rome.

Bello, Z. (2005) "Socially Responsible Investing and Portfolio Diversification," *Journal of Financial Research*, 28/3: 41–57.

Bodnar, G.M., Tang, C. and Weintrop, J. (1997) "Both Sides of Corporate Diversification: Value Impacts of Geographic and Industrial Diversification," NBER Working Papers, Working Paper 6224, Cambridge, Mass.

Friedman, M. (1970) "The Social Responsibility of Business is to Increase its Profits," *New York Times Magazine*, September 13.

Freeman, R.E. (1984) *Strategic Management: a Stakeholder Approach*. Pitman, Boston.

Freeman, R.E. and McVea, J. (2001) "A Stakeholder Approach to Strategic Management," in Hitt, M.A., Freeman R.E. and Harrison J.S. (eds) *Handbook of Strategic Management*, Blackwell, Oxford, pp. 189–207.

Freeman, R.E., Wicks, A.C. and Parmar, B. (2004) "Stakeholder Theory and the Corporate Objective Revisited," *Organization Science*, 15/3: 364–9.

Goss, A. and Roberts, G. (2006) "The Cost of Virtue: Corporate Social Responsibility and the Cost of Debt Financing," Working Paper, Schulich School of Business, York University.

Jensen, M.C. (2005) "Value Maximization, Stakeholder Theory, and the Corporate Objective Function," in Chew, D.H. and Gillan, S.L. (eds) *Corporate Governance at the Crossroads: a Book of Readings*, McGraw-Hill Irwin, New York, pp. 7–20.

Jensen, M.C. and Meckling, W. F. (1976) "Theory of the Firm: Managerial Behavior, Agency Costs, and Ownership Structure," *Journal of Financial Economics*, 3: 305–60.

Jensen, M.C. and Meckling, W.F. (2005) "The Nature of Man," in Chew, D.H. and Gillan, S.L. (eds) *Corporate Governance at the Crossroads: a Book of Readings*, McGraw-Hill Irwin, New York, pp. 87–102.

Margolis, J.D. and Walsh, J.P. (2001) *People and Profits? The Search for a Link between a Company's Social and Financial Performance*. Erlbaum, Mahwah, NJ.

Milevsky, M., Aziz, A., Goss, A., Comeault, J. and Wheeler, D. (2006) "Cleaning a Passive Index," *The Journal of Portfolio Management*, Spring, 110–18.

Orlitzky, M. and Benjamin, J.D. (2001) "Corporate Social Performance and Firm Risk: a Meta-Analytic Review," *Business and Society*, 40: 369–96.

Orlitzky, M., Schmidt, F.L. and Rynes, S.L. (2003) "Corporate Social and Financial Performance: a Meta-Analysis," *Organization Studies*, 24/3: 403–41.

Roberts, J. (2004) *The Modern Firm*. Oxford University Press, Oxford.

Roman, R., Hayibor, S. and Agle, B. (1999) "The Relationship between Social and Financial Performance," *Business and Society*, 38/1: 109–25.

Rubin, Amir and Barnea, Amir (2006) "Corporate Social Responsibility as a Conflict between Shareholders (March 10, 2006)". EFA 2006 Zurich Meetings.

Statman, M. (2005) "Socially Responsible Indexes: Composition and Performance," SSRN Working Paper Series. Available at SSRN: http://ssrn.com/abstract=705344

Waddock, S.A. and Graves, S. (1997) "The Corporate Social Performance–Financial Performance Link," *Strategic Management Journal*, 19: 303–17.

Wheeler, D. (2003) "The Successful Navigation of Uncertainty: Sustainability and the Organization," in Burke, R. and Cooper, C. (eds) *Leading in Turbulent Times*, Blackwell, Oxford, pp. 182–207.

Wheeler, D. and Davies, R. (2007) "Why Corporate Governance Rankings do not Predict Future Value: Evidence from Toronto Stock Exchange Listings 2002–2005," in Benn, S. and Dunphy, D. (eds) *Corporate Governance and Sustainability: Challenges for Theory and Practice*, Routledge, London.

9
Building the Case for Long-Term Investing in Stock Markets: Breaking Free from the Short-Term Measurement Dilemma

Steven Lydenberg

Introduction

Many voices have been raised in recent years extolling the virtues of long-term investing, and condemning the short-termism in today's stock markets. Pillars of our financial and business community – including the CFA Institute, the Business Roundtable, the Conference Board, the United Nations, the World Economic Forum, and the Aspen Institute – have all prescribed the long term as a cure for our short-term ills. An excessive focus on short-term profits has various detrimental effects. It causes corporate managers to misallocate assets. It introduces dangerous volatility into financial markets. It means society must divert productive resources to repairing environmental and social damage done in the headlong pursuit of profits. In a 2006 report, the Conference Board speaks for many when it describes the dangers of the short term:

> On a macro-economic level, short-term visions are the cause for market volatility and the instability of financial institutions. From the micro-economic standpoint, they undermine management continuity and expose a public company to the risk of losing sight of its strategic business model, compromising its competitiveness. In addition, the pressure to meet short-term numbers may induce senior managers to externalize a number of business costs (i.e., the cost of a state-of-the-art pollution system), often to the detriment of the environment and future generations.[1]

There are a host of useful remedies for the excessively short-term outlooks of the financial and corporate communities. These include:

- reforming the reporting of quarterly corporate earnings and the compensation incentives of analysts and managers;
- broadening fiduciary duties;
- including social, environmental, and corporate governance issues into stock analysis and institutional investors' mandates;
- increasing nonfinancial disclosure;
- creating best-practice guidelines for pension funds;
- revitalizing education on the virtues of the long-term approach.

Despite widespread concern, little real change is taking place. Financial professionals are aware of the trap in which they are caught. They can see ways out of it. But they are unable to act in ways that substantively change their practices. As Alain Leclair, president of the French Association of Financial Management, has put it: "We [...] face a dilemma. In practically all aspects [of investing], although everything ought to direct us to adopt a long-term approach, we are forced to measure and act in the short term."[2] We might call this the "short-term measurement dilemma." It goes to the heart of why long-term investing is currently so difficult to implement. When the market is valued according to a short-term measurement – that is, stock prices – and when managers' performance is measured against these prices, then long-term investing becomes impossible. In particular, the liquidity, or ease of trading, in today's stock markets contributes to the short-term perspective. Stock market prices are measured daily, hourly, and by the minute. A market that offers participants instantaneous opportunities to measure and act on their price-based worth – that allows them to jump in and out of stocks at little cost on the slightest bit of news or slimmest of rumors – deprives them of a perspective from which to measure the value of the companies over years or decades.[3]

Investors and corporate managers clearly can see the detrimental effects of this short-term perspective. What they cannot see, and what is keeping them from change, is a clear definition of an alternative long-term investing system and a system for implementing it. Without these two things in hand, real change will be impossible. All the pieces for solving this puzzle are already on the table. Yet the change that is implied by a shift to the long term involves a new way of thinking for a financial community of tremendous size and power. Change inevitably will meet with resistance. This chapter proposes a simple, clear definition of long-term investing and explores its practical implications. This should bring new approaches to the financial world, which will create true value and avoid the pitfalls of short-term price speculation. Although this chapter does not deal with the similar problem of short-termism for managers in the corporate world, the dilemma and its possible solutions run parallel to those suggested here.[4]

A comprehensive definition of long-term investing must address three issues:

- the benefits of holding stocks for long periods of time;
- the incorporation of environmental, social and corporate governance (ESG) factors into investing; and
- the willingness to add value to investments.

The definition proposed here incorporates these three elements. It is as follows:

> Long-term investors speculate on the value of corporations to society and the environment, while simultaneously seeking to enhance that value at the company, industry, and societal level.

This definition is intended to steer investors clear of the detrimental focus on price, and to emphasize value. It works because the wealth corporations create is more than stock price. It corrects the conception that investors can function only as price takers, not value makers. It stresses that, like investors in other asset classes, stock investors have the capability – and the responsibility – to add to the social and environmental, as well as the financial, value of their investments. To do so, long-term investors in the stock markets must engage management on important social and environmental issues and set clear standards – that go beyond relative price – on how to allocate their investments. We will look at the three components of our definition, one at a time.

9.1   The value of long holding periods

Much of the despair about short-termism focuses on day traders, arbitrageurs, profit maximizers, and others who think the road to fortune lies in moving quickly in and out of stocks. As the Conference Board noted, the 40-plus participants in its summit on short-termism were unanimous on this point: "stock investment speculation is a major cause of short-termism." If speculation on price is the cause of the disease, why should a simple remedy – buying and holding stock for long periods of time – not be the cure? For many in the investment world, "buy long and hold long" is a sufficient definition of the long term. However, this definition does not go far enough.

Indisputably, holding stocks for longer periods of time can bring investors great financial benefit. Long holding periods reduce transaction costs and save on tax liabilities. But simply buying and holding for a longer period is not enough to create a stock market where a long-term view and speculation on value predominate. Two widely practiced, but somewhat contradictory, buy-and-hold strategies in today's markets demonstrate why this is true:

- *Index investing* involves buying a broadly diversified basket of stocks and holding them for long periods of time. Its underlying assumption is that you cannot beat the market.
- *Value investing* involves selecting individual stocks that the market has not correctly priced and holding them for long periods. Its underlying assumption is that you can beat the market.

Neither captures the essence of the long term firmly enough to escape from the short term of our current marketplace. A closer look at index investing confirms this point.

Index investing is one of the most widely practiced investment techniques in the stock market today. It consists of buying diversified baskets of stocks and holding them more or less forever. Common benchmarks in which indexers invest are the Standard & Poor's 500 and the Russell 1000 indexes. These two indexes consist of the largest publicly traded stocks in the United States as measured by price. Literally thousands of other indexes capture various other markets and market segments around the world. Institutional investors today have invested trillions of dollars in these index funds. Stock indexes are usually capitalization weighted – that is, the size of the holdings of each stock in the index is determined by its market price multiplied by its number of shares outstanding. Because index investors hold stocks for an essentially unlimited time, it seems logical to consider them the embodiment of long-term investing. Indeed, many pension funds that use indexing strategies consider themselves long-term investors. However, simply holding stock for a long time does not guarantee that one is free from short-termism. As Simon Zadek has observed: "When pension funds say they are long-term investors, what they mean is that they have rolling investments in largely indexed linked funds. To speak accurately this makes them *perpetual investors* making short-term investments, forever."[5]

Or more accurately, indexers are exactly as short term or as long term as the stock market is at any given moment. When indexers buy and sell stock, they do so at whatever the market price is that day, without attempting to determine if these stocks are overvalued or undervalued. They therefore reflect, and indeed amplify, any pricing irrationalities of the markets at any given time. If there is a speculative bubble, if stocks are wildly overvalued or undervalued, indexers participate in that irrational exuberance or despair to exactly the extent of other market participants. Professor Alfred Rappaport goes to the heart of the problem of index investing when he notes that "Index funds make no independent contribution to allocatively efficient prices because indexing requires no valuations."[6] Indexers make no attempt to determine the value of the stocks they are purchasing because they believe that stock price and the value of corporations are one and the same. Their most fundamental belief is that investors cannot beat the market by making educated guesses about when stock price deviates from underlying value. They just buy the market. Indeed, the only way for indexers to add value to their portfolios is to reduce transaction costs.

By abandoning any attempt to actively value the market, indexers make it more speculative in two ways. First, they increase the percentage of speculators in the marketplace by withdrawing themselves and others who might potentially be interested in long-term valuation from the setting of stock prices, leaving that role to short-term speculators. Second, they force even those managers left in the market who are attempting to value stocks with a view toward the long term into mimicking whatever prices may be set by the short-term speculators. As one fund manager and participant in the World Economic Forum's working group explained, "As long as client [e.g. pension fund trustees] mandates require us to deliver performance benchmarked against short-term market tracker indexes, we will of course remain short term in our outlook."[7]

If we want stock markets to assess the long-term value of corporations, index investors will be of no help. We must look elsewhere. One place is to the value investor. Value investors are long term in their perspective and help counteract the short-termism of today's markets. They are stock pickers who evaluate the underlying, intrinsic value of a company, which they usually define as its long-term earnings potential, and compare that to today's stock price. Because earnings potential over the long term is their measure of value, value investors usually buy and hold. Put differently, because the markets can take a long time to come around to value investors' point of view, they tend to hold for long periods of time. Warren Buffett, the chief executive of Berkshire Hathaway and a widely recognized long-term investor, has reportedly asserted that his favorite holding period is "forever."[8]

The great virtue of value investors is that they are willing to take an alternative view of the intrinsic value of a corporation to that of the short-term markets. They sell when they think stocks are overpriced and buy when they believe they are undervalued. They can counterbalance the wild swings of markets that are purely speculative – markets that overshoot because investors become irrationally optimistic or pessimistic about what companies are worth. If long-term investors can predominate in the market, they can send signals to managers about which corporations are allocating their funds in an economically productive way and which are not. It is therefore crucial, as Keynes has wisely observed, that those with a long term predominate in the marketplace.[9]

If this function of the long term in the marketplace is so important, why is the market not set up so that value investors can predominate? One might think that value investors would be rewarded for their diligence and the wisdom of their approach, that they would consistently turn in superior performance results to their irrationally speculative peers, and that institutional investors would rush to place their funds in the hands of such wise and productive managers. The answer is both paradoxical and discouraging. Value investors in the aggregate cannot, *by definition,* turn in better price-based performance results than the indexers over long periods of time. Although a select few active managers may be able to beat the markets consistently, institutional investors find it difficult to justify making substantial use of them as a whole.

Index investors derive great satisfaction in pointing out that if value investors' returns are measured against the performance of capitalization-weight benchmark indexes, on average and over the long haul they cannot "beat the market." For this reason, indexers assert that value investors do not add value. This is devastating for advocates of long-term investing. It is also the reason that the "short-term measurement dilemma" is real and difficult to resolve. This dilemma for value investors arises because, although some value investors will always beat the index benchmarks, it is impossible for them in the aggregate to beat price-based market averages all the time. Two considerations make this inevitable. First, it is logically absurd to imagine a market where some managers outperform all the time and others underperform all the time. No intelligent investor would stay forever with a manager who underperforms all the time. Underperforming managers will either lose their clients and go out of business or change their tactics. Once managers' performance is measured against market prices set by counterbalancing buyers and sellers, by definition, half will outperform and half will underperform over time.

Second, value managers must incur an extra cost that index investors do not pay. That cost is research. This means that indexers have a cost advantage in the marketplace that will cause them to outperform over time and on average. Value investors, each trying to beat the performance of the others, must actually research the companies in which they invest. As hard as it is to believe, indexers do no research at all. Without this expense, index investors on average and over the long haul inevitably outperform the active value managers. Indexers, by definition, will outperform those who set the prices because they do not have to bear the cost of the research necessary to set those prices. As John Bogle, the founder of the Vanguard mutual fund company and a fierce advocate of index investing, has succinctly put it, "For all investors as a group, then, beating the market *before* costs is a zero-sum game; beating the market *after* costs is a loser's game" (emphasis in original).[10] In other words, the market is a zero-sum game: some participants gain at the expense of others, with none adding any true value. In such a market, those who incur costs by trying to determine the value of companies will inevitably underperform those without these costs.[11] Keynes, an advocate of the long-term approach to investing, was despairingly articulate on this point:

> Investment based on genuine long-term expectation is so difficult to-day as to be scarcely practicable. He who attempts it must surely lead much more laborious days and run greater risks than he who tries to guess better than the crowd how the crowd will behave; and, given equal intelligence, he may make more disastrous mistakes. There is no clear evidence from experience that the investment policy which is socially advantageous coincides with that which is most profitable.[12]

The long-term value investors about whom Keynes is speaking will always find themselves at a competitive disadvantage in today's stock markets and never predominate as long as their performance is measured against stock price. Long-term value investors cannot escape from the price-based measurement trap because it is price, as related to long-term earnings potential, by which they still judge their own performance. Their investment time horizon may be "forever" – or Judgment Day, another horizon line by which Buffett likes to calculate the earnings power of corporations – but price is still the ultimate measurement of returns.[13] Thus, the "short-term measurement dilemma" cannot be resolved by simply looking to long-term earnings potential. Other factors must be introduced if we are to give the long term a deeper meaning and more influence in our markets today.

9.2   The materiality of social and environmental factors

In determining the value of corporations, it is vital for long-term investors to consider factors other than price and earnings. Environmental, social, and governance (ESG) factors inherently impose a longer-term perspective. They take into account issues well suited to a long-term perspective, and these issues often cannot be clearly tied back to price. Any definition of the full potential of long-term investing must incorporate these factors. ESG-based evaluations of companies reach beyond those from traditional stock analysts because they encompass the less tangible aspects of a company's value. Generally, ESG factors relate to a company's relations with its stakeholders such as employees, customers, communities, suppliers, and the environment. Specifically, they include issues such as workplace safety, employee training, product quality, charitable giving, vendor labor standards, carbon emissions, and pollution prevention. These factors can lead to the exclusion of particular companies from investment consideration when they fail to meet certain stakeholder-specific standards. In addition, ESG considerations can help evaluate the role of whole industries in a sustainable society. Involvement in the production of weapons of mass destruction or tobacco, for example, might lead to exclusion.

Some ESG factors can be directly related to a company's stock price and some cannot. Those that can be tied to stock price are usually referred to as financially "material." Those that cannot are sometimes referred to as factors that have "nonfinancial materiality."[14] Another way of describing these nonfinancially material ESG factors is to use the economists' conception of positive or negative externalities, describing them as factors that create costs or benefits that cannot be translated easily into market price. However they are described and whatever their relationship to materiality, ESG factors are inherently long term in nature and contribute to the definition of long-term investing.[15]

ESG factors help direct the market to the long term because they frequently focus on issues where risks and rewards are best measured in years and decades, not months and quarters. Environmental issues with such long-term horizons include climate change, ozone depletion caused by industrial chemicals, development of alternative energy sources, changes in environmental regulation, environmental life-cycle analysis for products, energy efficiency, and the effective implementation of company-wide environmental management systems. Social issues with similarly long horizons include the availability of clean water in the coming century, the adequacy of labor standards at suppliers in developing nations, the incorporation of women and ethnic minorities into corporate workforces, the balancing of the pressures of the workplace and the demands of family life, investments in a highly trained workforce, and support for community economic development.

A growing number of investors state clearly that they consider ESG factors as relevant to their investments and corporate valuation. For example, Asset Management Working Group in 2004 reported that at the nine major brokerage houses that they commissioned for analyses of the role of ESG factors in stock valuations, "Analysts agreed that environmental, social, and corporate governance criteria impact both positively and negatively on long-term shareholder value."[16] In an encouraging development along similar lines, a number of major investment houses increasingly are hiring in-house staff to promote the integration of ESG research into their analyses for the mainstream investment community. Among the mainstream investment banks, insurance companies, and asset managers that now have in-house "green teams" that work with their traditional stock analysts on valuations issues are Citigroup, Goldman Sachs, Societé Générale, Henderson Global Investors, F&C Investments, Morley Asset Management (Aviva), and Insight Investment (HBOS). Mainstream investors and analysts are, generally speaking, incorporating ESG factors because they believe doing so will make them better stock pickers in the long run. In this sense they are like value investors, looking for buying and selling opportunities when ESG factors show that a company's intrinsic value has deviated from its current price.

It should be noted that simply because ESG factors look to the long term, they do not automatically protect the stock markets from short-term price speculation. In fact, the more ESG factors become incorporated into current price/earnings models, the more likely they are to fall prey to the short-term speculation those models produce. This is true because highly liquid markets invite speculation when price is the only consideration. Take, for example, the investment opportunities offered by the development of alternative energy sources. The exact prospects for wind-power companies are unknown today, but that does not keep the markets from speculating on them and driving their stock prices up sharply. In France in early 2007, for example, strong performance of wind power and other green stocks prompted a *Le Monde* story headlined "Is There a Green Stock Bubble?"[17]

While some ESG factors clearly are related to stock price, other ESG factors clearly cannot be related to the price of individual stocks or the market valuation of whole industries. This type of factor can be described as nonfinancially material or as an externality. Externalities are costs (or gains) that are borne (or shared) by those not involved in a particular transaction. In other words, externalities are costs and benefits that are not captured in the marketplace and cannot be measured by price. An example of a negative externality would be the health damage that tobacco products cause, costs that are borne by society. A positive externality would be the cost of training employees in skills that they could then take elsewhere. Ironically, considerations of externalities can, in theory, lead to investing in companies that cause harm and to shunning companies that produce societal benefit. Jeremy Siegel reports that the best performing US stock of the past 75 years has been Philip Morris (now Altria).[18] Furthermore, Siegel argues that investors are not rewarded for investments in companies that enhance productivity in the economy. Once a factor that has been an externality – carbon emissions, for example – becomes priceable in the markets, it will no longer be an externality. As long as price is the measure of stock value, markets cannot account for externalities. This is simply a restatement of one of the most painful aspects of the "short-term measurement dilemma."

However, if investors make their primary concern the economy as a whole, not the price performance of a single stock or industry, many of the complications of factoring in externalities disappear. This is the argument for the concept of universal investing, initially propounded by Robert A.G. Monks and Nell Minnow, and subsequently elaborated by Professors James Hawley and Andrew Williams.[19] Universal investors can be defined as pension funds or other institutional investors so large that they are invested across all asset classes. Universal investors essentially "own the economy." It does not profit them to invest in a company that increases earnings by externalizing environmental or other social costs onto other companies or the economy. The company's earnings may rise, but that gain will be offset by losses at other firms that will affect the investor's portfolio. As Hawley and Williams put it:

> For a universal owner, and thus for its beneficiaries, the whole may well be greater than the sum of its parts since long-term profit maximization for the portfolio of a universal owner involves enhancing

not just return on a firm-by-firm basis, but enhancing productivity in the economy as a whole. This approach to the role and responsibility of universal ownership simply takes two basic ideas, externalities and portfolio theory . . . and combines them.[20]

By factoring in ESG externalities, long-term investors remain aware of the effects of their investments on the economy as a whole. Being able to factor these externalities into assessments of positive and negative effects on the environment and society depends, of course, on the availability of data. Progress on disclosure of this data is being made by the ground-breaking work of such organizations as the Global Reporting Initiative and the United Nations Global Compact. Progress on the analysis of this data is being pioneered by research firms such as Trucost who are figuring out how to measure potential long-term costs. Investors who factor in both financially and nonfinancially material ESG factors can be said to be long-term investors. Those who only factor in financially material, price-related ESG factors will not, however, entirely escape from the traps laid by price-based performance measurements. Those who factor in the nonfinancially material externalities will need to take one additional step to act like a long-term investor in the deepest sense. That step is to "add value" to their investments by actively discouraging negative externalities and encouraging positive ones.

9.3   Adding value to investments as the key to the long term

The final piece of the puzzle of defining long-term investing is about investors using ESG factors as a tool to add value to the companies in which they are investing. This value can be reflected in many different ways. It may show up in short-term stock price appreciation, long-term price appreciation, the creation of intangible company assets, the enhancement of reputation, increased prosperity for local or national economies, enhanced trust between corporations and society, a healthier and more sustainable environment, or many other benefits for society and the environment. It is this willingness to include value enhancement as a legitimate part of the investment process that allows long-term investors to escape from the dictates of price-based benchmarks. Value can be added at the industry, societal, or environmental levels by minimizing negative externalities (avoiding companies or industries with ESG risks), or by maximizing positive externalities (emphasizing companies or industries that make long-term investments in their stakeholders).

Adding to the value of investments is not a radical idea. In certain asset classes other than equities, investors are expected to add value. Venture capital investors and private equity managers, for example, actively manage the firms in which they invest, placing representatives on boards of directors, hiring and firing top managers, or making strategic management decisions. Similarly, real estate investors frequently invest in the properties they own to enhance their value in the marketplace. The stock market, however – because of its liquidity and because investors are separated from the managers of the corporations in which they invest – does not lend itself easily to value creation by investors. That is not to say that such value creation is impossible. When Solomon Brothers was embroiled in a major scandal involving illegal trading in the bond market, Warren Buffett as a major long-term investor agreed to take a seat on the company's board to help restore confidence. But Buffett is not likely to argue that this is a model that should be widely replicated.

A more widely accepted example of value creation by investors is that of relationship investing. An example is the work of Robert A.G. Monks through LENS Investment Management (now LENS Governance Advisors) and Ralph Whitworth through Relational Investors LLC. Such relationship investors take substantial stakes in companies they believe have performed poorly and use their influence to improve the corporate governance of these firms. More generally, institutional investors such as public and union pension funds have in the past 15 years increasingly sought to add value to their investments by urging changes in corporate governance. For example, the Council of Institutional Investors each year creates a "Focus List" of companies whose poor financial performance can be helped by governance pressure from its members. A similar list is maintained by the California Public Employees Retirement System (CalPERS). Relationship investors say their strategy pays off financially. From 1992 through 2000, when it closed shop as a money management firm, LENS' portfolio outperformed the Standard & Poor's 500 Index.[21] Similarly, Brad Barber, in his 2006 study of the activism program of CalPERS, says that CalPERS imprecisely estimates the wealth creation from its shareholder activism to be $3.1 billion between 1992 and 2005.[22]

However, if stock price appreciation is the only goal of relationship investing, investors are back in the trap of short-termism. They are no different from those they often criticize, the hedge funds and private equity firms that seek to add short-term value to their investments through cost cutting. These are the venture capitalists that German government officials described as "locusts" and whose managers are portrayed in the press as heartless, short-term profiteers. What distinguishes the value created by relationship investors such as LENS and CalPERS is that they add value, not only to their particular investments but to the stock markets in general, by raising the standards of corporate governance. They often seek to create models of best practice and to create more honest and transparent financial markets.

This form of engagement with corporate management has its parallels on the environmental and social sides. Socially responsible investors with a long-term view seek to better the management of firms in part to improve their financial performance, but also to create models of best practice that can be replicated and bring broad societal benefit. They are creating positive externalities from which other investors and society may benefit. These externalities can be created either through engagement with companies on ESG issues or by setting ESG standards for investment selection. These two tools function somewhat differently, but both can add value at the corporate, industry, and societal level. Engagement on ESG issues follows the pattern of engagement by activist relationship investors. By engaging on issues such as carbon emissions, vendor standards, and equal opportunity employment, long-term investors seek to add value not only to a particular company's operations but to those of its industry as a whole.

This engagement can take the form of private dialogue with corporations, or more public confrontations. At the company level, for example, Domini Social Investments joined with other investors and nonprofit organizations to successfully pressure Procter & Gamble to introduce a line of fair-trade coffee, a dialogue that ultimately resulted in the launch of P&G's Millstone line of fair-trade coffees. On an industry level, a coalition of responsible investors representing trillions of dollars in assets has come together under the aegis of the Carbon Disclosure Project to urge emissions disclosures by the largest corporations in the world. A similar coalition has formed under the banner of the Extractive Industries Transparency Initiative, to urge companies to disclose payments to governments, particularly in the developing world. In the US, the Investors' Network on Climate Risk is a coalition of institutional investors working with US energy companies and utilities.

In the United Kingdom, engagement is now a widespread practice among large money management companies committed to sustainability. Among the major firms committed to substantial engagement programs are Insight Investment (part of HBOS) and Morley Fund Management (Aviva). These firms communicate with hundreds of companies on dozens of social and environmental issues each year. F&C Asset Management – one of the earliest and most thorough proponents of engagement – offers a separate investment management product called "responsible engagement overlay," or "reo". Through this service, F&C will engage corporate managers on sustainability issues, whether or not F&C actually manages the client's funds. In 2006, F&C recorded 268 milestones, or instances in which "a company improves its policies, procedures, or performance following engagement by F&C's Governance and Sustainable Investment (GSI) team."[23]

A second means of adding value is standard setting. Whereas mainstream investors will purchase any stock if the price is right, long-term investors let consideration of ESG factors limit or focus the number of companies in their investment universe. These investors can limit their universe, for example by eliminating industries such as tobacco and nuclear weapons that externalize costs onto society. In addition, they can seek to add value by shunning companies that do not meet internationally recognized labor standards or whose sustainability practices are subpar. They also can focus their investments on companies that address emerging ESG issues such as alternative power generation, access to water, health, or sustainable agriculture. The most dramatic example of how standard setting by investors can add unquantifiable value to society was that of the South Africa divestment movement of the 1980s and early 1990s. At that time, institutional investors around the world joined in a broad campaign to help dismantle the apartheid legal system in South Africa.

This standard-setting and divestment movement by institutional investors was made possible by the Sullivan Principles, devised to assess the quality of labor practices in that country. These principles served as the basis for exclusion of companies by investors when firms failed to meet levels of acceptable performance. The long-term goal of these standards, however, was not improved financial performance. The goal was the creation of a just society. The Sullivan Principles have been a positive model for an ever-expanding series of standards and principles. The Ceres Principles were launched in the late 1980s explicitly to do for environmental issues in the US what the Sullivan Principles had done for labor practices in South Africa. More recently, labor standards for specific industries as diverse as apparel, toys, cocoa, and rugs have been widely promulgated. Environmental standards and best ESG practices have been developed for the mining, construction, and banking industries.

Long-term investors broadly defined use of these standards to help assess the value of companies and base their investment decisions in part on these assessments. In doing so, these investors are not only seeking to identify companies with superior prospects for long-term financial performance. They also are seeking to achieve three additional goals:

- avoid companies that pose long-term ESG risks to society;
- help create positive externalities that benefit society; and
- take a constructive part in a broad societal debate about the relationship between corporations and society.

When KLD's Domini 400 Index or the FTSE4Good Global Index series exclude manufacturers of nuclear weapons from their investable universe, they are not only avoiding companies with long-term ESG risks, but also are weighing in on the question of negative externalities. This question is not one that markets can resolve, nor is it the intention of these indexes to solve these problems. Instead, their exclusion policy is an implicit recognition that international governmental initiatives are needed to address negative externalities. Social investors' efforts take place within the context of broader movements for change. They are not aiming to create long-term value on their own, but in conjunction with other players in society.

A desire to add value to investments in the public equity markets cannot be accounted for by current theories of investment management. It is beyond the scope of this chapter to discuss the relationship between modern portfolio theory (MPT) and a fully developed theory of long-term investing. However, it can be observed here that MPT addresses issues of holding period (longer is more efficient because you cannot beat the market by active trading) and ESG factors (matters of personal taste should not be factored into purely financial investment decisions). MPT is essentially silent on the issue of whether investors in the stock market can add value to their investments. In addition, the value created by long-term investing as defined here contrasts sharply with the value that either short-term speculators or classical long-term value investors create. Short-term speculators arbitrage away short-term anomalies in the market. Long-term value investors minimize transaction costs, save on taxes, and capitalize on long-term market anomalies. The latter in particular can be said to reward corporations that are using their assets most efficiently to drive up earnings and hence stock price. Neither, however, addresses the question of externalities and the ability of investors to add value to their overall portfolio by minimizing the negative externalities and maximizing those that are positive. Keith Ambachtscheer, a noted pension consultant, recently has suggested that the next step in the development of MPT might be the consideration of how investments can be used to create broad societal wealth. Ambachtscheer describes how investment can realize *"the promise of a higher rate of societal wealth creation"* as *"the biggest prize of all."*[24]

Conclusion: implications of the definition of long-term investing

The implications of the broad definition of long-term investing envisioned here are substantial. This definition, although simple in form, implies three essential changes: a fundamentally different approach to assessing the value of companies; adopting active steps to increase the value of investments; and developing new means of measuring and managing ESG risks and rewards.

How long-term investing affects selection of investments

Long-term investors will make active investment choices when they perceive that the value of companies or industries differs from that implied by today's price-driven markets. In some regards, these investment decisions will resemble those made by traditional value investors. In two notable regards, however, they will differ. First, they will take ESG factors and externalities into account. Second, based on ESG factors, they will exclude individual companies and whole industries from their investment universes, regardless of cost. Consequently, from the perspective of the price-determined benchmarks that dominate today, they may appear more speculative and risky than traditional investors. This apparently increased level of risk arises both because the longer out investors look the more speculative they necessarily become, and because ESG factors call for a mixture of art and science in their evaluation. These valuation techniques are a radical departure from today's mainstream. They imply a separation of price from value that can, under certain circumstances, be absolute. That is, for these long-term investors a stock can be seen as worthless at any price.

Augmentation of value

Long-term investors seek to add value to their holdings in ways that are not solely related to price. These value-enhancing tactics include engagement and standard-setting practices such as one-on-one dialogues with management, participation in coalitions of investors addressing social or environmental issues, alliances with stockowners concerned about corporate governance, advocacy for the adoption of standards for social and environmental behavior, exclusion of companies from investment consideration, and participation in public policy discussion. This active approach to adding value is a radical departure from today's mainstream. Most investors in today's stock market believe their role is to reflect value, not to create it. Those that seek to create value do so solely by capitalizing on market or management inefficiencies, seizing mispriced stocks or pressuring management to maximize short-term profits. Both approaches are essentially part of short-term, zero-sum games where no value need be added to society. Long-term investors approach value creation as a more collaborative effort between corporations and society. Whether the issue is apartheid in South Africa, CEO compensation, energy conservation, or equal workplace opportunity, value-creating stockowners look beyond questions of price to questions of just and sustainable societies.

Measurement and management of ESG risks

Finally, long-term investing will depart radically from current investment practice in its measurement of risks and rewards. By seeking to minimize ESG risks and maximize positive externalities, long-term investors inevitably confront issues that markets have difficulty pricing. They cannot remain content to have their performance over the long term measured solely against price-based benchmarks. They must seek to assess value through other measurements.[25] This involves the assessment of how in the long term companies can best add value to society. Such value can be difficult to measure in ways other than price, but that difficulty must be overcome if long-term investing is to become reality. As Keynes wisely observed in *The General Theory of Employment, Interest and Money*, it matters greatly whether the long term or the short term predominates in our financial markets.[26] This observation is no less true today than it was 70 years ago. If short-termers predominate, the social and environmental risks posed by corporations will go unmanaged. Given the size and power of our financial markets, and their increasing influence over the social and environmental quality of our lives, it is crucial that long-term strategies ultimately prevail.

To some, today's laser-like focus on price as a measure of value might make the dominance of the long term seem an unrealistic dream. Given the power and vested self-interests of those currently at the steering wheel, the prospects of turning this ship around seem dim. Yet relatively simple changes in the definitions of what finance should do, and a clear vision of how to implement these changes, can alter the fundamental nature of the system. It starts by recognizing that the decision to equate value with price inevitably leads to short-termism. When we see this, the means to create a more value-based marketplace become more apparent. If we incorporate progress in financial risk management to increase value in the present, and build on growing understanding of the environmental and social factors that enhance our common future, we should be able in relatively short order to change the behavior of investors. Finally, incorporating the long term into equity investing is only the start, not the end, of our journey. Similar approaches to the long term can be developed for other asset classes as well. Real estate, venture capital, private equity, cash, bonds, and commodities – all are subject to similar questions about the short and long term. The long term matters across all aspects of our financial activities. Progress in one asset class will support progress in all. Through this process, long-term investment can move from a goal devoutly wished for by some to a reality incorporated by all.

Notes

1. M. Tonello (2006) *Revisiting Stock-Market Short-Termism*. The Conference Board, New York, p. 42.
2. C. Gollier and A. Leclair (2006) "Avant propos, pourquoi l'ISR a-t-il besoin de recherche universitaire? Regards croisés," *Revue d'Économie Financière*, no. 8, p. 14.
3. J.M. Keynes (1997) *General Theory of Employment, Interest and Money*. Prometheus Books, Amherst, ch. 12.
4. J.R. Graham, C.R. Harvey and S. Rajgopal (2005) "The Economic Implications of Corporate Financial Reporting," *Journal of Accounting and Economics*, 40/1: 3–73.
5. World Economic Forum (2005) "Global Corporate Citizenship Initiative," in cooperation with AccountAbility, *Mainstreaming Responsible Investment*, January, p. 19.
6. A. Rappaport (2005) "The Economics of Short-Term Performance Obsession," *Financial Analysts Journal*, 61/3: 66.
7. World Economic Forum (2005), op. cit.
8. J.J. Siegel (2005) *The Future for Investors: Why the Tried and the True Triumph over the Bold and the New*. Crown Business, New York, p. xi.
9. Keynes (1997), op. cit.
10. J.C. Bogle (2005) *The Battle for the Soul of Capitalism*. Yale University Press, New Haven, Conn., p. 159.
11. As Peter Bernstein has pointed out, index investors do not actually believe that the market is a zero-sum game. They just act as if it is. They believe that the economy, like a rising tide, will benefit all players in the stock market. They believe in betting that the tide will rise, but not on betting that one ship will rise faster than another – see P. Bernstein (2005) *Capital Ideas: the Improbable Origins of Modern Wall Street*. John Wiley & Sons, Hoboken, pp. 120–1.
12. Keynes (1997), op. cit.
13. See the Berkshire Hathaway 2005 Annual Report, p. 19.

14. J. Sabapathy (ed.) (2006) *Accountability Forum: Material Futures,* "Editor's Note," Issue 11, Fall, p. 6.

15. Space considerations preclude a full discussion of issues of materiality here. Many alternative definitions of the concept exist. For example, material information has been defined by the US accounting profession as that which would affect the investment decisions of reasonable investors. In the UK, information is deemed material if it is relevant to considerations of a business's prospects for success. Alan Knight, the head of Standards and Related Services at AccountAbility, has described materiality as, among other things, encompassing "issues likely to be important now and in the future." Jed Emerson and Tim Little have argued that issues of materiality are often *"subjective, based upon the particular goals of a given investor"* (J. Emerson and T. Little (with contributions from Jonas Kron) (2005), "The Prudent Investor: the Evolution of the Long-Term Investor", Generation Foundation, working paper, Washington, p. 4). Whatever the definition, however, a distinction can be made between materiality that relates directly to stock price and materiality that is useful in broader valuations.

16. UNEP Finance Initiative Asset Management Working Group, *The Materiality of Social, Environmental and Corporate Governance Issues to Equity Pricing,* 11 sector studies by brokerage house analysts at the request of the 2004 Report.

17. J. Porier (2007) "Existe-t-il une bulle des valeurs vertes?" *Le Monde Argent,* April 1–2, p. 2.

18. Siegel (2005), op. cit.

19. R.A. Monks and N. Minnow (2000) *Watching the Watchers: Corporate Governance in the 21st Century.* University of Pennsylvania Press, Philadelphia; J.P. Hawley and A.T. Williams (2000) *The Rise of Fiduciary Capitalism: How Institutional Investors Can Make Corporate America More Democratic.* University of Pennsylvania Press, Philadelphia.

20. Hawley and Williams (2000), op. cit.

21. See LENS website at http://www.lens-inc.com

22. B.M. Barber (2006) *Monitoring the Monitor: Evaluating CalPERS Activism,* November. Available at SSRN: http://ssrn.com/abstract=890321

23. F&C Asset Management, *2006 Corporate Responsibility Report,* p. 6.

24. K. Ambachtscheer (2005) *Financial Analysts Journal,* January/February, 61/1.

25. Various alternatives to today's capitalization-weighted benchmark indexes exist. These include those weighted by financial factors other than price. Robert Arnott's fundamental indexes (Arnott) and Jeremy Siegel's indexes keyed to dividend payments (Siegel) are two such examples. Other examples including indexes such as those maintained by KLD Research & Analytics, Dow Jones and SAM Group, and FTSE4Good, use social and environmental criteria to limit the universe of stocks included in price-weighted indexes. These alternatives are steps in the right direction for those interested in long-term investing.

26. Keynes (1997), op. cit.

Part III
Is a Paradigm Shift Underway?
Three Pioneering Reflections

10
Financing Agriculture in Developing Countries: Governance Models Promoting Sustainability

Solène Morvant-Roux

Introduction

Seventy-five percent of the world's poor live in rural areas where their survival depends mainly on agriculture that is exposed to the risks of climate, changes in the market and is characterized by relatively weak profitability (World Bank 2007b). To develop their productive activities, agricultural households face numerous constraints including access to finance. Most of the farmers in developing countries are actually excluded from the banking systems. The number of people in Africa or South Asia working in agriculture and possessing bank accounts does not exceed 5 or 6 percent, whereas in the developed countries, agriculture banks early on played a major role in modernizing agriculture and incorporating farmers into the banking system.

In the countries of the southern hemisphere, the interventionist logic that prevailed during the 1960s and 1970s (the "old rural finance paradigm") has been broadly criticized for its inability to consider the realities of a situation, its costs and finally its ineffectiveness in dealing with real needs. The trend toward market regulation as the best vector for social justice was naturally adopted by public policy. However, the results of years of financial liberalization and the strong growth of microfinance over the past 30 years raise questions regarding what had appeared to be a universal solution: structured financing offered to poor and marginalized populations, particularly those living in rural areas, is still insufficient. Despite the importance of growth in the agriculture sector for reducing poverty,[1] more often than not the sector has only marginally enjoyed access to financial services (credit, savings, insurance, etc.). In this context and to correct the imbalances that have developed, a new grouping of the players in civil society, the private sector and government has emerged.

Given the uniqueness of agricultural finance, the current trend is toward a less dualist approach that does not disavow the basis for the change in the paradigm, and particularly the goal of sustainability of the sector; what needs to be identified are intermediate approaches that allow a number of diverse public and private players to interact. The approach which was developed in the 1990s and is based principally on contractual innovations, has given way to innovations in terms of methods of governance. The dynamics of restructuring public financing institutions in various regions, particularly in Latin America, have shown promise. Accordingly, the effectiveness of public policy can be improved through the establishment of innovative partnerships linking the public and private sectors, as numerous encouraging examples in the agricultural system have shown.

10.1   From the old to the new paradigm in rural finance

10.1.1   From the failure of the interventionist approach of the 1960s and 1970s to the promises of the new paradigm in rural finance of the 1980s

The old rural finance paradigm of the 1960s and 1970s was based on public authorities' desire to facilitate access to rural finance. The objective was to promote agricultural development by modernizing agriculture. The most common approach involved direct government intervention via state-owned development banks and direct donor intervention in credit markets with favorable terms and conditions like soft interest rates or lenient guarantees. However, this system was costly and unsustainable, due to poor repayment, and ultimately did not have the desired effect on the development of agriculture production (Meyer 2007). Beginning in the 1980s, the failure of a credit system which until then had been based exclusively on public intervention gave way to a new plan leading to a renewed approach to rural and agricultural finance in the developing countries. Depending on the countries, the context was characterized by the closing or privatization of state-owned development banks, the liberalization of the sector and the development of microfinance.

The new paradigm for rural finance developed mainly around contractual innovations that favored new forms of collateral, various schemes to encourage repayment, the social and geographic proximity of the financial intermediary, etc., all aimed at ensuring the continuity of the financial intermediaries with a view to developing financial intermediation.

In addition, the roles of the players have been redefined, particularly that of public intervention. Above and beyond the support provided in the form of public subsidies when rural credit institutions are being created (in particular for microfinance), public institutions have been structured with an emphasis on sector regulation, with legal frameworks specific to microfinance gradually being developed; along these lines, specific legislation called the "Parmec Law" was adopted in West Africa in 1993 related to the regulation of mutual or cooperative savings and loan institutions. The law gradually took effect in all the countries of the West African Economic and Monetary Union (WAEMU).[2]

10.1.2 Supply continues to be insufficient or not adapted to specific needs

Despite the hopes raised by this new approach to rural finance in developing countries, and in particular the emergence and strong growth of the microfinance sector,[3] we must admit that the supply of financial services to the agriculture sector has remained inadequate and most often only imperfectly meets the needs of farmers. If we look at microfinance, it is characterized by large disparities among countries and even within the territory of certain nations. Some countries attain very high degrees of penetration (the case of Bangladesh), while other regions (in particular sub-Saharan Africa) show much lower rates. Moreover, major disparities exist within countries, between urban zones and outlying suburbs and the rural areas which more often than not remain marginalized. Microfinance is mainly concentrated in urban areas and outlying suburbs which are easier to serve, and among the rural institutions the part of the loan portfolio intended for financing agricultural activities varies greatly. In India, in 2006–7, 8 percent of the loans granted by the microfinance sector directly financed agriculture and 14 percent went to animal husbandry. The remaining 78 percent was distributed among household consumption, funding microenterprises and commerce. Moreover, microfinance provided practically no credits for agriculture, mechanization, irrigation and land development (Pillarisetti 2007).[4]

The revolution in microfinance that emerged during the 1980s and 1990s was thus generally limited to urban areas in most of Africa and South America. Even when it did reach rural areas, as in certain regions of Asia, it was generally reserved for rural microenterprises. The institutions that work with microenterprises and in urban areas clearly proved to be less effective in developing a package to cover the financial needs of agriculture. The rural and urban clients of microfinance are generally located in densely populated, low-income areas, and where the economic activity is not agriculture. At the same time, with the liberalization of the banking sector, the removal of government has not been compensated by growth of the commercial banking sector in rural areas and even less toward increased financing of agriculture. On the contrary, many banks have even closed their rural branches (Zeller 2003). Thus, despite the available data, which is relatively general and mixed and only concerns certain geographic areas, we have to admit that agriculture remains inadequately funded or that supply most often meets the needs of agricultural producers[5] only imperfectly. This situation is essentially due to the fact that the financing of these activities is on the whole more costly, riskier, and less profitable. Above and beyond the difficulties that are usually pointed out when financial services are to be established in rural areas, agriculture presents a certain number of specificities that financing schemes must understand and take into consideration.

Agriculture is distinct from other sectors of economic activity in several respects. The factors that hinder the development of financial services made accessible to family agriculture are numerous and have been well identified: the location of these activities in isolated areas characterized by low population density and lack of infrastructure,[6] a dependence on climate conditions and the temporality of production cycles, the seasonality of income, and in a more general manner, the limited proportion of monetary revenue, the volatility of prices for agricultural products, less reliable guarantees from both the legal and economic perspectives, etc. Efforts needed to better understand the financial needs of farmers combined with the risks associated with these activities thus constitute additional obstacles to establishing a financing package for agriculture. In addition, the interest rates applied by financial intermediaries to cover the costs engendered by the services they offer and to protect themselves against risks have often been incompatible with the low profitability level associated with financing agriculture.

It is not an accident that faced with these constraints, institutions established in rural areas experience greater difficulty in being financially profitable and must often resort to public subsidies. Pressure on profitability imposes strategic choices on these institutions which generally lead them to neglect rural areas and agriculture, preferring to establish themselves in urban areas and the outlying suburbs where they are exposed to strong competition from for-profit organizations (Servet 2008). The logic of the market, combined with the many contractual innovations that have been promoted by the new paradigm, have not fulfilled all the promises to the rural world and more particularly to agriculture that finance would be forthcoming. Therefore, institutions that work with microenterprises and in urban areas have definitely proved to be less effective for developing a package that could cover the financial needs of agriculture. Entrusting the financing of development to private resources and players should not totally supplant public action which alone is capable of promoting a certain level of collective consistency indispensable for these operations and for the development goals they claim to serve (Servet 2008). Between the "all powerful state" and the "all powerful market," the challenge is to see that the allocation of resources is directed toward those sectors of activity considered conducive to improving the productivity of farmers and the living conditions of local populations.

In this context and faced with the specific characteristics of financing agriculture, the current trend is beginning to take a less dualist approach. Without abandoning the fundamental reasons for changing the paradigm, and in particular the sustainability of the sector, what is needed is to identify the intermediate approaches that will allow a large number of diverse public and private players to interact. The current trend actually stresses the limits of a monolithic theory of division between public and private, and encourages a redefinition of the scope of action and the respective roles of government, the private sector and civil society (Bouquet 2007). The approach which is based mainly on contractual innovations (required collateral, ways to encourage repayment and financial products) and upon which the new paradigm for rural finance has been developed, has left room for innovation in terms of governance. Above and beyond the institutional model which is not by itself the sole determining factor, a certain equilibrium among the various players is sought, and this is desirable. This balance should help to avoid the errors of the past.

10.2   Creating original methods for interaction among the players

Faced with this new paradigm for rural finance, public financial institutions initially lost all legitimacy in terms of participating in the structuring of a financial package in developing countries (Gonzáles-Vega 2003). The limited interest of the private sector for rural areas and low-income borrowers is once again stimulating thought as to how the different players complement one another. Original and varied methods of governance for rural financial institutions have thus been developed in different regions.

10.2.1 Development banks converted to engines of agricultural development

In contrast with the dominant ideology, the debate in Latin America and in certain Asian countries no longer simply consists of questioning the relevance of creating or maintaining public financial institutions, but trying to make them work more effectively and ensuring that they best serve the development goals entrusted to them. In Latin America, there are 108 development financing institutions (DFIs), 32 of which offer loans for agriculture, either because they were established with this objective or because they usually finance various sectors of economic activity. Recent changes in some of these institutions have taught us some interesting lessons. The issue of the effectiveness of these organizations has actually led to the promotion of private sector participation through governance that aims at limiting political interference, a factor that renders these institutions fragile. The experience of Banrural SA in Guatemala is interesting from two perspectives: the innovative character of its governance structure matched with financial performance goals. Banrural SA resulted from the restructuring of Bandesa, the Guatemala public bank for agricultural development. The most credible alternative at the time (first half of the 1990s) and the one supported by several multilateral agencies was the outright privatization of Bandesa. However, the restructuring of Bandesa by local players caused other options to emerge aimed at creating a new model, while at the same time preserving certain characteristics inherited from Bandesa which were conducive to its mission of promoting development; this mission would have been compromised if the privatization option had been chosen.

The model of governance at Banrural SA is original in several respects. In the first place, Banrural SA is a mixed-capital bank in which the public sector holds 30 percent of the shares, with the remaining 70 percent held by private shareholders: the cooperative movement (20 percent), farmer organizations (20 percent), and various private shareholders (NGOs, microentrepreneurs, etc.) hold the last 30 percent. This model allows each of the shareholder categories to elect their leaders during general meetings. The composition of the management committee thus remains representative of the different categories of shareholders. The result is a system that requires permanent negotiation and a search for consensus among the shareholders. At an operational level, the bank works via two channels: either directly through its branches located in almost all the major cites of the country (its primary business); or indi-rectly through a refinancing line of credit which targets those entities involved in microfinance (NGOs or cooperatives) operating in isolated areas (its secondary business). Since it began to offer this line of credit, Banrural SA has managed to serve more than 75,000 rural clients through over 150 local financial organizations.

Of all the original characteristics of this model, we draw attention to two: firstly, the possibility given to civil society organizations to invest in the new bank, thereby offering these entities greater opportunities to be considered and recognized in the public sphere; and secondly, the pos-sibility for the state through the executive branch – as a shareholder – to exchange its ideas for rural development strategy with the management committee, and to promote the work of the bank as a way to support and enhance government program initiatives. Overall, Banrural SA appears to be an exemplary institution from a profitability and coverage perspec-tive, and it provides for balance between the various shareholders: the state, cooperatives, indigenous or farmer organizations, and nonprofit organizations.

The profile of the development bank in Latin America in which the public sector still plays a significant role has thus changed a great deal during recent years. There are now various formulas for development banks in the agricultural sector, ranging from exclusively public entities specializing in agriculture, to refinancing, mixed-capital or multisector institutions. This multiplicity of potential responses to the obstacles lim-iting finance in the agricultural sector reveals a number of attractive alternatives. Between institutions controlled by the public sector which are generally dependent on the current administration in power, and pri-vatization, there are various alternatives for reform that can bring about change within the governing structures of those entities dedicated to financing development. These alternatives allow the best advantages of private initiative to be enhanced while preserving the positive aspects of those entities involved in development that are supported by the power of the state (which we differentiate from the government in place at any particular time).

It should be pointed out, however, that in terms of the participation of clients/members of these financing institutions, where they are involved in governance (which is not the case in Chile, Argentina, Peru or Colom-bia), their role in determining the kind of financial services offered is more often than not marginal. In Mexico, agricultural representatives play a political role but are not involved in determining what financial services are offered. Once again, the experience of Banrural SA Guatemala is an exception with its real convergence of, on the one hand, the participation of customers of the institution in its governing body, and on the other, managers who are convinced of the importance of responding in the best possible way to the needs of customers in order to ensure the viability of its services.

Other experiences of restructuring financial institutions which have aimed at creating a financial product adapted to the constraints of the agricultural sector have occurred in a number of Asian countries. The example of the BAAC in Thailand (Bank for Agriculture and Agricultural Cooperatives) deserves to be mentioned. Governance of the BAAC with majority ownership controlled by members of the government (99 percent of the shares are in the hands of the Ministry of Finance, and the remaining 1 percent is held by agricultural cooperatives) does not shield it from emphasizing those short-term strategies that may characterize governmental institutions and which may go against a medium-to-long-term stability essential for constructing a sustainable product. On the other hand, the restructuring has concentrated more on business profitability, and the emphasis placed on attracting savings has considerably reduced the dependence of the institution vis-à-vis external sources of finance. In 2003, the BAAC reached 5.3 million households or close to 92 percent of all agricultural households in Thailand.

In India, the NABARD (National Bank for Agriculture and Rural Development) initiated its institutional development from below, through a DAP (development action plan) prepared for each category of rural financial institution (RFI) – cooperative banks, regional rural banks, etc. These reforms of the financial sector through the DAPs also led a large number of institutions to change their systems and procedures, their credit and deposit programs as well as their methods for managing human resources, all in the interest of improving their profitability while ensuring that their credit programs were broadly distributed. Even if the initial results were not particularly successful, a large number of these institutions (district central cooperative banks as well as regional rural banks) managed to be profitable while maintaining loans for agriculture (Pillarisetti 2007).

The linkage between national banks dedicated to agriculture and microfinance institutions also proved to be productive in Mali where support of the National Bank for Agricultural Development (Banque Nationale de Développement Agricole – BNDA) in the form of a refinance facility, allowed these institutions to reduce their liquidity risks. A study carried out by D. Seibel showed that Kafo Jiginew, the network of savings and loan cooperatives, used lines of credit and savings accounts from the BNDA or from other commercial banks to reduce annual cash flow fluctuations due to the seasonality of agricultural activity (Seibel 2008). As a general rule, we should underline the preponderant place of producers' organizations as the favored interlocutors in the process of establishing financial schemes for funding agriculture in the countries of the southern hemisphere. Their participation in the governance of financial institutions could be fostered.

The Federation of NGOs in Senegal (FONGS) has encouraged participation in the governance of the National Bank for Agricultural Credit of Senegal (Caisse Nationale de Crédit Agricole du Sénégal – CNCAS) due to an acquisition of 4 percent of the bank's capital which allowed it to have a seat on the bank's board of directors in order to secure the only instrument of agricultural finance. An additional goal was to influence the rural finance policy of CNCAS and in particular to ensure the development and sustainability of finance in rural areas. This strategy has led to notable advances in the area of rural and agricultural finance:

- expansion of CNCAS's network and increased proximity to rural producers;
- reduction of interest rates from 18 to 7.5 percent;
- the beginning of a dialogue regarding linkages between CNCAS's network and decentralized endogenous savings and credit cooperatives.

The examples presented above, however, illustrate that the idea of a unique organizational model adapted to the specific characteristics of financing agriculture does not correspond to reality as we know it. Selecting the institutional model in strategies for accessing financial services is not the sole determinant. In fact, above and beyond development financial institutions, there are many models which contribute to financing agriculture: self-help groups, savings and loan cooperatives or even private capital companies. What emerges is that the forms of governance of development financial institutions, as seen particularly in Latin America, bring the private sector together with civil society in the governing structures; they combine to provide support (principally in the form of refinance facilities) and to structure the financial sector; this interesting compromise strengthens and stabilizes the sources of finance for agriculture. These experiences have led to a better coverage of the needs of this economic sector by emphasizing the demands of short-term profitability that are compatible with the agriculture sector. The role of the state in financing agriculture is therefore bound to change. Beyond the functions related to sovereignty, which confine its action to developing a legal and regulatory framework,[7] its intervention is always justifiable, especially when there is concern for equity among the different categories of the population. Without being too intrusive, the goal of public intervention should thus be to stimulate and support the private sector.

In fact, research has identified the advantages associated with public banks in emerging economies. What we see is a greater involvement in those sectors which traditionally have not benefited from the services offered by commercial banks (such as small farms, women and small businesses) as well as a greater stability and permanence of their commitment to these sectors of economic activity or segments of the population compared to private banks (see, *inter alia*, Vogel 2005; Micco and Panizza 2005). Public subsidies also allow the most disadvantaged groups to be reached (Balkenhol 2007). More generally, to the extent that the problem of agricultural finance consists of uniting proximity, innovation and diversification, and risk reduction, other methods of interaction have been experimented with in the agricultural sector.

10.2.2   New methods of interaction in the agricultural sector

From this viewpoint, the fact that not only financial institutions, but also all the players in the industry (producers, suppliers, buyers, processors) face numerous risks justifies coordination efforts in order to reduce these risks. Consequently, through strategic alliances we are now witnessing more reflective thinking by all parties aimed at bringing together the comparative advantage of each category, stimulating mutual dynamics and reducing risks for all players. Several initiatives aiming to strengthen interaction between these two sectors are underway. The objective is to build long-term relationships and reduce risk for the different actors: producers, borrowers, buyers and processors. These partnerships come in different forms:

- some focus on one link in the value chain (for instance, partnerships between MFIs[8] and storage facilities, or between MFIs and exporters);
- others address the chain as a whole (Danone's business model in Bangladesh);
- partnerships may be direct or indirect, i.e. incited by a third party such as an NGO, which plays the role of a catalyst, facilitator and sometimes service provider.

There are recent examples of value chain actors playing the limited role of "virtual guarantor," in which case a producer's mere association with a large buyer or processor, for instance, serves as a sign of creditworthiness in the eyes of financial institutions. The value chain actor may also be directly involved in financial transactions, providing producers credit services, a more traditional approach (Gonzales-Vega et al. 2006). There have been experiments in different types of interaction and they can be grouped under the three following headings.

(a) MFI multiparty contract – producers/input suppliers/buyers

This type of interaction was developed by the Caisse d'Épargne et de Crédit (CECO) in Ivory Coast; this bank was established in 1991 and today has over 5000 shareholders/members. In order to limit the risks to the MFI, as it guarantees producers of irrigated rice and cashew nuts access to inputs and a stable market, CECO adopted the following strategy. On the basis of identified profitable agricultural sectors, CECO selects partners who will contribute to the system and bring it credibility (suppliers of inputs, service providers, processors, etc.). The line of credit is not deposited directly with the borrower, but the services rendered and access to inputs is directly billed to CECO which will be repaid once the harvest has been sold (Touré 2007).

(b) Integrated production and commercialization model

The Grameen Danone Foods Ltd. Project in Bangladesh is a partnership between Grameen Bank and Danone (Ardoin 2007) designed to produce and distribute yogurt locally, and incite local consumption of the product. Danone is responsible for building the factory and producing the yogurt. The MFI, Grameen Bank, facilitates financial access at two levels:

- upstream, with milk producers who supply the factory, thus guaranteeing a stable supply for Danone;
- downstream, with the women in charge of distributing (retail sales) the product and creating a new commercial niche.

(c) Fair trade

The fair trade model offers producers not only viable and predictable commercial channels for selling produce at prices that cover production costs (investment and labor), but also financial support. However, this prefinancing does not fully meet the financial needs of the industry: insufficient volume, risks and inadequate forms of collateral, administrative problems in the organizations of agricultural producers (Lapenu 2007). Most of the initiatives taken to establish alliances between the financial sector and players in the food processing industry are relatively recent, in particular the alliances with the agroindustrial sector. More time is needed to evaluate their effectiveness. Do they really lead to a reduction in risks? Does the alliance allow for a more balanced sharing of risks between the MFI, the agroindustrial sector and producers? It is important to emphasize that these partnerships do not provide solutions to the issue of the profitability of certain kinds of agriculture, in particular food production for home consumption by farm households or sold locally, neglected for more profitable agricultural products (coffee, cocoa, cotton, rubber, tobacco, etc.). Consequently, less profitable activities are excluded from the numerous alliances that are emerging in the safe sectors. Some experiences have shown that segmentation occurs among those types of agricultural activity that are economically profitable (the case of CECO in Ivory Coast). The question of financing activities that have low profitability, particularly food production, is still open and requires more thought along with public policies that are favorable, consistent and developed in concert with all players involved.

Conclusion

Given the limits of the two models – state and market – alternative approaches have emerged and should be looked at more closely. Parallel to this, the international economic situation is bringing agriculture, particularly in developing countries, back to the center of the world's concerns: agricultural prices are rising and satisfying the food needs of a planet experiencing strong demographic pressure can no longer be guaranteed. In this context, the major problem of meeting the food needs of the Southern countries must be ensured by regional producers. But under what conditions could rural areas meet this growing demand? For the farmers in the southern hemisphere, this context offers opportunities but in order to seize this historic good fortune, they need to invest in and increase their production. That implies having access to the appropriate credit and insurance systems. Faced with these challenges, the state has a strong role to play in supporting schemes for financing agriculture.

Among the current initiatives, some are promising but we still need time to evaluate the effectiveness of the new forms of partnerships as well as the public policy tools to meet the diverse financial needs of agricultural producers. Research and analyses carried out to date have been specific and do not lend themselves to generalities. The studies devoted to the role of the state rarely take into account the specificities of agriculture, so their scope is therefore limited. Cross-analyses at a regional level are of great value because, without being prescriptive, they lead to the identification of experiences that offer solutions and can thus guide the decisions of the different players.

Notes

1. "[...] GDP growth due to agriculture contributes at least twice as much to the reduction of poverty as does GDP growth from the non-agricultural sector" (summarized from World Bank 2007b).
2. In Bolivia, those involved in rural finance have mobilized to adapt regulations in the financial sector so that they take into account the specific characteristics of the sector. Indeed, adapting the regulations constitutes a crucial issue for improving access of farmers and the effectiveness of the financing mechanisms for several reasons: qualification and evaluation standards adapted to an agricultural portfolio; specialized projection standards for the agricultural portfolio; finally, standards acknowledging the sector as strategic and specialized to ensure that producers participate and have access to the assets of the microfinance institutions (Marconi 2007).
3. Annual growth of the sector between 1997 and 2005 was over 30 percent (Daley-Harris 2006). However, this figure hides large disparities between countries and within the territory of individual nations.
4. However, it should be emphasized that certain networks adopt can-do approaches to cover the financial needs of farmers. Such is the case of the Confederation of Financial Institutions (CFI) in West Africa. An analysis of loan terms granted by the network over three sample years (1998, 2001 and 2004) shows a considerable change in medium-term loans (those maturing between 12 and 36 months) from 5 percent in 1998 to 36 percent in 2004. Even if the issue of covering needs is still current and significant regional disparities persist, these results are encouraging.
5. Data provided by the CFI network once again goes against the trend observed in numerous contexts, since 40 percent of the loans granted by institutions in the network in 2006 were for financing agricultural and fishing activities. The rest of the portfolio was divided between crafts (8 percent) and trade and services (52 percent). These results are encouraging despite the significant regional disparities. Indeed, within the WAEMU the figures are 19, 21 and 60 percent for trade (Ouedraogo and Gentil 2008).
6. Current experiments using new information and communication technologies can provide a certain number of solutions to the problem of geographic isolation and low population density (Ivatury 2006).
7. There is much reticence about direct public intervention in the financial market; some fear market distortion and its negative repercussions on the sector of associations and cooperatives, which voluntarily try to cover the demand for financial services in rural disadvantaged areas.
8. MFIs: microfinance institutions.

References

Ardoin, J.L. (2007) "Analyse du Business model Grameen Danone Food Ltd au Bangladesh," paper presented at the international conference "What Can

Microfinance Contribute to Agriculture in Developing Countries?", Paris, December 4–6.

Balkenhol, B. (ed.) (2007) *Microfinance and Public Policy: Outreach, Performance and Efficiency.* Palgrave Macmillan, London, 196 pp.

Bouquet, E. (2007) "Construir un sistema financiero para el desarrollo rural en México. Nuevos papeles para el Estado y la sociedad civil," *Revue Trace*, no. 52, June.

Daley-Harris, S. (2006) *State of the Microcredit Summit Campaign*, Report 2006, Microcredit Summit Campaign, Washington.

González Vega, C. (2003) "Deepening Rural Financial Markets: Macroeconomic Policy and Political Dimensions," paper presented at the conference "Paving the Way Forward: an International Conference on Best Practices in Rural Finance", Washington, DC, June 2–4.

Gonzalez-Vega, C., Chalmers, G., Quiros, R. and Rodriguez-Mega, J. (2006) *Hortifruti in Central America: a Case Study about the Influence of Supermarkets on the Development and Evolution of Creditworthiness among Small and Medium Agricultural Producers.* AMAP Micro Report, no. 57, Development Alternatives Inc. and the Ohio State University.

Ivatury, G. (2006) "La technologie au service de systèmes financiers inclusifs," CGAP, Focus note, no. 32, January.

Lapenu, C. (2007) *Evolutions récentes dans l'offre et les stratégies de financement de l'agriculture. Echanges d'expériences et synthèse bibliographique.* RFM/FARM, Paris, 25 pp.

Marconi, R. (2007) "Adaptation de la réglementation aux conditions du financement agricole et rural," paper presented at the international conference "What Can Microfinance Contribute to Agriculture in Developing Countries?" Paris, December 4–6.

Meyer, R. (2007) "Microfinance Services for Agriculture: Opportunities and Challenges," paper presented at the international conference "What Can Microfinance Contribute to Agriculture in Developing Countries?" Paris, December 4–6.

Micco, A. and Panizza, U. (2005) "Public Banks in Latin America," background paper prepared for the conference "Public Banks in Latin America: Myth and Reality," IDB, Washington, February.

Ouedraogo, A. and Gentil, D. (eds) (2008) *La microfinance en Afrique de l'Ouest: Histoires et innovations.* CIF-KARTHALA, Paris, 308 pp.

Pillarisetti, S. (2007) "Microfinance for Agriculture: Perspectives from India", paper presented at the international conference "What Can Microfinance Contribute to Agriculture in Developing Countries?" Paris, December 4–6.

Seibel, D. (2008) "Self-Reliance vs. Donor Dependence: Linkages between Banks and Microfinance Institutions in Mali," in Pagura, M. (ed.) *Expanding the Frontier in Rural Finance: Financial Linkage and Strategic Alliances,* Practical Action Publishing, Rugby, pp. 147–68.

Servet, J.-M. (2008) "Inclusion financière et responsabilité sociale: production de plus values financières et de valeurs sociales en microfinance," *Revue Tiers-Monde*, forthcoming.

Touré, G. (2007) "Impact de la microfinance en milieu rural: expérience de la caisse d'épargne et de crédit d'Odienné," paper presented at the international conference "What Can Microfinance Contribute to Agriculture in Developing Countries?" Paris, December 4–6.

Vogel, R. (2005) "Costs and Benefits of Liquidating Peru's Agricultural Bank," USAID–EGAT–AMAP.

World Bank (2007a) "India: Taking Agriculture to the Market." Internal Report 35953-IN, World Bank, South Asia Sustainable Development Department, Washington, DC.

World Bank (2007b) *World Development Report 2008: Agriculture for Development.* Washington, DC.

Zeller, M. (2003) "Models of Rural Financial Institutions," paper presented at the conference "Paving the Way Forward: an International Conference on Best Practices in Rural Finance," Washington, DC, June 2–4.

11
Innovative Investments for Sustainability: Solutions for the Twenty-First Century

Andy White

11.1 Global mega-trends

Why are some of the world's most forward-thinking, aggressive and successful financial institutions moving to differentiate themselves through their environmental, social, and governance (ESG) capabilities? Global hypercompetition, accelerated by a "perfect storm" convergence of powerful global mega-trends, has created both challenges and opportunities for investors which are quite literally unprecedented. In order to confront those challenges and seize the opportunities, investors will need both a radically different mindset and an entirely new arsenal of analytical tools. Traditional, accounting-driven investment analysis appears to have reached the limits of its usefulness. As recently as the mid-1980s, financial statements were arguably capable of capturing 75–80 percent of the true risk profile and value potential of major corporations.

According to New York University accounting guru and business professor Baruch Lev, however, by the early twenty-first century that figure had dropped to less than 20 percent on average. This tectonic shift reflects the inexorable transformation of developed economies to the point where wealth is now created primarily by knowledge and other intangible assets, rather than by land, factories, physical labor, or even finance capital. Intellectual capital has become the most important factor in creating wealth; ergo, identifying and managing it has become the single most important driver of competitive advantage and sustainable value creation. Yet accounting statements have almost no light to shed on these "nontraditional" value – and investment risk – drivers. As we move deeper and deeper into the era of knowledge value and intangibles, conventional balance sheets and profit and loss statements are capturing less and less of a company's true value, investment risk, and competitive potential.

What is needed instead is a new, more dynamic "iceberg balance sheet" approach, one which focuses investor and senior management attention where it properly belongs: on the roughly 80 percent of companies' true value which cannot be explained by traditional, accounting-driven securities analysis. In short, one which provides a focus on leading indicators of company performance, not trailing ones.

Indeed, my own research firm, Innovest Strategic Value Advisors, forewarned of the current subprime crisis by analysing bank lending through an ESG prism. When Innovest first uncovered that the US subprime sector was on the brink of a trillion dollar collapse it was somewhat by accident. Our finance sector expert, Greg Larkin, was initially researching data about microfinance funds, and was surprised to find that even though microfinance funds consist entirely of financially at risk poor people, default rates were generally under 2 percent; in the subprime sector defaults were usually closer to 5 percent. Greg was trying to find if there was a subprime originator which used a microfinance business model to manage credit risk, when he uncovered some extremely alarming trends about the residential mortgage market in the US.

The first trend is that loan originations for people with impaired credit, no credit history or unlawful immigration status grew fivefold between 2001 and 2005 to reach $625bn. This surge was fueled by a booming residential real-estate market, unprecedented liquidity, and the proliferation of new risk management instruments like credit default swaps. Forty percent of mortgage-backed securities (MBSs) issued in the first half of 2005 were linked to subprime originations, up from 6 percent in 2003. We suspected that such rapid growth probably meant that underwriting standards were being compromised.

The second trend was that there was no data which indicated that poor people could afford these loans. That is, this surge would make sense if it corresponded with a surge of poor people becoming prosperous. But the opposite was true. Payrolls were stagnant, and data indicated that consumers were increasingly overstretched. Household savings rates (savings as a percentage of disposable income) were negative for the first time since the Great Depression. (This meant that consumer expenditure was booming because of an overextension of credit as opposed to an increase in real wages.) We then found an economic relationship that was a harbinger of the doom to come. For about ten years every time there was a downturn in the household net savings rate, net charge-off rates on retail loans would shoot up by an almost equal and opposite

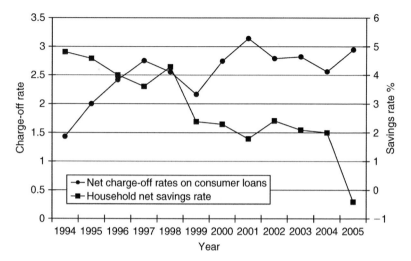

Figure 11.1 US net charge-off rates on consumer loans vs household net savings rate
Source: Innovest

amount. In other words, as people's savings were depleted they were increasingly unable to repay their loans to banks. Being that household savings were now negative, we thought we might be at the tipping point (see Figure 11.1).

The question that we kept coming back to was how were all of these poor people suddenly able to afford homes while their wages and personal finances were rapidly deteriorating? The answer we came up with to that question was that they could not. In the subprime sector there is (or at least, should be) a pretty simple rule of thumb for investors: if a borrower cannot afford the home that they covet with a fully amortized, fixed rate mortgage then they probably cannot afford that home – period. What we discovered was that over the past six years banks found a way to bypass this constraint and still hit their quarterly targets by offering loans which had a low fixed rate for a few years which then reset to recoup the capital that the borrower would have spent if the loan were fixed rate and fully amortized. A recent chart released by Crédit Suisse calculates that subprime adjustable rate mortgage originations reached $1.5 trillion, and only 39 percent of those mortgages have so far reset. By taking this loan the borrower essentially gambles that his income will increase by between 20 and 30 percent in three years in order to be able to cover the mortgage reset. (Or, more likely, the terms of the loan are not completely clear and the reset is a big surprise.) The quality of the mortgage-backed

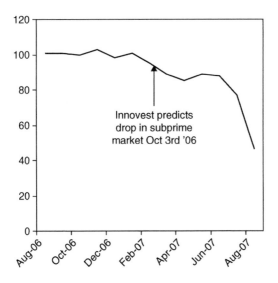

Innovest predicts drop in subprime market Oct 3rd '06

Figure 11.2 Subprime mortgage-backed securities' performance
Source: Markit, Nomura.

security linked to this borrower was and still is an equivalently risky bet. However, these assets were packaged into mortgage-backed securities and sold off to the capital markets for a fee, so it was off the bank's balance sheets and in some unsuspecting pension fund or structured investment vehicles (SIVs). The likelihood of these assets surviving are equivalent to the odds of the borrower's income increasing enough to cover the cost of his reset mortgage (i.e. not good).

What does this say about Innovest's analysis? We analyzed the subprime sector from a different angle than Wall Street and the City and because of that actually had a better sense of that market's intrinsic value than the "experts" did (see Figure 11.2). We looked at subprime in order to assess its impact on poverty in low-income consumer demographics. The only question we asked was, will poor people be better or worse off because of these loans? Can they afford this debt? And the answer was a resounding "no." Wall Street's primary question was how can we make as much money as possible in the residential real estate market and the answer they came up with was subprime. Ironically there was more money to be made through our analysis.

Increasingly, then, it is this unseen part of the "value iceberg," that much larger portion below the surface, which contains the primary drivers of the company's future value-creation capabilities, risks, and unique comparative advantages.

There follows a selection of the key global mega-trends which are making the case for the iceberg balance sheet analysis even more compelling:

1. *Depletion of natural resources.* Today humankind is using resources in a way that is not sustainable. Our outtake or depletion of forests, clean water, topsoil, fish stocks, etc. is larger than the regenerational capacity of the planet.[1] This threatens long-term prosperity and security in a world where the population is estimated to reach 9 billion during the twenty-first century. In just a few decades, wars may be fought over access to clean water.

2. *Growing urbanization.* Midway through the first decade of the twenty-first century, the world is rapidly approaching a situation where, for the first time in human history, more people will live in cities than rural areas. The year 2008 will mark this historic moment and the future of this urban millennium very much depends on the decisions made today in preparation for such continued growth.[2] Over the coming decades, virtually all of the population growth in the world will take place in urban environments, resulting in a situation where approximately 2 billion additional people will live in cities by 2030.[3] As a result, the demand for investment in urban solutions that can improve quality of life without consuming excessive natural resources will increase over time.

3. *Rising energy needs.* Parallel to this trend, global energy and natural resource use is increasing rapidly, with energy demand expected to increase by more than 50 percent by 2030 if current trends continue.[4] By 2020 China is estimated to be the world's second largest consumer of energy, India the sixth and the Asia-Pacific region is predicted to consume more than one-third of the world's energy.[5]

4. *Global warming.* According to scientists we must reverse a more than 150-year-old trend of almost exponential growth of CO_2 emissions globally within less than a decade in order to avoid a climate catastrophe. The window of opportunity is approximately eight years.[6] This view is shared by almost all significant world leaders and businesses. Translated into concrete action this would require Western countries who are the biggest emitters to set an example and reduce their CO_2 emissions by 80–90 percent before 2050.

5. *Tightening of regulation.* Increasingly, policy-makers at the national and state level are recognizing that clean technologies can be a valuable asset in creating jobs, improving environmental performance, and promoting national security and resource independence.

6. *Global policy action.* With the entry into force of the Kyoto Protocol and European Trading Scheme (ETS) in February 2005, the global cleantech industry received a powerful shot in the arm. Mandatory caps on European greenhouse gas (GHG) emissions, coupled with voluntary programs the world over, have spurred significant R&D and project finance investments in low-carbon technologies and related products, services, and markets.
7. *Capital markets acceptance.* In the past two years, some of the biggest and most respected names in the banking, private equity, institutional, and corporate arenas have made significant investments or commitments to cleantech businesses or markets. All of these players forecast cleantech in some shape or form to be one of the most important industries of the twenty-first century. Recently, many large corporations have been taking a public stance of supporting the cleantech agenda, like General Electric's watershed Ecomagination™ initiative plans to generate $20 billion in annual sales by 2010 from ecoefficient products and services such as wind turbines, fuel-efficient engines, energy-efficient appliances, solar energy panels and water treatment systems.

11.2   New investment ideas for the twenty-first century

11.2.1   Innovation is a key value driver

One of the best ways to tackle the challenges created through the global mega-trends outlined above is through innovation.

Innovation is a vitally important theme for companies and investors but is an area that historically has been low on the corporate governance agenda. Larger corporations have often been reluctant to launch new, niche market solutions, for fear of undermining their core revenue streams from traditional products and services. But in a global economy, with tightening environmental regulations, where consumer values are changing – leading to new demands for environmentally friendly products – and with competition increasing from emerging market countries such as China and India, large multinational companies are having to reconsider the business-as-usual scenario. The management editor of UK newspaper *The Independent* wrote recently that "innovation is the most important thing companies do." And the highly respected London Business School, recognizing that conventional management is "squelching on its foundations," established MLab in 2006, a management innovation laboratory. According to MLab, management is "stuck," and "is still firmly anchored in version 1.0." MLab has been set up to create a new management model that rethinks organizations from top to bottom, in light of today's knowledge and conditions, Management 2.0 in fact. So there is a strong argument for developing a toolkit to properly analyze innovation potential.

11.2.2   Failure to innovate represents a business risk

While innovation adds value, innovation may also have a negative or destructive effect. Organizations that do not innovate effectively may be at a disadvantage to those that do and so innovation typically involves a degree of risk. Companies look to innovation to open new streams of revenue, stay ahead of competitors and justify price increases. But nine out of ten innovations die in the pipeline, and about three-quarters fail after launch. Searching for growth, the temptation is to pump out more and more innovative ideas in hope of finding a few big winners – often an expensive and ineffective approach. As such, innovation should be of interest to investors: a risk that should be correctly analyzed and priced into any stock.

A key challenge in innovation is maintaining a balance between process and product innovations, where process innovations tend to involve a business model which may develop shareholder benefits through improved efficiencies, while product innovations develop customer support, albeit at the risk of costly R&D that can erode shareholder returns. R&D alone may be a poor indicator of the degree to which companies successfully innovate. An innovation rating, by contrast, signals the extent to which management is able to develop and implement successful innovation strategies.

11.2.3   Environmental technology at the heart of innovation

Innovation in environmental technologies is of the highest importance because of rising regulations and market constraints and increasing awareness of the environmental impacts of businesses. As a key success factor in obtaining or maintaining a license to operate, in gaining a competitive advantage or preserving a reputation, the environment is definitely at the forefront. In addition, taking a resource-based view, a proactive environmental policy within companies ultimately requires a structural change in production and delivery processes. This redesign involves the development, acquisition and implementation of new technologies and may lead to economic advantages vis-à-vis competitors. Environmental technologies to improve processes and products are all around us: wind turbines and solar panels, cleaner cars, biofuels and certain washing powders, recycling systems for waste or water, etc. These are technologies designed to prevent or reduce environmental impacts, at any stage of the life cycle of the product or activity.

The specific applications we now find in environmental technologies stem from older ideas about cleaning up dirty industries to more recent ideas of pollution prevention. The shift has parallels to that of alternative medicines where the adage that prevention is better than cure reigns. Environmental technologies currently include technologies that address the following broad themes:

1. *Dirty industry modifications.* Technologies that clean up previously dirty industries where pollution is already released. For example, technologies that remediate contaminated land (e.g. soil surveys and purification solutions of Nippon Steel).
2. *End of pipe.* Technologies that reduce or control environmental harm or externalities associated with industrial manufacturing. Examples include filters or scrubbers on smoke stacks (e.g. Alstom emissions reduction technologies and scrubbers to remove SOx, NOx) or catalytic converters on car exhaust.
3. *Clean substitutes.* Provide cleaner substitutes to existing technologies or materials, often using the same infrastructure. Examples include biofuels like ethanol or low toxic auto paints (e.g. Bayer's new waterborne automotive coating system).
4. *Efficiency.* Enhance efficiency of existing processes so that fewer inputs used lead to reduced outputs. Examples include energy-efficient lighting (e.g. Philips Green Flagship products) and building materials that enhance thermal efficiency.
5. *Pollution prevention.* Eliminate pollution, for example, using sensors and monitors to optimize process inputs in order to reduce NOx or other emissions (e.g. Johnson Controls products).
6. *Industrial ecology.* Models of efficient use of resources, energy and waste in a system setting using closed-loop design. An example of this would be taking waste, energy or other materials and turning it into a feedstock (e.g. BASF Verbund initiative).

11.2.4 Two types of innovation to consider

Innovation within a business context refers to revolutionary or incremental changes to products, processes or services. Incremental innovations are a step forward along a technology trajectory, or from the known to the unknown, with little uncertainty about outcomes and success, and is generally in the form of minor improvements made by those working day to day with existing methods and technology (both process and product), responding to short-term goals.

Breakthrough, disruptive or radical innovations mean launching an entirely novel product or service rather than providing improved products and services along the same lines as currently. The uncertainty of breakthrough innovations means that seldom do companies achieve their breakthrough goals this way, but when breakthrough innovation does work, the rewards can be high. And in between these two types, we have "substantial" innovations which provide greater opportunity to add value, as they engender the creation of business opportunities that are likely to lead the industry and provide a competitive advantage to the company developing them.

In the organizational context, innovation may be linked to performance and growth through improvements in efficiency, productivity, quality, competitive positioning, market share, etc. All organizations can innovate, including large-scale companies and not just small, start-up firms. Innovation is of interest to investors because it is a key driver in effectively growing market share and therefore nurturing revenues.

11.2.5   The innovation investment logic

There is increasing evidence showing that superior performance in managing environment is a useful proxy for superior, more strategic corporate management, organizational agility and responsiveness and therefore for superior financial performance and shareholder value creation. The business value of innovation is well recognized. Most leading companies emphasize their innovation focus and strengths in external communication and for internal motivation. Although notoriously difficult to measure, the premise that effective innovation creates company value – in terms of additional sales or profits – is now generally taken as a given.

Research by Arthur D. Little[7] has shown that innovative firms achieve on average a six-times-higher earnings before net interest and tax (EBIT) margin, and a growth rate that is 13 percent higher, than those of the underperformers. Leading companies also understand the importance of being seen to be innovative, because a reputation for being innovative enhances a company's reputation – among investors, customers, business and government partners, staff and target recruits – and thereby generates additional value.

One recent prize-winning[8] study examined the link between environmental innovation and financial performance. The research[9] conducted for the period 1995–2003 shows that stocks with a high "ecoefficiency rating" (i.e. Innovest corporate ecoefficiency score) outperformed the low-rated stocks. Based on Innovest ecoefficiency scores, the study constructed and evaluated two portfolios that differed in ecoefficiency. The high-ranked portfolio provided substantially higher average returns than its low-ranked counterpart over the period 1995–2003. Such an outperformance could not be explained by industry or country specifics, investment style or market size.

A similar study published in the *Journal of Asset Management* (*JAM*)[10] also concluded that the ecologically enhanced versions of the quantitative strategy were superior to those of a baseline portfolio, although all the active strategies exceeded the benchmark for the time frame tested, even after accounting for transaction costs and incorporating style constraints. The research found that the information ratio on the portfolio was most significantly improved when the extreme ratings were incorporated into the process. The results of this analysis support the assertion that sensitivity to environmental issues, particularly for the top performers, may enhance returns of an active strategy over time.

11.3   New marketplace dynamics

11.3.1   Case study – the automotive sector

The automotive sector is one where innovation has a major role to play in determining the longer-term success of the main market protagonists. The following case study, taken from an Innovest automaker sector report published in 2007, demonstrates the level of innovation analysis that is now possible in helping to evaluate current and future company performance.

Tightening fuel economy regulations

Fuel economy regulations are tightening in all major auto markets as a result of climate change concerns and discontent over gasoline prices. This section discusses the current state and outlook for fuel economy regulations in major markets.

The European Union has entered into voluntary agreements with automobile manufacturers' associations, including the European Automobile Manufacturers' Association (ACEA) and the Japanese Automobile Manufacturers' Association (JAMA), to achieve fuel economy averages of 140 CO_2 g/km (~40 mpg) by 2008–9 and 120 CO_2 g/km (~43 mpg) by 2012 (see Figure 11.3). While meeting this nonbinding standard is

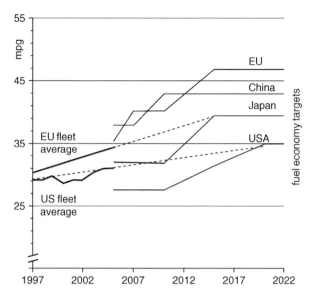

Figure 11.3   Chart of fuel economy standards in major markets

voluntary, the proclaimed inability of many European automakers to meet this standard is likely to prompt a regulatory response. Regulations (and voluntary agreements enforced by threat of regulation) have already been introduced in various European countries, including the United Kingdom and Spain, that would impose fines on automakers exceeding 120 CO_2 g/km after 2012.

The United States, where corporate average fuel economy (CAFE) regulations have been nearly unchanged since introduced in 1975, is extremely likely to make dramatic increases in fuel economy standards. A revised CAFE bill passed in the Senate in June 2007 and looks set to pass, possibly with some minor loosening, in the House. California has preempted new CAFE standards through statewide fuel economy regulations of its own, which are currently being challenged by automakers in US courts. The law has been copied by a number of states including Connecticut, Massachusetts, Vermont, Rhode Island, Maine, New Jersey and New York. Automakers have signaled they may prefer a uniform environment of slightly higher federal standards than a state-by-state hodgepodge of local standards. The tightening of fuel economy regulations presents a market-altering challenge to the auto industry. Companies that have developed the capacity to build fuel-efficient

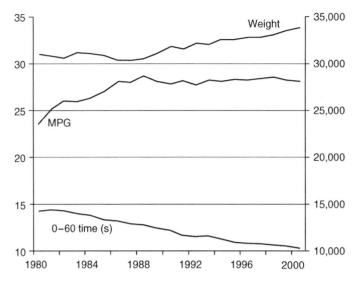

Figure 11.4 The 2005 fleet fuel economy for the major automakers in the US market. Efficiency gains were spent on speed and safety, not mileage
Source: Honda Motors. Graphic style modified.

engines will benefit not only from higher sales but also from minimal regulatory burden. Companies unprepared for fuel economy regulation will be subject to significant fines and gas guzzler taxes for their fuel-intensive fleets.

Comparing fleet fuel economy

In the US, lax government intervention to mandate fuel economy regulations since their introduction in 1975 has allowed the market to be dictated entirely by consumer preference. Therefore, technological advances over the last 25 years have focused primarily on improving speed and safety. As such, 0–60 acceleration times have decreased and automobile weight has climbed steadily but fuel efficiency has remained stagnant. Had cars not gotten faster and heavier, the technological innovation would put the US fleet at ~35 mpg today. Figure 11.4 shows the 2005 fleet fuel economy, averaged across cars and trucks, for the major automakers in the US market.

As fuel economy legislation advances and consumer preferences reflect high gas prices, the strategic priority of fuel efficiency is increasingly obvious. As more R&D funds are dedicated in this direction we expect that fuel efficiency will improve significantly in the coming decade. Automakers focused heavily on the US market are generally less prepared for consumer preferences for fuel economy, and are increasingly challenged by the current trends.

The EU entered into voluntary compliance agreements with automaker associations in 1998, requiring companies to improve fleet fuel efficiency or face regulation, leading to a steady improvement in European fleet fuel economies. Members of the ACEA committed to reducing average CO_2 emissions from new EU car sales to 140 CO_2 g/km by 2008 – a 25 percent reduction over 1995 levels, and the Korean and Japan Automobile Manufacturers' Associations (KAMA and JAMA) committed to do the same by 2009. Currently only Renault, PSA, Fiat and Ford are on track to be in compliance with the directive, while 75 percent of automakers are off target. In response to the failure of these voluntary compliance directives, the EU is likely to see binding legislation, mandating aggressive reductions in fuel efficiency.

Evaluation of alternative power trains

Not all alternative power trains will prove lucrative investments. Innovest examined the costs, technological challenges, infrastructural requirements, efficiencies, sustainability forecasts and carbon profiles of each major alternative power train in order to assess the commercial feasibility of each technology and the timeframe on which it is likely to be in commercial production. Biofuels in particular stand out as a technology Ford and GM are betting heavily on but which we see as a very short-term solution as it provides little price relief to consumers at the pump.

Five-year market scenario

This section presents a scenario for the changing mix of power trains for cars and light trucks in three global market segments: the US, EU, and rest of the world (ROW). This long-term scenario is based on original research and incorporates shorter-term forecasts from organizations such as JD Power & Associates. Based on the analysis below we find the following companies in advantageous positions vis-à-vis bringing new power trains and serving growing markets: in the US we see DCX, VW, and BMW benefiting from the growth of diesel, and Toyota, Honda, and to some degree GM and Ford winning for hybrids. The EU is likely to experience less change than the US, but we see Fiat, Peugeot, and Renault as benefiting from the push for higher fuel efficiency. Finally, in terms of seizing positions in the fast-growing emerging markets, we see VW and Honda as leaders in China. Renault is focusing on getting a Logan successor and is in talks with Bajaj to expand to India. Of the major automakers Fuji, Hyundai, Porsche, Harley-Davidson, and Mazda are the least exposed to these growth trends. These companies face a shrinking market share as other firms better capitalize on growth drivers.

The following sections describe the scenario and model used to project future alpha movement derived from the predicted growth or shrinkage of market share.

Modeling growth in the auto sector

We have defined a scenario for the global auto market growth; the model is characterized by heavy growth in the ROW segment, which includes Japan but de facto implies growth from China and Asian markets. The scenario also highlights the increasing role of diesel and hybrid power trains. Global passenger vehicle demand (cars plus light trucks) is expected to grow 4.8 percent annually. Global auto production was 70 million units in 2006 and will be ~91 million units in 2012. This growth will be disproportionately driven by emerging markets. Annual growth in the US will be 2 percent, in the EU 3.4 percent, and in ROW 8–10 percent. This implies that the US and EU will become slightly less important markets, shrinking slightly, while the ROW segment will expand from 40 to 46 percent of the market (see Figure 11.5).

After defining this scenario a substitution rate was assembled for each automaker. This substitution rate was used to allocate new vehicles to each manufacturer. For example, of each new 100 hybrid vehicles sold in the EU in the five-year scenario these new sales were allocated to each manufacturer based on this substitution rate. The substitution rate is

$$R_m^P = S_m \cdot K_m^P$$

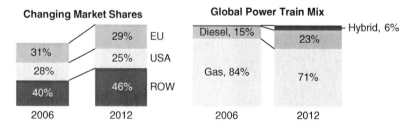

Figure 11.5 Regional growth in the auto market

Note: Lefthand bar chart shows absolute number of vehicles in the bar widths and market share percentages overlaid in text.

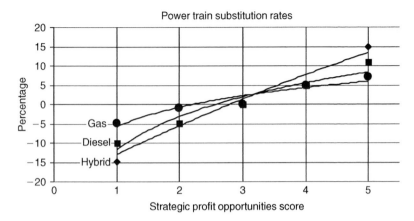

Figure 11.6   Substitution rates based on power train scores

where each manufacturer *m*'s substitution rate *R* for each of the three power trains *p* (gasoline, diesel, and hybrids) is the company's market share *S* multiplied by an adjustment factor *K* particular to Innovest's rating of that manufacturer's power train score. The adjustment factors used for *K* are presented in Figure 11.6. A high score for hybrid power train development is considered to be more advantageous for capturing market share than a high score in gasoline engines.

Limitations of the scenario

This scenario intentionally focuses on one aspect of the auto market, namely the growing importance of high-mileage power trains. It does not address other important factors in determining stock performance in the sector; one of these factors is labor costs. The scenario is presented to illustrate how fuel economy trends will impact the competitive landscape.

Scenario results

The output of this scenario is a forecast market share for each manufacturer. In the scenario each company's global market share changes based on the company's exposure to each geographic market segment (since the different segments grow at different rates) and the company's scores in strategic power train development as explained with the substitution rate above (see Table 11.1).

Comparison of power train development and commercialization

We have evaluated each company to determine which, and how much, each company is investing in each next-generation power train

Table 11.1 Scenario winners and losers

	Global market share (%)		Market share change (%)	
	2006	*2012*		
Denway	7.9	9.4	1.5	Winner
Toyota	13.4	14.6	1.2	Winner
Suzuki	3.1	3.6	0.5	Winner
MMC	1.9	2.2	0.3	Winner
Hyundai	5.6	5.9	0.3	Winner
Isuzu	1.0	1.2	0.2	Winner
Maruti	0.9	1.0	0.1	Winner
Honda	5.4	5.5	0.1	Winner
Fiat	3.5	3.6	0.1	Winner
Fuji	0.9	0.9	0.0	Winner
Mazda	2.0	2.0	0.0	Winner
Nissan	5.3	5.3	0.0	Winner
Porsche	0.2	0.1	−0.1	Loser
BMW	2.1	2.0	−0.1	Loser
VW	8.7	8.5	−0.2	Loser
Peugeot	5.1	4.9	−0.2	Loser
Renault	3.7	3.4	−0.3	Loser
DCX	7.2	6.5	−0.7	Loser
Ford	9.1	7.7	−1.4	Loser
GM	13.2	11.7	−1.5	Loser

technology. In Table 11.2, a dark circle means the company is a leader in this technology; a white circle means the company has indicated no serious plans to commercialize the technology. The circle quarters reflect the amount of priority placed on each technology, so second-tier priorities for large automakers with large R&D budgets could be given more points than the top priorities for smaller automakers.

Carbon intensity of manufacturing

The manufacturing of automobiles is an energy-intensive process with significant cost implications as tighter regulations on greenhouse gas (GHG) emissions loom. Innovest monitors each company's GHG emissions performance. In this section we provide GHG emissions data for those companies which report, and we also frame the potential cost implications assuming a high-end carbon price of €30 per tonne of CO_2. Figure 11.7 compares the financial implications of CO_2 (plus CO_2 equivalent) emissions for the 13 companies in the sector which disclose their

Table 11.2   Who's betting where on power trains

Company	Gas	Gas Hybrid	Diesel Hybrid	Clean Diesel	Plug-in/ Battery	Hydrogen
Honda	●	●	○	◔	●	●
GM	◕	◕	◔	◔	◕	●
DaimlerChrysler	◔	◕	◑	◕	◑	●
Renault	●	◑	◑	●	◔	◕
Nissan	◔	◔	○	◑	◔	◕
BMW	●	◑	◑	◕	◑	◕
Toyota	●	●	◑	◔	●	◔
Ford	◑	◕	◑	◑	◑	◔
VW	◔	◔	◔	●	○	◔
Peugeot	●	○	●	●	◔	◑
Yamaha	◔	◑	○	◑	◔	◑
Fiat	●	◑	◑	●	◑	◑
Suzuki	○	◑	○	◕	○	◑
Hyundai	◕	◑	○	◔	○	◑
Mitsubishi	◕	◑	○	◕	●	○
Fuji Heavy	◑	◔	◑	◔	◔	○
Bajaj	○	○	○	○	◔	○
Isuzu	○	○	●	◕	○	○
Mazda	◑	○	○	◑	○	○
Porsche	◔	◑	○	○	○	○
Denway	○	○	○	○	○	○
Maruti Udyog	○	○	○	○	○	○
Harley-Davidson	○	○	○	○	○	○

Source: Innovest.

emissions. Emission reporting is not yet standardized; companies differ in whether they report only direct emissions or also include indirect emissions.

The wide range of GHG emissions intensity across the sector reveals that significant risks and opportunities exist for shareholders, between companies with proactive carbon management strategies and ones that fall behind the curve. Industry leaders, such as Honda, Nissan and Renault, have already established targets to reduce the amount of GHGs generated by their production, logistics and office activities on a global scale. GM's exceptionally high carbon emissions, however, implies a poorly managed manufacturing process that could hurt earnings once regulation is passed mandating a reduction in GHG emissions. The company is attempting to correct its high carbon emissions and has announced an ambitious goal to reduce CO_2 emissions by 40 percent from its North American manufacturing facilities by 2010, compared to 2000 levels.

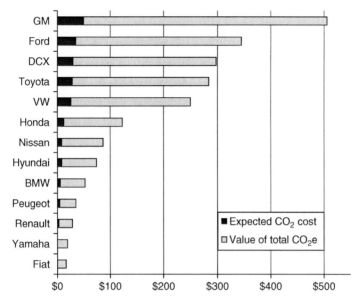

Figure 11.7 Potential cost of CO_2 emissions at €30/tonne emissions cost. Calculations are based on the latest figures available for each company's Scope 1&2 emissions set forth under the reporting guidelines of the GHG Protocol. Expected reduction cost is based on assumed 10% reduction requirement

Table 11.3 shows each company's CO_2 emissions; the value of these emissions assuming emissions could be traded on an emissions exchange market for a price of €30 per tonne; the likely financial liability of the company's emissions assuming a mandated 10 percent emissions reduction; and finally this likely liability expressed as a percentage of FY06 net income.

GM and Peugeot's carbon emissions costs, represented as a percentage of their 2006 net income, are well above the rest of the sector. GM has low net income and high CO_2 emissions. Although the percentages listed do not reflect the actual price necessary to comply with a particular reduction scheme, they do communicate the fact that the top two companies' emissions profile makes up for a larger fraction of their annual income than industry peers.

In analyzing the CO_2 emissions between each company, one caveat investors should keep in mind is the comparative nature of the reported information. Often the wide differences between each company's performance is a result of the inconsistency in reporting standards. The lack of a standardized international carbon-accounting framework makes it

Table 11.3 CO_2 emissions and potential CO_2 emissions liability

	CO_2 emissions (Mt)	Value of CO_2 emissions ($ million)	Likely CO_2 cost ($ million)	Likely CO_2 cost (% of net income)
GM	12.3	454.3	50.5	25.5
Peugeot	0.8	31.4	3.5	15.0
DCX	7.2	268.1	29.8	7.0
VW	6.1	225.3	25.0	6.9
Hyundai	1.8	67.5	7.5	5.5
Yamaha	0.5	17.5	1.9	3.0
Ford	8.4	310.3	34.5	2.7
Toyota	6.9	255.4	28.4	2.4
Honda	2.9	110.1	12.2	2.4
Nissan	2.1	78.3	8.7	1.9
BMW	1.3	47.3	5.3	1.3
Fiat	0.4	14.7	1.6	1.1
Renault	0.7	25.4	2.8	0.7

Source: Innovest research, Carbon Disclosure Project 2005 (www.cdproject.net). Expected reduction cost is based on assumed 10% reduction requirement.

difficult to carry out accurate comparative analysis. Companies within different regions often have different reporting guidelines as to what constitutes direct and indirect emissions. As Innovest's database of reported emissions extends over time, this will allow more comprehensive conclusions to be made. For the most accurate carbon management analysis, investors should refer to the individual profiles for each company and to Innovest's Carbon Ratings Platform.

11.3.2   Climate change and innovation – an alpha driver

Using this carbon ratings platform, we conducted a rigorous financial performance study to test empirically the proposition that companies with superior carbon management practices and strategies can financially outperform their peers (the proxy used here for "financial performance" was share price performance with dividends reinvested – "total return"). In order to isolate the possible existence and size of any "carbon risk premium," the impact of other, more traditional, investment factors was eliminated through quantitative techniques.

It should be noted that the analysis used in this study is not a so-called "static back-cast." That is, the Q2 2007 Carbon Beta ™ company ratings were not simply back-cast and assumed to have been the same in 2004 and thereafter. Instead, we have used Innovest's time series database of

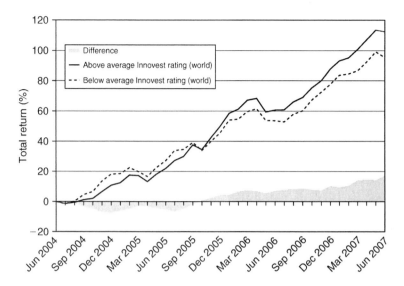

Figure 11.8 Carbon Beta™ performers vs laggards globally

company ratings for each month and as company ratings were changed over time, those "live" ratings were used in the study. This approach provides a much more robust set of results than a simple, static back-cast.

In all comparisons made between any two portfolios, or between any portfolio and an index benchmark in this analysis, data was adjusted for sector and regional effects. That is, the weights in each group were adjusted to match the industry sector and geographical distribution of the constituents of the peer group. Unless otherwise stated, all sector and regional exposures correspond to those of the leaders group of the comparison in question. That is, for comparing global carbon leaders vs laggards, for instance, the latter group was reweighted to match the same industry and geographical distribution of the constituents of the former group. In doing this, we have neutralized any effect that could distort the comparative performance of a portfolio due to regional regulations and competitive conditions in a specific market or industrial segment.

11.4 The research results

Carbon risk variance from one industrial sector to another requires different managerial responses and strategies for companies – both to hedge their risk exposure and to take advantage of the different profit opportunities from operations, products and services that climate change can potentially bring. Consequently, for Innovest, companies positioned as top carbon performers have a higher expected return in comparison with the overall market benchmark and, moreover, with same sector companies judged to be "carbon laggards." Three-year empirical stock market research using Innovest's Carbon Beta™ model reveals that, in fact, this is the case. As expected, the "carbon beta premium" varies considerably, both by industry sector and by region. Companies rated under the Carbon Beta™ platform as top carbon performers surpassed the return of companies rated as below average from June 2004 to June 2007 by an annualized rate of return of 3.06 percent (a cumulative total return of 81.85 percent compared to 72.67 percent).[11] This is shown in Figure 11.8.

Notes

1. Living Planet Report 2006, www.panda.org/livingplanet
2. http://www.unfpa.org/swp/2007/english/introduction.html
3. http://www.un.org/esa/population/publications/WPP2004/WPP2004_Volume3.htm
4. http://www.iea.org/Textbase/nppdf/free/2006/Key2006.pdf
5. Manning, Robert A. (2004) "The Asian Energy Market: a New Geopolitics?" *Asian Energy Markets Dynamics and Trends*, Emirates Center for Strategic Studies and Research, Abu Dhabi , p. 31.
6. http://environment.guardian.co.uk/climatechange/story/0,,2073006,00.html
7. Arthur D. Little, "Integrity + Innovation = Sustainable Performance," http://www.adl.com/index.php?id=191
8. Moskowitz price: http://www.socialinvest.org/resources/research/moskowitz.cfm
9. Guenster Derwall and Koedijk Bauer (2005) "The Eco-Efficiency Premium Puzzle," *Financial Analysts Journal*, 61.
10. Kimberly Gluck, CFA, State Street Global Advisors (2004), *Journal of Asset Management*, 5/4: 220–2.
11. The selected period was chosen due to the fact that it was only in 2005 that the first significant carbon restricting regulation took place in Europe. Therefore, it is most likely that the market started capturing the climate change effects on the perceived value and risk of a company and sector at this time. For the purposes of this study, "top carbon performers" were defined as those achieving an Innovest Carbon Beta™ rating of BBB "investment grade" or better.

12
Financialization: Limits and Ways Out

Paul Dembinski and Federica Viganò

Introduction

Western societies find themselves today in a paradoxical situation in relation to finance. In the workplace Western man is simultaneously exposed to the pressure of efficiency and the risk of unemployment, both for the sake of stock-market prices; in his private life, as a consumer, he is harassed by consumerist temptations and payment obligations; and finally, as a human being and in some cases parent, he attempts to resist all these pressures and preserve an area of independence and truth – a haven of humanity, so to speak. Financial logic underpins all these pressures. But why is there all this pressure, which can sometimes lead to physical or mental violence? Supposedly, it is all in his best interests! Western man is the ultimate beneficiary of the forthcoming fruits of financialization – provided, of course, that he puts all his daily energy into ensuring the smooth running of the economic machine in which he has invested all his hopes (and all his money). Under the terms of the economic pact that underpins Western society, today's saver/shareholder will, when he retires, enjoy the fruits of his years of work. It is this prospect of a life of leisure that explains the sacrifices free societies accept in order to accumulate financial value.

The material progress achieved over the past two centuries owes much to the Western world's ability to save and invest. The industrial revolution took place and has continued in successive waves up to the present day thanks to financial techniques that have enabled savings to be invested on a large scale. Throughout most of this period, savings were used for projects which were certainly profitable but did not have financial performance as their main goal. Finance was a necessary but not sufficient means toward other ends. It thus admitted its inability to

225

determine goals. More recently, when infinite multiplication of assets becomes an end in itself, an ultimate goal that predominates over all others, finance becomes a tyrant. Although fear of the future leads to precautionary behavior and accumulation of resources, it tells us nothing about how to use these resources (except in emergencies). "How to spend it?", the title of the glossy supplement to the world's leading economics and finance journal, the London *Financial Times*, reflects this inability of "assets" to give meaning to existence. The question of how accumulated wealth is to be used cannot be divorced from that of meaning. It is no accident that ostentatious philanthropy and patronage are now so fashionable. It is therefore natural to return to the dilemma "Finance – servant or deceiver?"[1] by asking some questions about meaning.

Is finance a means to an end, or an end in itself? Where are we today, tossed back and forth between the thankless nature of finance as a means and the euphoria of finance as an end? Financialization is dragging the West, and with it the rest of the world, into the arms of finance the tyrant. Is this an endless deterministic process guided by the iron hand of human history, a process that contains its own inherent limits – or an open-ended process that can be contained if we have the will and the strength to do so? Three aspects of the problem will be discussed here: (1) the three limits inherent in the financialization process; (2) its external limits; and (3) possible ways of intervening to curb it.

12.1   Internal limits to financialization

12.1.1   The specter of sterility

Financial transactions provide a way for noncaptive partners in a relationship to escape from it by objectivizing the value that was hitherto built into it by markets, through prices. It is therefore not surprising that efforts to "enhance value" are part of the arsenal of those who seek to get out of relationships with a profit and those who make their living from transactions. All the transactional "noise" is, in principle, external to the actual relationship. The potential, or value, of a relationship is known above all to the partners on whom it depends. They are happy with their relationship and do not need to shout about it from the rooftops. Since the relationship is by definition open to the future and since the future depends (among other things, of course) on the partners' trust, loyalty and commitment, it has no objective value that is independent of the partners. It is thus an untransparent reality, one that is both fertile and fragile. Financialization involves large-scale exploitation of relationships for transactional purposes. This process will have a direct impact on relations between partners in relationships. They will become more cautious, and less willing to commit themselves to new relationships.

What happens in a relationship when one of the partners starts looking for ways to get out of it? As soon as the captive partner becomes aware of this, he will develop a sense of insecurity which will erode trust and may even lead him to adopt cunning retaliatory or countervailing strategies. Such behavior will deprive the relationship of part of its substance and its development potential. The resulting masquerade will have potentially devastating economic and social consequences and may ultimately destroy the relationship altogether. The commitment on which fertility, growth and multiplication depend in turn depends on trust. Investment projects presuppose and rely on cooperation and hence trust between the partners – in other words, lasting relationships. The root of all investment is openness, acceptance, trust and even self-denial in the hope of return and profit. All of this is only possible in a lasting relationship. Failing this, distrust of the future, and of the other partner, is likely to prevent cooperation, and creativity, by freezing them into a mechanical sequence of tit-for-tat transactions. This will destroy any potential for cooperation. A relationship is by definition a succession of imbalances which, as in the process of walking, makes it more dynamic and increases its potential. The prospect of transactions makes relationships sterile and leaves the economy and society less flexible. This is what happens when, instead of trusting in the other partner's ability to rebalance the relationship if necessary, each partner is looking for ways to get out of it.

What is the point of establishing new relationships if distrust is growing? When distrust increases, each partner seeks to protect himself and to control the other partner's activities and performance. This makes the relationship economically less efficient, increasing its costs and reducing its productivity. Any relationship that is merely formal will rapidly cease to be profitable. The limit will be reached when the costs of monitoring or supervising each other approach what the relationship can reasonably be expected to produce. At this point the relationship becomes sterile. When distrust is widespread, there can no longer be any cooperation, or creativity, or innovation. Economic sterility looms. This is the first of the limits inherent in financialization. Sterility surely reaches its height when financial relationships are established not because of their creative potential but merely so that they can be valued by a market and then resold. Such extreme exploitation of relationships for transactional purposes was condemned in early 2007 by the Bank for International

Settlements, which termed it the "originate and distribute" strategy. Before the subprime crisis of mid-2007 gave it a moral dimension, this condemnation was a purely technical one, on the grounds that purchasers of securities had no knowledge of the underlying relationships. When relationships are established merely for transactional purposes, we are dealing with a clear inversion of ends and means. As the subprime crisis and the financial instruments created in its wake make only too clear, a good deal of financial innovation in recent years has involved precisely this kind of inversion.

12.1.2   Complexity

The spread of transactions involving increasingly sophisticated components of economic reality has made the whole system a good deal more complex. Transactions and the underlying relationships are more and more strictly regulated and cannot be understood, or realized, without whole teams of qualified intermediaries. This increased complexity is due to several factors. Today's computer and database resources make it possible to grasp increasingly refined elements of finance and to carry out sophisticated transactions with almost infinite precision. The handling of vast sums to accuracy of mere hundredths of a percent requires an extremely complex technological and regulatory apparatus. The market mechanism is fragile. To preserve its theoretical efficiency, modern society has hedged it about with an increasingly dense set of rules and procedures. The difficulty of correctly diagnosing recent upheavals, such as that caused by the long-term capital management crisis in 1998, is partly due to the dense network of linkages. So complex has the system become that even the best-informed players, including central banks, are unable to grasp it. The web of risks and conditional contracts is so complicated that global finance is increasingly treated as a compact, total entity – an anonymous process – in which individual players' autonomy is reduced to almost nothing.

Even the most sophisticated player cannot cope with this complexity, and individual operators attempt to mark out the terrain by establishing procedures that will at least enable them to grasp specific segments of finance. This is true for sustainability indicators as well as for corporate social responsibility metrics that are developed today by civil society and rating actors. Governments do likewise, laying down standards and regulations in specific areas and imposing them on operators. Yet the complexity remains. Mere proceduralization accompanied by strict division of responsibilities cannot cope with it, for finance is an intrinsically innovative activity and markets are not, by definition, open areas. Although proceduralization has revealed its limits, especially in times of crisis, it is still the only method used both at institutional level and throughout the system. Despite attempts to channel developments, the changes described above are inevitably turning modern finance into an anonymous process – a plane with no pilot and a huge number of passengers.

Like distrust, the complexity of modern finance, with its hidden, unpredictable risks and frailties, is the second limit inherent in financialization. Beyond a certain point, growing complexity could plunge financialized societies into chaos – as some of the scenarios in mathematical catastrophe theory indeed suggest. According to this theory, the most complex systems may find themselves out of control as a result of minute changes. Researchers have used such theories of complexity to explain the collapse of various societies in the course of history, suggesting, for example, that excessive complexity was a major factor in the collapse of social orders such as Ancient Rome.[2] On the one hand, complexity is a source of efficiency and precision; on the other, it is a source of fragility and management and monitoring costs. When costs – which today are largely socialized – exceed efficiency gains, financialization will no longer serve any economic purpose. Things will then go into reverse, but the process is likely to be messy.

12.1.3 Concentration of economic power

Financialization is based on, and in turn amplifies, concentration of economic and financial power. The emergence of savings silos such as pension and investment funds has created mega-players who are able to handle unprecedented sums, thus greatly speeding up the development of financial transactions and so fueling the financialization process. To control their costs, particularly intermediation and management costs, these mega-players have encouraged the emergence of intermediaries of similar size. Liquidity has been channelled toward the largest markets, which are the only ones capable of absorbing it, and stock-market capitalization in the OECD countries has skyrocketed as a result (as has the volume of transactions and commissions). Thus, there has been a consolidation of large intermediaries, and remunerations have been greatly polarized. The same process is equally evident among quoted very large companies (VLCs), the hubs of the real economy.

It is clear that the moral, technical and social legitimacy currently enjoyed by the principle of proportional remuneration of capital has, for purely mathematical reasons, speeded up the concentration process. Today, this process has been further boosted by financialization, with its vast number of transactions. Ideologically, this trend has been justified by the doctrine of shareholder value. The beneficiaries are financial intermediaries and foremen in businesses, and only to a marginal extent the final recipients – present and future pensioners. Financialization has not increased their pensions or reduced their contribution periods, but in the meantime some directors and intermediaries have seen their incomes rocket. This concentration of economic power would seem mainly to involve Northern countries, but appearances are deceiving. The globalization of their supply and distribution networks means that listed VLCs now influence the economies of both the North and the South. The concentration of resources and the main economic levers in the hands of so few has not gone unnoticed by the starving masses of the South. While the North will soon only be working to guarantee its pensions, the South can still barely earn its daily bread. Although a few Southern countries have managed to keep up with the lead group, such inequality cannot continue to grow without eventually triggering a response of some kind – expulsion, rejection or outright aggression.

The recent and widely noted emergence of sovereign wealth funds has given the North good cause for concern. Massive investment by these funds in banks weakened by the 2007–8 crisis may herald a new inversion of trends. It may turn out that the new shareholders do not revere shareholder value and intend to use their newly acquired power for purposes other than simply increasing their assets. This may be one way in which other goals, including political ones, will start to challenge and threaten financialization on its own turf. The same could be said – but with many qualifications – about the emerging investment vehicles organized around the philosophy of sustainability and corporate social responsibility. However, their "firing power" is, for the time being, much smaller and less focused than that of sovereign funds. Concentration of economic power in the hands of a small number of financial players, including sovereign wealth funds, threatens the future of financialization, for it suggests that growing inequality may no longer be tolerated. As the history of the world has shown, the affluence and dogmatic arrogance of the few may eventually become unbearable to the excluded masses.[3] Thus the growth of inequality, as reflected by a large number of national and international measures, should be seen as a possible limit to financialization.

12.2   External limits to financialization

Besides the limits inherent in financialization itself, the process may also run into external obstacles. Three of these deserve brief mention here: the widespread sense that life has lost all meaning; the erosion of ethical principles; and the sense of ethical alienation and helplessness. These obstacles may well be inherent in human nature.

12.2.1 Transactions: beyond conflicts of interest

Anything goes in the pursuit of financial efficiency, including things which seemed unacceptable only a few years ago. The long list of scandals and dubious practices exposed by the media shows that today's "winner-take-all society"[4] has less and less time for losers. The struggle for economic survival is almost bestial, sometimes suggesting a Hobbesian war of all against all. In such a society, the weak, the naïve, the gullible, the less well educated and immigrants are not objects of sympathy, but targets for marketing and opportunities for others to make money.

Confrontation and aggressive pursuit of profit are emerging in areas in which trust-based relationships prevailed until recently – areas in which commissioned agents were supposed to act in their clients' best interests. This is the case in all areas in which knowledge is asymmetrical, and hence in most service sectors. Doctors, lawyers, accountants, sales advisors – even asset managers – traditionally had a moral duty to defend their clients' interests, if necessary at the expense of their own monetary interests. This duty was part of their professional ethics and hence was passed on from generation to generation, and at the same time it was founded in the prevailing moral principle that people should not exploit each other. Agents torn between loyalty to their wallets and loyalty to their clients were thus internally equipped to resist temptation. Today, as a brilliant analysis by Tamar Frankel has shown, things are changing: in professions which were until recently based on respect for clients' interests, there is a growing shift toward strictly contractual relationships. Such a change only makes sense if the partners have equal knowledge – which is clearly not the case with professions specifically based on know-how and expertise. This shift toward contractualization, which is a form of transaction, is part of a wider trend that is pushing relationships into the background.

This trend further strengthens the agent's position, for once the contract is signed his only duty is to perform the tasks specified in it. At that point, the question of whether the client understands its meaning and scope becomes irrelevant. This trend toward contractualization of all services is part of professionals' pursuit of legal cover and their wish to shed the ethical principles that formerly required them to defend their clients' or patients' interests.[5] It leads to situations in which trust-based relationships can be abused quite legally. Trust and service no longer count – only transactions matter. If the trend were to persist, it would erode one of the cornerstones of civilization: the idea that the strong have a moral duty to take care of the weak. This minimum duty of care is the basis for society and for solidarity. As Albert Tévoédjrè has indicated, the rise of transactions may, unless it is contained by ethics, undermine the very foundations of society:

> The ills of the industrial civilization have their origins in the principles applied at grass-roots level in order to increase production and profit: concentration and specialization [...] From the moment industrialization "specializes" the individual, every time the economy switches from use-based to exchange-based, one sees the family reduced to its most simple expression. The accumulative society certainly enjoys an extraordinary ability to take things over [...] But can the society itself be said to truly exist?[6]

In a book that caused a sensation at the time, George Soros recalled that even the most perfect market could end up destroying the social nexus unless it was contained in a firm cultural and ethical corset.[7] But nowadays a mechanism reigns whereby trust is systematically exploited by transactions performed solely with a view to capital gains. This value-extracting process driven by financialization is having a destructive impact on society. It is feeding an unhealthy self-perpetuating pattern, for no one wants to lose out. This race for transaction premiums may irreversibly blight the social fabric. From a societal as opposed to purely economic point of view, efficiency gains that can be quantified in terms of increased national product must be set against their destructive effects on society, which are very real, even though unquantifiable and almost invisible. The only way to stop this process of erosion is to take action to put relationships and transactions back where they belong.

12.2.2   Ethical alienation

The spread of procedures and regulations is intended to organize society as rationally and efficiently as possible – to make it predictable, standardized and controllable. Proceduralization – which simply means chopping up relationships into separate segments, or transactions – is part of an attempt to depersonalize processes and make roles interchangeable. If there is a detailed procedure for everything, it no longer matters whether Tom, Dick or Harriet is pressing the keys or performing the transactions. Use of procedures also means that responsibility is broken up into pieces for each separate stage of the procedure. All those involved are thus well aware of their "own" responsibility and feel no need to think about the meaning of what they are doing, i.e. the meaning of the chain of procedures in which they are involved. Ultimately, no one feels responsible for the overall result, but everyone feels an exaggerated technical responsibility for his or her particular segment. No longer knowing why they are doing what they do, they become mere operatives who simply obey their superiors rather than use their common sense and their instincts. In a compartmentalized world that prevents them from seeing the big picture, they tend to withdraw into themselves and stop thinking, obeying authority either because they are afraid or because they can no longer rely on their own survival instincts.[8] Totalitarian regimes have never demanded that everyone should believe in all their ideas, but have simply required people to obey authority and carry out precisely defined tasks in meticulous detail – a phenomenon described in numerous works on Nazism and Stalinism.[9]

Finance, with its promise of an utterly risk-free society, is not actually totalitarian, but it is certainly "totalizing." Its complexity makes it very suitable for division of responsibility, which insulates players from the consequences of their acts. This is because (a) markets dissolve individual operators into the broad mass, which by definition relieves them of responsibility, and (b) finance, which involves manipulation of symbols in its purest form, is kept remote from its consequences by technology and by its language of ratios and percentages. Above all, players are insulated because they work in the closed environment of finance, where they feel more powerful than other economic players.[10] Finance is thus unquestionably a fertile breeding ground for "ethical alienation." Like Marx's workers, who are alienated because the pursuit of industrial efficiency denies them contact with the end product of their labor, manipulators of symbols are bound by rigid procedures and can easily become indifferent to the meaning and implications of what they do. In many cases ethical alienation becomes a habit – especially since the rewards are so high. Several decades ago, Stanley Milgram showed that ethical abdication is a typical feature of situations in which people obey authority. Yet the market economy is in theory based on free interaction between players, whereas in practice it is the product of free societies. The spread of ethical abdication among people who claim they are acting under the pressure – and in some cases the *authority* – of impersonal forces, and hence of behavior similar to that analyzed with such acuity by Stanley Milgram, is therefore particularly disturbing.

12.2.3   A sense of helplessness

Ethical alienation – the abandonment or loss of criteria other than those of efficiency – leads to a sense of helplessness. This paradoxical feeling is clearly expressed in the French documentary *Ma mondialisation.*[11] In an economy theoretically based on freedom of choice, it is striking to see that all the real-world players say that they have no choice, and hence that they are acting under duress. This is because the all-out pursuit of efficiency is driven by implacable anonymous processes. It is presented not only as a benefit, but as the sole criterion for behavior. This piece of sleight of hand allows it to take over the area reserved for goals and eventually to be perceived as the only true motive for human activity. Technology is a field in which the efficiency ethos can easily become entrenched. Yet the implacable logic of technological responses increases people's sense of helplessness. In the same way, markets – the mass of nomadic shareholders – impose their "sentiment" on individual operators and drag them along with them. The only way to overcome this feeling of helplessness is to reformulate the problem – not just in terms of "how?" (a purely technical question) but also in terms of "why?" (a question which takes account of goals). Although this is not easy, it is essential if we are to escape from the technical totalitarianism that is feeding on this widespread sense of helplessness.

The end of religious and moral control over the economy coincided with Adam Smith's recognition of economics as a separate discipline. The end of social control over the economy was proclaimed by writers such as Karl Polanyi, who described the end of the "embedding" of the economy in society as a "great transformation." In the last quarter of the twentieth century, globalization finally ended political control over the economy and finance. The financialization process is not only the culminating phase of this development, but also marks the establishment of economic thinking as the predominant paradigm. Today, economics and finance are not only free from metaphysical, societal and political control, but, in the absence of any countervailing forces, have come to prevail over metaphysics, society and politics. Given the current predominance of financialization, calls for political control to be reestablished over the economy are little more than pious hopes or idealistic incantations that seem unlikely to be heeded any time soon.

12.3   Resisting the financialization process: priorities for action

Yet, however powerful financialization may seem, it is not some deterministic historical "law" whose progress cannot be halted. People's sense of helplessness is thus not entirely justified, although not everything is possible and what is possible cannot be done at once. In today's world, financialization has solid intellectual, social, institutional and regulatory foundations. Over the past quarter-century it has become an integral part of everyday life in the West, and indeed the whole world – for other cultures have offered no resistance to the efficiency ethos and its battery of statistical indicators.[12] Yet financialization is merely one of many possible organizing principles, and it represents a choice which, if taken to its extreme, is a threat to both humanity and society. As this analysis shows, there are other, currently less prominent principles which could take its place – among them the notion of the common good.

There is a permanent confrontation between various ways of thinking at every level of the social system: at the micro-social level of everyday behavior and decisions, at the level of established mechanisms and at the level of institutions. Despite appearances, social and economic reality is not fixed, but is influenced at the margin by individuals' day-to-day decisions. The changes that have led to financialization will be halted only if they run into internal resistance or external opposition. Given the current predominance of financial thinking, the only kind of resistance strong enough to undermine it is one based on the question of meaning. The sustainability concern is a partial answer to the lack of meaning prevailing in the financial activities. The idea of meaning as the sole antidote to the implacable logic of technology has been forcefully expressed by Jean-Baptiste de Foucauld in the following terms:

> To opt for meaning [...] is to acknowledge that, available and present within us, there is a spirit, a moral awareness, a wish to love and to give that are peculiar to man – something whose origins and purpose we do not know for certain, but which we must carry, develop and affirm in the face of all opposition, against absurdity, stupidity and injustice and at our own risk, simply in order to be ourselves.[13]

Accordingly, the last sections of this chapter will be devoted to the search for ways to resist.

Some fragmentary avenues concerning the various modes of causality whereby financialization has managed to permeate society will be briefly explored here. Perhaps the most powerful and fundamental process analyzed here is the slow maturation of ideas. It took more than two centuries for the efficiency ethos to become the dominant, unquestioned paradigm and world view in the modern era. Our first priority for action should therefore be to resist this paradigm's attempt to monopolize meaning – for meaning is first and foremost a question of ends, and only then of means. The aim, then, is not to make financialization more moral, but to make it subservient to ends that respect human dignity and human nature.

12.3.1   Challenging financial ethics

There have been countless ethical initiatives to make finance "more moral." They have all resulted in various professional codes of financial ethics, on which a number of now classic books have been published.[14] This approach to the issue of financial ethics – or rather ethics in finance – involves finding methods and regulations that will make financial transactions "ethical." The focus is thus on the way in which transactions are performed: measures to combat insider trading and increase transparency, the duty to keep partners informed, and the fight against corruption and trickery (as in the recent option backdating scandal). Each of these problems is important in itself, particularly as regards market organization and regulation and the establishment of compliance procedures within businesses.[15] This is a key concern for all the institutions whose job is to ensure the integrity of markets and transactions. Yet, the sole purpose of all these measures is to make transactions as mechanically "flawless" as possible. Most current efforts to promote financial ethics focus on these issues.

In fact, the technical quality of transactions is a side issue. The socioeconomic fabric may be undermined by the expansion of transactions at the expense of relationships. Putting too much energy into micro-regulatory issues may distract attention from the main threat that financialization poses to the system, namely that relationships are becoming sterile. Micro-regulation of markets and their environment will not suffice. In a lonely crowd of individuals linked only by transactions, the common good is an irrelevant and meaningless notion.[16] All that politicians have to do at present is regulate, i.e. use procedures to prevent collisions between the countless market players, in much the same way as road traffic is managed.

12.3.2   Encouraging long-term relationships

Financialization has become predominant through the gradual replacement of relationships by transactions. This process creates distrust, generates supervision costs and eventually makes cooperation, creativity and long-term commitment almost impossible. Relationships, and the common good, can only exist in the long term. In other words, the pressure of financialization is a threat to relationships. The only way to resist this pressure is to encourage long-term relationships. On this point there is a full convergence with the idea of stable and active "shareholdership" as put forward by some institutional investors active in the CSR framework. In the case of joint-stock companies, "golden shares" are under pressure throughout the world because they imply that different groups of shareholders – stable, strategic shareholders on the one hand, and nomadic shareholders looking for a quick killing on the other – should be treated differently. However, the advantage of this arrangement was that it introduced a filter between the real economy and the turmoil of finance, allowing businesses a degree of strategic independence. The fact that some businesses are now being "delisted" and that others are issuing fewer financial reports suggests that less exposure to stock-market neurosis may be good for them.

Emphasis on the long term may be reflected in working relationships, remuneration and even rewards for loyalty. Working relationships must involve more than just negotiation of legal conditions. Relationships that are not based on trust will remain hollow in both economic and human terms, and will become mere formal links with little or no potential.[17] Rather than encourage formal relationships, it is important to make arrangements that will encourage trust within socioeconomic relationships. There have already been some innovative steps in this direction, from "solidarity finance" to microfinance projects and responsible investment initiatives based on long-term relationships between shareholders and businesses.[18] Lasting relationships are also important when it comes to taxation, which is the material expression of taxpayers' links to particular parts of the world. There should be bonuses for staying in one place rather than, as is now the case, for moving around (tax breaks for newcomers). Taxation must break out of the present vicious circle of distrust, in which taxpayers see governments as robbers and governments treat taxpayers as lawbreakers. All initiatives in this area should be reinforced and more firmly tied to their philosophical and ethical underpinnings, which need to be better known and understood. One relationship that should be restored as soon as possible is international solidarity, particularly full-fledged, no-strings-attached development aid – a topic that has vanished from international agendas, at least under that name.

Greater emphasis on long-term relationships does not necessarily require legal or regulatory action. The point is to reward faithfulness and loyalty to places, individuals, projects and ideas, rather than lure people with the prospect of easy pickings. Effective action will depend on individual behavior based on firm conviction. Transactions reflect a systematic preference for an "elsewhere" (in time or space) that liquidity can supposedly bring within our reach, at the expense of the here and now. Yet, despite all the achievements of modern communication technology, it is only in the here and now that the human spirit – and, of course, the common good – can truly blossom. Besides duration, proper relationships depend on the partners not being too far distant from one another – and not just in geographical terms. If relationships are to be strong and fruitful, the partners must know each other personally. This is not the case in many present-day relationships, in which the links are purely legal ones and the partners cannot see each other's faces. This deprives the relationships of some of their dynamism. If relationships are to predominate once more, they must become literally closer and less anonymous, with a reduced role for intermediaries.

12.3.3   Changing the system of remuneration

Remuneration has been one of the most powerful vehicles for financialization. The number of intermediaries and others keen to earn commissions on transactions has rapidly expanded. This system of remuneration distracts people's attention from the intrinsic quality – including the moral quality – of their work and encourages them to focus instead on how others will see them. It also encourages greed and ruthless pursuit of gain, distracting attention from the quality of people's behavior and focusing instead on its effects. A system of remuneration that will encourage long-term relationships and increase the quality of professional conduct will certainly help reduce the pressure of financialization on the marketplace.

Finance serving the common good is not a chimerical vision. It is a possible outcome of many convergent actions and decisions taken today by a variety of concerned actors. Many of them share a sense of systemic urgency. The emerging "sellers-take-all-society" based on infectious greed is a deadlock, not a viable long-term perspective. In order to encourage such actions and provide them with a kind of broad-picture framework, the Observatoire de la Finance – a Geneva-based think tank – recently issued an appeal in the form of a "Manifesto for finance that serves the common good." Its full text is reproduced in the following concluding chapter.

Notes

1. This is a title of a forthcoming book by Palgrave Macmillan.
2. Tainter, J. (1988) *The Collapse of Complex Societies*. Cambridge University Press, New York, 250 pp.

3. Ziegler, J. (2005) *L'empire de la honte*, Fayard. Paris, 323 pp.; and Hollenbach, D. (2002) *The Common Good and Christian Ethics*. Cambridge University Press, Cambridge, 270 pp.
4. Frank, R. and Cook, R. (1996) *The Winner-Take-All Society*. Penguin Books, New York, 288 pp.
5. Frankel, T. (2002) *Trust and Honesty*. Oxford University Press, New York, 264 pp.; and Dembinski, P.H. (2004) "Conflits d'intérêts: le déni de l'éthique," in *Rapport Moral sur l'Argent dans le Monde 2003–2004*, Association d'Economie Financière, Paris, 450 pp.
6. Tévoédjrè, A. (1978) *La pauvreté, richesse des peoples*. Les Editions Ouvrières, Paris, p. 33.
7. See the review of *The Crisis of Global Capitalism* in *Finance and the Common Good/Bien Commun*, 2: 56–60, spring 1999.
8. Milgram, S. (1974) *Obedience to Authority: an Experimental View*. Harper and Row, New York, 224 pp.
9. See in particular Haffner, S. (2002) *Defying Hitler: a Memoir*. Farrar, Straus and Giroux, New York, 309 pp.; and Deselaers, M. (2001) *Und Sie hatten nie Gewissensbisse?*, Benno Verlag, Leipzig, 424 pp.
10. Dembinski, P.H., Bonvin, J.-M. et al. (2000) "Les enjeux éthiques dans les activités financiers", in *Finance and the Common Good/Bien Commun*, 3: 6–21.
11. Perret, G. (2007) http://www.filmsduparadoxe.com/mondialisationcat.html
12. Thomas Crump's *The Anthropology of Numbers* (Cambridge University Press, Cambridge, 1990, 197 pp.) shows that extreme quantification is the prerogative of Western culture, and explains that it was able to spread across the globe so easily because other cultures had no "antibodies" to the invasion of statistics and the concomitant notion of efficiency.
13. De Foucauld, J.-B. (2002) *Les trois cultures du développement humain*. Odile Jacob, Paris, p. 41.
14. Boatright, J.R. (1999) *Ethics in Finance*. Blackwell Publishing, Boston, 224 pp.; Melé, D. (1998) *Etica en la actividad financiera*. Ediciones Universidad de Navarra (EUNSA), Pamplona, 250 pp.; Koslowski, P. (1997) *Ethik der Banken und der Börse*. Mohr Siebeck, Tübingen, 118 pp.
15. Thévenoz, L. and Bahar, R. (eds) (2007) *Conflicts of Interest: Corporate Governance and Financial Markets*. Kluwer International, Leiden, 416 pp.; Plender, J. (2003) *Going off the Rails*. John Wiley & Sons, London, 282 pp.
16. Riesman, D. (1950) *The Lonely Crowd*. Yale University Press, New Haven, 386 pp.
17. Villette, M. (1996) *Le Manager jetable*. La Découverte, Paris, 186 pp.
18. See the following issues of *Finance and the Common Good/Bien Commun*: "Investissement socialement responsable," no. 8, autumn 2001; "Economie et finance solidaires: Chimère ou nouveau défi ?" no. 21, autumn 2004; "Europe: La microfinance se fait une place," no. 25, autumn 2006. See also Balkenhol, B. (2007) "Microfinance: Performance and Efficiency," *Finance and the Common Good / Bien Commun*, 28–29: 147–51.

13

Conclusion: Manifesto for Finance that Serves the Common Good

Observatoire de la Finance

The current financial turbulence, whatever its immediate effects, is systemic in nature. It is the symptom of steadily increasing pressure that is undermining the material, social, and intellectual aspects and ethics of the liberal socioeconomic system. In a recent report, the Observatoire de la Finance carried out an extensive analysis of this transformation. There is a real risk that if pressure is not reduced, it will deflect the market economy from its primary vocation, that of promoting the dignity and well-being of humankind.

Society is never set in stone; it is characterized by an ongoing quest for the arrangements best adapted to a given time. Today is no exception. During the last 30 years, finance has constantly increased not only its share of economic activity, but also of people's *Weltanschauung* and aspirations. The greater practical and conceptual role of finance sometimes goes by the name of "financialization." The Observatoire de la Finance dedicated its last report to the analysis of the multiple dimensions of financialization. The report shows how financialization has transformed both our economy and our society by increasingly organizing it around the search for financial efficiency. Today, pushed to its extremes, this tendency is coming close to its breaking point.

The diagnosis

By the mid-1970s, most Western countries had linked their promises of pensions and retirement benefits to investments that depended on sustainable liquidity. The long-term viability of this model is dependent on the profitability of financial instruments. At the same time, other savings instruments were developed. This progressively exposed the so-called "productive" economy to the vagaries of finance, thereby producing an increasing need to devote more and more of the added value to the remuneration of the savings thus invested.

Pressures on the companies quoted on the stock exchange have been translated into other pressures in three complementary directions: on their staff to achieve ever-increasingly improved performance; on consumers, who came under increased pressure from sophisticated marketing techniques; and on the companies' suppliers and larger distributors as well as on many SMEs (small and medium-sized enterprises) in both the North and the South to achieve increasingly unsustainable results.

Though initially financial, the demand for financial results has trickled down through the entire economic system and become an omnipresent part of the culture of everyday life. This evolution has now resulted in a paradoxical situation for Western societies. The system of capitalization and shareholder value, by imposing demands for the future, has compromised the present. This "radiant future" is proving to be as much of an illusion as the communist utopia.

This process of "financialization" has been facilitated by the political appeal of deregulation, as well as by "laws" and other "theorems" postulated by Nobel prize-winners. The "ethos of efficiency" has also been allegedly validated by "scientific" truths, and has progressively overcome moral and ethical resistance.

After over 30 years of "financialization," the state of the economic and social system is worrying on more than one count:

- "Financialization" has led to the almost total triumph of transactions over relationships. Contemporary finance has prevailed because it has carried to its ultimate the search for capital gains and instant results. At the same time, patience, loyalty, enduring relationships, and trust have been undermined, leading to increased distrust. The liquidity of financial markets is nothing more than a mechanical substitute for interpersonal trust;
- The ethos of efficiency has become the ultimate criterion of judgment. If pushed to the extreme, the preoccupation with efficiency leads to internal procedures that distribute tasks and responsibilities in an increasingly strict manner, until the point of "ethical alienation" has been reached. Employees lose their sense of meaningful employment and replace it by gainful employment;
- The ethos of efficiency, when disassociated from moral considerations, has led to the increasingly brutal expression of greed. This is obvious in the subservience of trust to transactions. Repeated acts of self-interest

can push any society to the breaking point. The free market, based on a sense of responsibility of its actors, is about to be replaced by a "greed" market – which will require escalating controls and costs, in both public and private spheres. This, in turn, will breed the unwillingness of the actors themselves to take responsibility for their actions.

Possible lines of action

This analysis suggests that the fundamental values of free judgment, responsibility and solidarity – which form part of the common good, and without which a free and humane society cannot exist – are under threat. The Observatoire de la Finance proposes three lines of action:

- Carry out a critique – in the positive sense of the term – of the *Weltanschauung* underlying contemporary economic and financial theories. This critique would include both their relation to social and economic realities and the conceptual and ethical dimensions of their underlying assumptions. This should lead to a challenge to the dogmatic preeminence of the preoccupation with economic and financial efficiency as well as to the reinstatement of ethical concerns and of the primacy of common good;
- Encourage the development of long-term commitments in all aspects of economic and financial life. Such commitments would slow or even reverse the destruction of relationships due to the current focus on extracting surplus through ill-considered transactions. This would be a huge undertaking with implications in several different fields: finance, taxation, salaried work, local development, etc.;
- Establish some way to loosen the stranglehold which the unrealistic promise of retirement benefits currently brings to bear on productive activity. This will require great political courage, since the professional interests of financial intermediaries could be at stake. However, it is crucial since it is increasingly obvious that pension promises are unrealistic, and that the pursuit of strategies to earn the returns demanded are undermining the ethical basis of capitalism. But the work must be undertaken before the threatened breakdown of the current saving and pensions system becomes a reality.

Appeal

The above text aims to alert men and women of goodwill to a serious threat to the economic and political freedom we treasure. This threat is the result of having succumbed to the illusion that "private vice" could contribute to "public virtue." While "private vice" may give the impression of increasing economic efficiency, this is at the cost of the very basis of society: trust, respect and solidarity. It has now become indispensable to take our future in hand – to walk out, to slam the door of the apparently golden prison of financial promises, to free humankind from the illusions of "financialization," and to set it to work for the betterment and dignity of all.

The *Finance and the Common Good/Bien Commun* reviews, as well as the Observatoire de la Finance's website, are at your disposal.

Please send your contributions to: manifeste@obsfin.ch

Index

Note: Figures and tables are indicated by 'fig.' or 'tab.' before the page number.